ERP Systems Implementation in Manufacturing: An Analytical Approach

Dr. Amar Rajendra Mudiraj

INDIA • SINGAPORE • MALAYSIA

Contents

Chapter 01

Research Introduction

1.1 Introduction

Enterprise resource planning (ERP) is business process management software that allows an organization to use a system of integrated applications to manage the business and automate many back-office functions related to technology, services and human resources. ERP software integrates all facets of an operation, including product planning, development, manufacturing, sales and marketing.

Business management software-usually a suite of integrated applications, that a company can use to collect, store, manage and interpret data from many business activities, including: – Product planning, cost and development, Manufacturing or service delivery, Marketing and sales, Inventory management, Shipping and payment

ERP is an acronym for Enterprise Resource Planning; a term that is used for business management systems which are designed to integrate the data sources and processes of an entire organization into a unified system. A key element is the use of a single database to store data for the various system modules.

ERP is not some kind of software; this is an ideology. Some companies build applications that work according to this ideology, called ERP solutions. But there is something more there... the developers of such solutions build their application implementing some best business practices in it, and this is one of the most valuable features of ERP systems. The so-called know-how is the most common thing that many of the small businesses out there lack. And this could be the difference between the successful, fast flowing company and the average company. At some point of the life cycle of an enterprise, the need of such a system becomes inevitable. The earlier managers understand this, the better. As the company grows, its control becomes more and more difficult task. An integrated solution, like ERP software, could be really helpful in this situation. Maharashtra is one of the largest and richest states in India Maharashtra is third most urbanized state with urban population of 45% of whole population Maharashtra has been in the forefront of economic development and is the economic power house of the country. With its proactive policies, the State continues to occupy the dominant position amongst the industrially advanced States in India. In accordance with the provision of Micro, Small & Medium Enterprises Development (MSMED) Act, 2006 the Micro, Small and Medium Enterprises (MSME) are classified in two Classes:

1.1.1 Manufacturing Enterprises

The enterprises keep in the manufacture or production of goods pertaining to any industry specific in the first agenda to the industries (Development and regulation) Act, 1951) or occupying plant and machinery in the procedure of value addition to the final product having a different name or nature or use. The Manufacturing Enterprises are defined in terms of venture in Plant & Machinery.

1.1.2 Service Enterprises

The enterprises engaged in providing or depiction of services and are defined in terms of investment in equipment. The enterprise belongs to Medium scale enterprise, if investment in plant and machinery is more than 05 crore rupees but does not exceed 10 crore rupees.

1.2 Objective of the Research: –

To Study the significance of Operational, Managerial, Financial, Technical feature of ERP in the Organization.

To Analyze the Benefits of Operational, Managerial, Financial, Technical facet of ERP in Selected Medium Scale Manufacturing Units in Maharashtra.

To Understand & investigate the Impact of Operational, Managerial, Financial, Technical aspects of ERP in Manufacturing Industries for enhancing effective Decision making with special reference to Selected Medium Scale Manufacturing Units in Maharashtra.

To Analyze the Different ERP Module implementation adopted by Medium Scale Manufacturing Units in Maharashtra.

To compare the different ERP's implementation and critical factors in Selected Medium Scale Manufacturing Units in Maharashtra.

1.3 Hypothesis:

H0: – There is No Significant Impact of ERP system in the Improvement of the Work Competency of the Employee in the Manufacturing Units
H1: – There is Significant Impact of ERP System for Bringing the Work Competency improvisation in the employees of the manufacturing Units.

H0: – There is No Significant Impact on the Manufacturing unit's for obtaining Better Resource Utilization due to ERP Implementation.
H2: – There is Significant Impact on the Manufacturing unit's for obtaining Better Resource Utilization due to ERP Implementation.

H0: – ERP System Does Not Provided the Technology Support System That Conveys the Better Precision in the Decision Making.
H3: – ERP System provides Technology supports system that conveys the better precision in decision making.

1.4 Research Methodology

1.4.1 Introduction:

This chapter provides information on the research methods of this thesis. A descriptive / Qualitative / Survey Based research methodology was used for this study. A survey was administered to a selected sample from a specific Medium Scale Manufacturing Units identified by the Development Commissioner (MSME) Ministry of Micro, Small & Medium Enterprises, Mumbai and Nagpur Division. The term 'survey' is commonly applied to a research methodology designed to collect data from a specific population, or a sample from that population, and typically utilizes a questionnaire or an interview as the survey instrument (Robson, 1993).

Surveys are used to obtain data from individuals about themselves, their MSMU, or about ERP implementation process and impact on them and their manufacturing unit. Sample surveys are an important tool for collecting and analyzing information from selected individuals. They are widely accepted as a key tool for conducting and applying basic social science research methodology (Rossi, Wright, and Anderson, 1983). The survey research method has been chosen to determine the importance, Benefits, Impact and Critical Factors of Operational, Managerial, Financial, Technical aspects of ERP implementation medium Scale manufacturing Units (Industrial Zone-wise) in Maharashtra State. The sampling technique has been described followed by the measurement procedures. The data collection and data analysis are also included in this chapter. And lastly, the limitations of the thesis are discussed.

1.4.2 Sampling:

This research is based on purposive sampling technique, the alternative use of probability sampling is not considered due to limited time and resources. The researcher will make contact with potential respondents with the use of In-person visits to MSMU with discussion on telephone and e-mails for the participation of this survey research. The process will continue until the researcher has at least more than 50% respondents of total sample consider for the research willing to participate in this research. First the telephonic conversation has been used for the first talk, then sent an e-mail out to each respondent who give positive response to telephonic request. With a converging letter explaining the purpose of this research in-person visit on each MSME tried to make possible and collected the responses from the MSMU. Those MSMU who are not willing to provide time for in-person visit to their manufacturing units are e-mailed with converging letter explaining the objective of study and ask them to reply within three weeks. Each respondent will receive a summary of the research result for the participation.

The samples are selected on the basis of the knowledge, connection and judgment of the researcher in the Medium Scale Manufacturing Units (Industrial Zone-wise) in Maharashtra State. It is through the researchers personal and work relationships with the Individuals in medium scale manufacturing units and their references further units for same division or others to ensure the participation and completion of this survey. Most of them are Managerial, professionals and executives' companies. MSME, DC-MSME, Mumbai and Nagpur, updated industry news and events, personal experience and other information all help to form the basis for the selection and ongoing maintenance of samples. To maintain the quality and effectiveness of this survey research, the researcher chooses to have at least 50% of total sample size. The Managerial, professionals and executives' companies in this sampling are regarded to wealthy professionals that have sufficient knowledge and experience with ERP system implementation process and able to evaluate the merits or risks associated to an ERP on the MSMU. The research and study is based on primary data. The data is collected by applying standard questionnaire methods and personal interview conducted on 249 selected medium scale manufacturing units who have implemented ERP in their units and out of 249 only 145 (approx. 59%) medium scale manufacturing units are willing to share their responses for the research from all over the Maharashtra industrial zone-wise shown in Table 1.

Sr. No.	Name of Industrial Zone	Medium Scale Manufacturing Units who use ERP	Medium Scale Manufacturing Units Using ERP (Response Collected)	Percentage
1	Desh (Pune Div)	44	23	52.27%
2	Khandesh (Nasik Div)	30	17	56.67%
3	Koken (Mumbai Div)	84	44	52.38%
4	Marathwada (Aurangabad Div)	33	29	87.88%
5	Vidharabha (Nagpur Div)	35	19	54.29%
6	Vidharabha (Amravati Div)	23	13	56.52%
Total Manufacturing Units		**249**	**145**	**58.23%**

Table 1.1 Manufacturing Units Who Using ERP (Selected for Study)

Source:-(www.dsmsme.gov.in, www.maharashtradirectory.com/www.indianyellowpages.com/india/manufacturers/

In the present study, the selected Manufacturing unit's information like Number of Manufacturing Units Registered, Name and Industrial Zone wise count was collected from the MSME (Ministry of Small, medium Scale Enterprises), which is the Apex Body under the Central and State

Government Organization who prepare the Annual Report every year. The Present research has collected Total Population of 792 Medium Scale Manufacturing Units **(Source: MSME-2014-15 report).**

1. As per the title and objective of the research, we have start collecting brief survey via personal Visit, Organization's Website, Annual Report available on the respective portal and telephonic communication to check the Status of the ERP Implementation in the organization.

2. The outcome of the Pilot survey was to finalizing the sample size of Medium Scale Manufacturing Units who were using the ERP system as End-To-End Product for the manufacturing process and which connect all the stakeholder of the business process through ERP System Only.

3. The Pilot Survey found 249 Medium Scale Manufacturing Units out of 792 MSMU at different industrial Zones in the Maharashtra State (The Detail updated list of MSMU was prepared based on the brief pilot survey). Out of249 MSMU only 145 Manufacturing Units were shown the willingness in the Final Survey for the research questionnaire.

4. Hence 145 MSMU out of 792 MSMU approximately 18.30% of the total Universe

1.4.3 Measurement Procedures:

The method of e-mail survey is used in this research. This particular instrument has been chosen due to the unique characteristics of the study population and the efficiency of data collection. The survey will be consisted close-ended questions formulated aiming to ensure more in-depth information is provided. The questions are formulated based on the objectives, research question and hypothesis of this research. The questions will follow a logical succession starting with simple themes and progressing to complex issues to sustain the interest of respondents and gradually stimulate question answering. A cover letter is attached to the survey to explain the purpose of this research and its relevance, and to seek their agreement to participate in this research. Contact information of the researcher has been provided in case a respondent has any questions. The questions of the survey have been designed to test the five hypotheses of this thesis. The wording of each question has been organized according to the multi-dimension constructs for the measurements of each factor derived from previous research. The use of the e-mail system other than in-person visit, promotes efficiency and offers respondents to answer the survey at their own pace and convenience. The disadvantages include possible bias based on the researcher's judgment for sample selection and less spontaneous response.

The questions 37 Questions are organized into four sections. Section A of the survey includes 12 Questions on General Information about the Respondents and its MSMU, the questions are organized in each category namely, MSMU Name, Place (City), End Product, Year of Establishment, Annual Turnover, Name of Respondent, Gender, Designation, Total Work Experience and Income group. Section B of the survey includes 11 question on Fundamental Information on ERP System, namely as, ERP vender, Year of ERP implementation, year of ERP using in the Manufacturing units, re-engineering process status, total no of computer system in the unit, implementation strategy etc. in Section C, 7 Questions are asked on multi ranked answer (with multiple-choice) for identifying Managerial, Operational, Technical and Financial Critical Success factors of ERP implementation on manufacturing units, type of Training provided by the MSMU with the cost details of training cost in respect to the total ERP implementation budget. The last Section D includes 7 Questions; based to prove the Objectives and hypothesis attainments whereas, also try to identifying the Managerial, Operational, Technical and Financial benefits of the ERP system implementation on Respondents Manufacturing Units.

For calculating validity and reliability,

1. I have conducted a pilot study and survey in 10 different and Random Medium Scale Manufacturing Units in the form of Personal Interview Method of the Concern respondent who willingly participated in the survey and who are working professional and ERP Expert, Managerial, professionals and executives of the Medium Scale Manufacturing Unit
2. The respondents were selected based on their willingness, their work Experience on ERP System and Understanding of Overall Business process and manufacturing cycle through ERP System.
3. The Reliability of the Questionnaire was tested using Half Split Method, and applied Construct Validity. The Reliability of the Questionnaire also Validated and Reviewed by the ERP Expert for the Industries, Senior Academicians, Research Guide and Co-Guide with Experience Statisticians.
4. Out of 37 Questions which were splatted into three sections A – (General Information), B (Fundamental about ERP System), C (Objectives and Hypothesis based).
5. 19 Questions were found to be fully reliable often applied Half Split Method

1.4.4 Data Collection:

The feedbacks of the surveys are collected from the period between June-2018 to Dec-2020. The data has been recorded and updated simultaneously as responses are received. The results have been organized in the Microsoft Excel spreadsheet with the code sheet that has been developed to measure the attitudes from the data of the survey results. The data is organized into separate rows and columns with the assigned attitudinal score as mentioned previously in this chapter. The responses of each question have been assigned with numerical values for the data analysis.

1.4.5 Data Analysis:

The analysis of the survey data is processed using Microsoft Excel and the add-in software Analyze It like IBM SPSS Statistics Data Editor 2010 Ed. Collected data was compiled in MS-excel sheet, for analysis the collected data SPSS (Statistical Package for Social Sciences Ver. 20th) was used. The statistical analyses that have been conducted include: overall multi-dimension constructs measurement towards each factor descriptive statistics of frequency and percentile manner. The data is analyzing questionnaire wise and Reponses are get collected and interpretations done by using frequency and percentile of the frequency as compare to the total number of respondents. The Cross Tabulation or Cross Factors Analysis is used for the correlation between the industrial Zone-wise medium Scale manufacturing units towards each factor and the actual percentage of their occurrences with entire MSME and each zone wise. Tabulation and charts are provided for the ease of comparison between different categories. Other information related to respondents also designed by pie charts, Line charts and column charts for more pictorial description and analysis.

1.4.6 Limitations:

The main concern of conducting this survey research is the Sampling. Due to limited resources and time, only small portions of the Medium Scale Manufacturing Units in Maharashtra state are implemented ERP system are requested to participate in the survey. It is only through the researchers personal and work relationships with the MSMU to ensure the participation and completion of this survey.

Most of them are professionals and executives of units. The sample size may not accurately represent all MSMU, although most of the respondents are professionals and managerial level and therefore are more likely to have in-depth knowledge of the subject to provide accurate reflections. The resources from previous research and studies are very limited. There is very little information available on the subject of ERP implementation in medium scale manufacturing units and very less MSMU implemented ERP in their unit and there for the study also get restricted.

There are other ERP implementation features and activities that are also concerns of MSMU world-wide that are not discussed in this thesis. The aim of this thesis is to provide the general impact of ERP system implementation on medium scale manufacturing units in more insightful information. It is hoped that this thesis could provide more references for individuals' MSMU in decisions and ERP implementation process for the manufacturing units to advancement in their managerial, Operational, Technical and Financial Factors evaluation and improvement.

1.5 Summary of Chapter Schemes: –

Chapter 1. Research Introduction

This chapter will discuss the Introduction of the research, ERP system, global, national and Maharashtra market and industrial structure of Manufacturing industries, the chapter also describe the Objective of the study, Hypothesis, Scope, limitation, Benefits of study and research.

Chapter 2. Relevant Study & Literature Reviews

The chapter will discuss the various studies done in the past and recently on the ERP implementation in manufacturing industries. The literature review will cover the research article, papers, PhD thesis; new article right from the international to national level, the review will cover last 5 and more years for the highlight the study domain on the ERP implementation system in the manufacturing industries in all over the globe

Chapter 3. ERP System Fundamentals & its Relevance with Manufacturing Units

The section gives the details of the research methodology used for the study and detail of the sampling techniques and research world, where details of the sample, reason behind selecting only given sample is going to discuss. The details of the data collection and tabular formatted, chart and figures and going to be demonstrate in this section

Chapter 4. Data Collection, Observation and Interpretation.

This will be the core section of the Thesis where all the data analysis, observations and interpretations are going to be discuss, also provide some analytical tools and techniques for analysis of the given data on the various parameter on which the conclusion and recommendations are going to be discussed.

Chapter 5. Conclusions and Suggestions

This chapter concludes the research by providing some important conclusions basis on the observations and interpretations in the chapter4. basis on which some important recommendation will suggest to the Medium Scale Manufacturing Units, MSME and MIDC for future enhancement on those loopholes, gap which founds by this research.

Bibliography and References

This will give the detail list of the research article, reference books, website and other study materials which help to analyze the study and get the expected result from it.

Chapter 02

Relevant Study & Literature of Review

Introduction:

The purpose of this chapter is to present the previous efforts and findings in related areas. It presents an overview of previous research on ERP implementation in information systems. The significant developments related to ERP system relevant for the present research has been highlighted. For clarity, the literature has been classified into seven sections. In the first section of this chapter Definitions of ERP from various authors, books and other references are presented. Second part of this chapter deals with ERP fundamentals with try to highlighting basic ERP process. In the third section BPR i.e. Business process reengineering process review get analyze and try to discuss various authors opinions about the BPR process and its impact stories on various county and organization. The fourth section of this chapter ERP implementation process in manufacturing industries are get reviewed, with their implementation strategy and experience of different research and authors. In Section Five SME scenario gets observed and discusses, it reviews the researchers and their correspondence analysis about the small and medium sale enterprises structure and overview. In Section Six the process of ERP implementation in SME get reviewed with their implementation strategies, deployment approaches and the reviewed results from various studies and research, as the theoretical frameworks for this study. In the last section the overview of Post implementation of ERP thorough literature review of all the factors has been taken. It presents a critical appraisal of the previous work published in the literature pertaining to the area of ERP implementation in SME.

2.1 ERP definitions

ERP systems were named differently by different authors, some of them are enterprise systems, enterprise wide-systems, enterprise business-systems, integrated vendor software, and enterprise application systems, but however with no significantly different definitions [1]. **Rosemann (2001)** [2] defines ERP system as "customizable, standard application software which includes integrated business solutions for the core processes (e.g. production planning and control, warehouse management) and the main administrative functions (e.g., accounting, human resource management) of an enterprise.

According to D. P. Goyal (ERP managerial perspective)[3] ERP is the "Computer-based integrated information system, which is designed to process an organization's transaction and to integrate various functions/departments/divisions within an organization."

In "Textbook of ERP" Mahadeo Jaiswal & Ganesh Vanapali[4] say's "the ERP is An integrated, multidimensional system for all functions, based on business model for planning, control and global (resource) optimization of the entire supply chain, by using state-of-the-art IS/IT technology that supplies value added services to all internal and external parties.

- An integrated system that allows information to enter at single point in the process and updates a single shared database for all the functions that directly or indirectly depend on this information.

- An integrated suite of application software modules, providing operational, managerial and strategic information for an enterprise, in order to improve productivity, quality and competitiveness.

Marry Sumner in ERP book design the ERP definition as "An ERP system is packaged business software system that allows a company to "Automate and integrate the majority of its business processes; share common date and practices across enterprise; and produce and access information in a real time environment."

2.2 ERP Fundamentals:

Enterprise Resource Planning (ERP) systems have emerged as the centre of successful information management system and are considered as the backbone of organizations. In this global business scenario, organizations of any magnitude have either implemented or are in the process of implementing ERP systems in order to remain competitive. ERP can be regarded as highly integrated management information system having the capability to manage all aspects of business operations of organizations, which include production, manufacturing, sales, accounting, customer service, etc. According to **Gable & Stewart, (1999)**[5] ERP is increasingly becoming accepted platform for the small and medium scale industrial sectors and is viewed as one of the ways to achieve competitive advantage and to reengineer business process. **Wang et al., (2009)**[6] To achieve synergy across product lines, these businesses must implement a set of standard business applications and consistent data definitions across all business units. ERP packages are extremely useful for integrating a company at the global level and for providing a "common language" throughout the organization). Indian small and medium business is also affected with such scenario. However, the large establishments have attempted to tackle in their own way and it is the small and the medium scale enterprises (SME) that are showing their huge potential growth using ERP. Indian SMEs contribute well above 60% of country's gross domestic product (GDP) and, because of its potential growth ERP vendors are moving their attention towards small and medium business (SMB) by offering customized and cheaper solutions from both the organizational and technological point of view **Chen, (2001)**[7]. According to **(Mabert et al, 2001**[8]; **Koh & Simpson, 2007**[9]) SME creates the largest employment opportunities for the Indian population. India's SME sector is a vibrant, dynamic, flexible and productive entity, containing as many as 12 million units and employing around 30 million people. At the time of removal of quantitative restrictions under WTO in 2001, it was widely feared that this sector would collapse under the onslaught of global products. On the contrary, the sector quickly adapted and restructured itself to face the competition head-on. It embraced high technology, accepted norms of quality and competitiveness and continued to expand faster than the rest of the industrial economy. A vast majority of small and medium scale organizations have some significant constraints in their resources. While Indian SMEs overlook the benefits of integrating ERP systems stating that such ERP software are beyond their budgets as the reason, but there is no doubt that the implementation of ERP software can improve the company's performance as well. The awareness of implementing enterprise business application (i.e. ERP) among SMEs is less than 35%, as compared to over 80% for large organizations as per survey conducted by International Data Corporation (IDC). The critical influencing business drivers for SME segment increase the overall business efficiency, increase the capital and labor productivity and to reduce the fixed and variable cost. Research and survey by leading IT vendors clearly points out that the need for technology solutions is not only confined to metro cities in India but also business organizations operating from urban and Sub urban area also need ERP solutions as well. As all ERP vendors are focusing on this market, the Indian SME segment will have many alternatives to choose any one out of those having different competitive price. It has been found from the outcome of several researches that the implementation of ERP systems is more complex and expensive task for small organizations. According to **Leonard Simon (1997)**[10], the ERP paradigm shift is a result of demand from industries for flexible and integrated information systems and exploitation of information technology advancements such as Relational Data Bases, Client\Server computing, Object Oriented Network and Graphical User Interfaces to this end. **Rick, Mullin (1997)**[11] stated that the Integrated packaged software solutions are being built around common information technology standards and adaptable to specific industry to reduce training/running cost. Information networking and strategic alliances with suppliers or distribution channel partners or logistic operators have become a compelling need to reduce cycle times. Companies effected by world class competition, bench mark not only their products but also their key business processes. Therefore companies are no longer willing to automate existing processes blindly. Rather, wish to transform business processes with best industry practices. Information networking and strategic alliances with suppliers or distribution channel partners or logistic operators have become a compelling need to reduce cycle times.

According to **Parr and Shanks (2000)** [12], Vanilla implementation is safer option for the implementation with minimum customization. **Rao (2000)**[13] stated that 80 percent of the benefits of ERP came out of integration. There should be a clear policy to implement the ERP in the "VANILLA" form without the customization. **Grossman and Walsh (2004)**[14], has the view that the pilot phase is merely a prototyping phase. Once that phase is complete and all the data is loaded to the system then the stress testing must be performed to find out the critical factors which help in the implementation of ERP. According to **Peffers et al. (2003)**[15], senior managers have found CSF to be appealing for IS planning because they help justify the development of strategically important new systems, the benefits of which may be hard to quantify. ERP systems allow the integration of functions, divisions of businesses in terms of information exchange and flow, and the integration of business functions as diverse as accounting, finance, human resources, operations, sales, marketing, customer information and even the supply chain.

Mohammad et al. (2005) [16] stated that considering ERP implementation as an IT project is a risk itself. If the implementation is treated as a Project, the ERP system will never be implemented to its full capabilities. In such cases the business process will not be properly reengineered and aligned with the software requirements, and staffs swill resist. **Park and Kaushik(2005)** [17], the ERP project need to be based on an enterprise-wide design and it is not possible to start with pieces and then try to integrate the software component later on.

According to **Dezdar and Ainin (2011)** [18], In spite of the many benefits, there are number of problem in the adoption of ERP. A recent research reveals that more than 90% of ERP implementations have been delayed and required additional budget amounts. **Finney and Corbett (2007)** [19], has identified a gap in the literature which there is a need to identify the critical factors for the successful implementation of ERP in SMEs. **Wang et al. (2008)** [20], It is vital to identify factors leading to success of ERP systems implementation. According to **Dezdar and Ainin,(2011)** [21] Global ERP vendors are now trying to extend their market to companies in turns many developing countries are now implementing ERP systems, but there has not been much research on the success factors of ERP projects in these regions/countries.

2.3 Business Process Reengineering (BPR)

As mentioned before, there are two main options to implement ERP systems: modify an ERP system package to suit the organization's requirements or the implementation of an ERP system package with minimum deviation from the standard settings. However, ERP systems are built on best practices that are followed in the industry, and to successfully install ERP, all the processes in a company should conform to the ERP model. (**Davenport, 1998a; Sumner, 1999**)[22] Research has shown that even a best application package can meet only 70% of the organizational needs. According to **Melymuka, (1998)**[23] To take the full advantage of an ERP software, business process redesign is seen as a prerequisite. Business Process Reengineering was identified as critical success factors. (**Bingi et al. (1999)**[24]; **Holland and Light (1999)**[25]; **Sumner (1999)**[26]; **Sykes and Willcocks (2000)**[27]; **Rosario(2000)**[28], **and Kuang, Lau, and Nah (2001)** [29]) BPR is important factor that is constructed in the beginning of the project phase. Business Process Reengineering is strongly related with how suit is the ERP software chosen with current business process. (**Bingi et al., 1999)**[30]: Companies need to identify their current business structure and business process associated with their existing IT systems in the beginning of ERP project and relate this to the business process contained within ERP system.ERP software configuration is different from building a customized system because the development focus shifts from system analysis and design to software configuration. **Holland & Light, (1999)**[31] Companies should be willing to change the business process to fit with the software because software should not be modified as far as possible (**Sumner, (1999), Holland and Light (1999))**[32] further argued that the majority of system analysis and design effort had already been captured within the ERP software, and software modification can reduce the software functionality and increase in error possibility. **Rosario, (2000)**[28] The philosophy of the business process changes besides to align the business process with the software is to simplify the process so as to eliminate redundant activities.

2.4 4 ERP System Implementation in Manufacturing Units

Today many organizations are under pressure to meet the challenges of increasing competition. They need to be better, cheaper, and faster than the competition. ERP systems have come on the scene with a promise to provide a common database and to integrate business process, providing a seamless enterprise paradigm. ERP systems can save money, can improve efficiency, and can allow companies to remain competitive. Countless companies have implemented ERP systems and have been able to save millions of dollars in operating costs, reducing cycle times, maintaining continuous improvements, and increasing the overall efficiency of their businesses. Today manufacturers realize that many core processes that run their businesses are often best handled with an enterprise application package that is cheaper and more up-to-date than previous ones. However, integrated systems reduce the need to reconcile data across modules, support more extensive financial analysis, and allow for easier cross training of staff. The Internet represents the next major technology enabler, which will allow a rapid supply chain management even for multiple operations and multiple trading partners. It is very important to keep a good data base system for the customer to come back, and that is what this emerging generation of ERP is all about.

Syed M. Ahmed, Irtishad Ahmad, Salman Azhar and Suneetha Mallikarjuna(2007)[70] investigate the suitability and the implementation status of ERP systems in contractor firms. The methodology employed is a mix of literature review, market studies and detailed questionnaire survey. It is found that the majority of contractor firms have awareness about the ERP systems but very few organizations have so far implemented such systems. The major reason is that the implementation of any ERP system needs a huge investment in time, money and resources. However, when implemented to solve the right problems, these ERP systems can be a powerful tool for business improvement. The study shed light on the barriers to the implementation of ERP systems in the construction industry and also highlights valuable lessons learned and benefits gained by companies that have such systems in place."

Elisabeth J. Umble a, Ronald R. Haft b, M. Michael Umble (2003)[71] identifies success factors, software selection steps, and implementation procedures critical to a successful implementation. A case study of a largely successful ERP implementation is presented and discussed in terms of these key factors."

Fergal Carton and Frederic Adam, (2005) [72] an attempt to tease out the issues in the global implementation of ERP systems, they carried out a number of case studies at Irish manufacturing sites of multinational firms where management sought ways to defend their hard won local reputation for excellence and efficiency in the face of changes to the organization due to a corporate ERP implementation. Their study indicates that local managers are given too little scope and time to adequately adapt the template to their site and that the risk of productivity loss is quite high, at least in the short term. They conclude that mechanisms must be put in place to better understand how to accommodate local specificities whilst enforcing the required level of standardization."

Jan Olhager, Erik Selldin (2003)[73], presents a survey of ERP implementation in Swedish manufacturing firms, concerned with ERP system penetration, the pre-implementation process, implementation experience, ERP system configuration, benefits, and future directions. The ERP system cannot be considered to be an overwhelming investment for the enterprise. ERP systems primarily support the material and information flows and secondarily the financial flows.

Joseph Sarkisa, R.P. Sundarraj, (2003)[74] details the management of this implementation from a process-oriented perspective. The lessons learned from this effort help to support and further the academic and practitioner literature especially in the area of large-scale information systems management."

Majed Al-Mashari a, Abdullah Al-Mudimigha, Mohamed Zairib, (2003)[75] provides the guidelines on, the taxonomy is based on a comprehensive analysis of ERP literature combining research studies and organizational experiences. The taxonomy reflects the essential features of ERP systems, as being built based on the principles of business process management. Furthermore, it illustrates that ERP benefits are realized when a tight link is established between implementation approach and business process performance measures. This paper has presented a novel taxonomy of realizing and maximizing ERP benefits though a critical factor approach. The paper argues that ERP benefits are realized when a tight link is established between implementation approach and business-wide performance measures. The paper has discussed the concept of ERP as a pioneering, enabling and support system that is compatible with the requirements of modules business and that can help the effective implementation of the business process management principles. The paper agreed the ERP systems can yield to a wide array of benefits that are of a tangible and intangible nature. These are, however, heavily dependent on the approach adopted for the evaluation, selection and project management of ERP systems. To this end, a several critical factors have been identified and have been included to individually, within the paper.

Majed Al-Mashari, (2003)[75], "attempts to fill this gap by proposing a novel taxonomy for ERP research. Also presents the current status with some major themes of ERP research relating to ERP adoption, technical aspects of ERP and ERP in IS curricula. The discussion presented on these issues should be of value to researchers and practitioners. Future research work will continue to survey other major areas presented in the taxonomy framework, paper has presented a survey of research relating to some major ERP issues. The paper has illustrated taxonomy of ERP research that is believed to be covering the major issues in this important field. Much research is still needed to better understand the ERP phenomenon from a balanced perspective. Several themes have been discussed in this paper, and future work will continue to survey the other areas described in the framework. It is expected that the current and future work will collectively provide researchers and practitioners with a good reference to research and practice in this emerging field."

Joseph R. Muscatello, Michael H. Small, Injazz J. Chen,(2003)[76], adopts a multiple case study approach to investigate the implementation process in small and midsize manufacturing firms in the US. The research focuses on implementation activities that foster successful installations and are developed using information gleaned from our field studies of four projects. Avenues for future research are also suggested. The successful firms in our study had also concentrated significant effort on many of the planning, justification and installation practices that have been found to lead to successful adoption of MRPII and CRM. This suggests that there may be some common traits in the implementation of modern technologies, especially among the human-factors related activities."

Edward A. Duplaga and Marzie Astani, (2003)[77] interviewed IT and other personnel at 30 manufacturing firms of various sizes to discover the major issues concerning the implementation of enterprise resource planning (ERP). Among the conclusions reached, the authors were surprised to learn that smaller organizations implementing ERP with a "big-bang" approach proved more successful than larger firms using a gradual rollout. large companies tend to use a phased implementation strategy for their ERP systems, smaller firms tend to experience the same ERP implementation problems as larger firms. The number-one problem for organizations of all sizes was lack of ERP training and education, followed by lack of in-house expertise in ERP."

W. H. IP, C. L. LAI and C. W. LAU, (2004)[78] In this paper the authors attempt to overcome the lack of understanding and training of ERP in manufacturing industry. He propose an ERP training model which integrates with Web-based training to form the framework for training and learning. The model is simulated using System DynamicÐa powerful modeling and simulation methodology of Organization Learning and Training advocated by professor Forrester of MIT. The implementation of this model is described using an example from manufacturing industry. The results are illustrated with this lamp manufacturing company which indicated successful ERP implementation to achieve higher productivity and performances.

Sanna Laukkanen, Sami Sarpola, Petri Hallikainen, (2005) [79] "This paper investigates the relationship of enterprise size to the constraints and objectives of Enterprise Resource Planning (ERP) systems adoption. The survey data based on the responses of 44 companies indicates that significant differences exist between small, medium-sized and large enterprises in ERP system adoption. Specifically, the findings suggest that small companies experience more knowledge constraints than their larger counterparts in ERP adoption. Further, while being the most prevalent objective for ERP adoption in all the company groups, business development through ERP adoption is considered especially important by the medium-sized and large enterprises. Finally, the findings of the study suggest that instead of considering small and medium-sized enterprises as one homogenous group, the differences between these two groups of companies should be acknowledged in the future research."

2.5 Small and Medium Size Enterprise (SMEs):

Small and medium enterprises (SMEs) are considered as the backbone of the economy of many countries around the world. There is no single generalized definition for the identification of SMEs. **Ibrahim and Goodwin, (1986)**[32]Some of the most widely used criteria to identify SME include size, number of employees, sales volume, asset size and capital requirement According to the UK Department of Trade and Industry, SMEs include the organization that that have less than 250 employees and micro SMEs that have less than 10 employees. SMEs have certain characteristics that make them unique in comparison with large enterprises. Such SMEs usually are specialized in a particular field or tend to serve a particular market. ERP systems used to be a domain of large companies but now a day there is increasing number of small and mid-sized enterprises who are adopting ERP as well. There are some reasons for this trend which include a saturation of the market; most of the large organizations have already implemented an ERP system, increasing possibilities and need for the integration of systems between organizations and the availability. SMEs have been defined on the basis of various criteria such as the number of workers employed, volume of output or sales, value of assets employed, and the use of energy, etc.

Organization for Economic Cooperation and Development (OECD) defines establishments with up to 19 employees as 'very small', between 20 and 99 employees as 'small, from 100 to 499 employees as medium, and over 500 employees as large enterprises. However, many establishments in some developing countries with 100 to 499 employees are regarded as relatively 'large' firms. Multilateral Investment Guarantee Agency (MIGA) has recently developed a guarantee program, called the Small Investment Program (SIP) that is specifically designed for SMEs. MIGA defines SMEs, for coverage under this program, as firms with not more than 300 employees, value of assets not exceeding US $ 15 million and annual sales not exceeding US $ 15 million. The European Union defines SMEs as enterprises that have employees of less than 250, with a turnover not exceeding Euro 50 million. In India the SMEs are not well defined. The internal group set up by the Reserve Bank of India has recently recommended that the units with investment in plant and machinery in excess of Small Scale Industries (SSI) limit and up to Rs. 10 cores may be treated as medium enterprises . The US Small Business Act 1953 states that a small business concern is one that is independently owned and operated and which is not dominant in its field of operation. The size standards are broken by NAICS industry classification and are based on two things (a) size standards in millions of dollars; and (b) by number of employee. In most industries, 500 is the maximum for small businesses, though there are industries where a business can have 1000-1500 employees yet still considered "small business". The European Union makes a general distinction between self-employment, micro, small and medium sized businesses based on the following criteria:

In the Indian context the definition for micro, small and medium enterprises as per the Ministry of Micro, Small and Medium Enterprises MSME Development Act, 2006 stated that the entrepreneur can be classified as per ceilings on investment. This investment may be in plant and machinery (for manufacturing enterprise), on equipments or rendering services.

According to MSME Development Act, 2006, for enterprises to be classified as micro, small and medium enterprises are as follows:

1. Micro **Manufacturing Enterprises** Rs. 2.5 million/ Rs. 25 Lakhs (US$ 50,000) Micro **Service Enterprises** Rs. 1 million/ Rs. 10 Lakhs (US$ 20,000)
2. Small **Manufacturing Enterprises** Rs. 50 million/ Rs. 5 Crores (US$ 1 million) Small **Service Enterprises** Rs. 20 million/ Rs. 2 Crores (US$ 40,00,000)
3. Medium **Manufacturing Enterprises** Rs. 100 million/ Rs. 10 Crores (US$ 2 million) Medium **Service Enterprises** Rs. 50 million/ Rs. 5 Crores (US$ 1 million)

In Manufacturing Enterprises investment is based on (limit in Plant and Machinery), whereas, In Service Enterprises Investment limit in Equipments.

Small and Medium sized Enterprises (SMEs) are very important to economies of many developing countries. These units are the integral part of their economies. But these units face numerous challenges in implementing technologies such as Enterprise Resource Planning (ERP) systems, which includes a lack of human, financial and lack of technological resources to support such initiatives,

Rao (2000)[13], In recent times, many multinational companies have restricted their operations to partnering only those midsize companies that are using compatible ERP software. Hence, it becomes essential for many Indian SMEs to adjust their business model and adopt ERP software that is compatible with the large enterprises with which they deal. Indian SMEs are increasingly finding themselves attracted to ERP solutions and the associated benefits. Additionally, ERP systems are becoming a necessity in order to maintain relations with larger enterprises.

Somers and Nelson, 2001[80]**; Mabert et al., 2003**[81]**; Mandal and Gunasekaran, 2003**[82]**; Nah and Delgado, 2006**[83]. The literature points out significant differences between SMEs and large organizations. SMEs have relatively informal structures and culture. **Ghobadian and Gallear, 1996**[34]; SMEs top management is usually involved in day-to-day activities. **Gunasekaran et al., (1996)** [36], One major disadvantage of SMEs is lack of human and financial resources. Staff shortages at SMEs might even require production to halt during training. Skills upgrading may be needed, however SMEs often cannot afford extensive training .Furthermore, and they may face challenges in paying for major. According to Sun **et al.,(2005)**[37], indicated that such resource shortages might hinder project success. Regarding IT, SMEs seldom have dedicated IT staff.

(Adam and O"Doherty, 2000[38]**; Mabert et al., 2003**[39]**)**, Major projects face increased external and internal risks when compared to large organizations. Externally, SMEs are more fragile than large companies and face greater difficulty in obtaining credit such external risks can lead to project delays or even abandonment. Internally, SMEs may find it difficult to implement reengineering projects due to limited resources.

(McAdam, 2001)[40]: they may face greater challenges in adopting technology. Finally, the cost of an ERP implementation may be proportionally higher for SMEs than for large organizations. **Mabert et al., (2000)**[41], SMEs may be more severely impacted by unsuccessful implementations.

Muscatello et al., (2003)[42], Resource constraints, limitations of the infrastructure and capability are most likely the major challenges facing an SMEs to adopt ERP systems. However, the factors that are influencing ERP in large organizations vary from those influencing the Small – Medium – Enterprises.

Laukkanen et al. (2007)[43], Large organizations benefits from adopting and implementing ERP systems range from simple organized operational level business processes to strategic decision taking capabilities.

Seethmraju, 2008[44]**; Mabert et al., 2003**[45], the updated IT infrastructure play a vital role in ERP implementation in large organizations. The basic functional areas (human resources, production and manufacturing, sales and marketing, finance and accounting) do exist in the large organizations. While taking into consideration that the financial ability of large scale companies enables the large investment in IT/IS and can support the risks attached to such investment. These later issues have been considered particularly advantageous for major projects.

In their book **(Laudon and Laudon, 2009)**[46] define the most favorable ERP systems implemented in large organizations in order to be, Customer Relationship Management (CRM) system, Supply Chain Management (SCM) system, Enterprise Resource Planning (ERP) System, and Knowledge Management System (KMS). Major vendors for such systems are international vendor who excel worldwide such as Oracle, SAP, BAAN, Microsoft Great Plains, etc. In line with **(Seethmraju 2008)**[44], there is no clear identification of what defines the critical success factors for ERP implementation in large enterprises, the reason for this is that not only the implementation takes responsible for the ERP's success or failure. It is the whole adoption process which identifies implementation as part and different stages of implementations pre and post preparations, standardization and integration without implemented ERP systems.

2.6 ERP Implementation in SME

Christopher P. Holland and Ben Light (1999)[84] highlighted a case study analysis of the strategic context and implementation of a global ERP project in a multinational textiles group is presented.

Jeanne W. Ross,(2000)[85] examined the impacts of packaged ERP systems on organizations. Specifically, it was intended to identify how firms were leveraging their ERP environments to generate business value. Thus, he intended to identify firms that had gone live with one of the leading ERP packages (SAP, Baan, PeopleSoft, or Oracle) firm-wide or within a major division. All implementations included manufacturing modules and some combination of financial, sales and marketing, and other modules."

As organization-specific characteristics and contexts have been always important research aspects, they attracted researchers to investigate their implications on the ERP implementation process. A study presented a conceptual model that could help implementers, vendors, and consultants implementing SAP R/3 ERP to better understand the system expectations by SMEs in certain contexts or regions (e.g. Australia) **(G. Gable and G. Stewart 1999)**[86]. Since organization size and business complexity affect ERP implementations, it was reported that implementations in Irish SMEs are usually easier and shorter in duration than those reported in ERP literature **(F. Adam and P. O'Doherty 2000)**[87]. In **(H. Liang and Y. Xue, 2004)**[88], through adopting a vendor's perspective, they recommend that ERP systems need to be localized according to the local management features. SMEs' characteristics and culture play an important role in the success or failure of ERP implementations in Belgian SMEs **(C. Doom, K. Milis, S. Poelmans, and E. Bloemen,, 2009)**[89], while cultural issues did not play a major role in ERP implementations within Chinese SMEs **(Y. Xia, P. Lok, and S. Yang,, 2009)**[90]. Moreover, ERP implementation methodologies differ between different organization sizes and business complexities, as LEs are more reluctant to adopt a Big-Bang approach than SMEs **(V. A. Mabert, A. Soni, and M. A. Venkataramanan, 2003)**[91]. Further, a comparative analysis on ERP implementation rates and success, between different organization sizes and industrial sectors in Taiwan shows that ERP implementations in electronic and science industry SMEs are usually more successful than those in traditional industry **(J.-H. Wu and Y.-M. Wang, 2003)**[92] There is no agreement among the researchers about the definition and duration of implementation phase.

Walsham, (1995)[45] mentions that the term implementation "is sometimes used to mean technical implementation, namely ensuring that system development is complete and that the system functions adequately in a technical sense". At other times, it is used to refer to the human and social aspects of implementation, such as that the system is used frequently by organizational members or that it is considered valuable to them in their personal work activities or coordination with others.

According to Markus **(2000)**[46] ERP systems affect both the internal and external operations of an organization. The successful implementation and use are critical to organizational performance and survival ERP implementation brings with it tremendous organizational change, both cultural and structural. This is on account of the best practice business processes that ERP systems are based on. This calls for ERP implementations to be looked at from strategic, organizational and technical dimensions. The implementation thus involves a mix of business process change and software configuration to align the software and the business processes.

Holland and Light, (1999)[25] ERP system implementation issues have been subjected to ample research under various theoretical perspectives dealing with aspects like: attribute, adoption and implementation process **(Nandhakumar, Talvinen & Rossi, 2005; Butler & Pyke, 2003)**[93], project design or accomplishment **(Laframboise, 2002)** [94], organizational influence **(Westrup & Knight, 2000)**[95], predicting the probability of success **(Magnusson, Nilsson & Carlsson, 2004)** [96], advancement towards e-commerce **(Schubert & Leimstoll, 2004)** [97] says on the key factors for the implementation of ERP in large and SMEs. For developing countries like India ERP system is in its early stage. It has been found that reasons like limit of capital, non-availability of resources, poor management base, and dearth of IT expertise are seriously affecting the implementation and adaptation of enterprise system in India and other similar Asian developing countries compared to the developed countries. SMEs either do not have sufficient resources or are not willing to commit significant portion of resources to complex ERP implementation process.

(Buonanno, Faverio, Pigni, Ravarini, Sciuto & Tagliavini, 2005)[47] SMEs are more fragile than large companies and the adoption of ERP is no longer limited to large scale enterprises. Several academics and practitioners have tried to capture the main reasons for failure or success of ERP implementations. **(Lindley, Topping & Lindley, 2008)**[98] Most of the analyses focus on the issues that contributed to failures than those contributed to success. If all these factors are controlled and managed so that they are phrased as positive factors that contribute to success and the factors that appeared mostly on the lists include: Top level management support, User training and education, Project management, clearly defined goals and objectives, Project team competence, and Change management.

((Upadhyay & Dan, 2008, 2009)[48]**. Rana Basu, Parijat Upadhyay, Manik C. Das, Pranab K. Dan(2012)**[49]**)**, SMEs face pressures from various corners that include competition from global vendors, new regulatory compliance requirements that would come up every year requiring complying with and providing information to government agencies, needing to strengthen products and services, at the same time, physical expansion need to be taken care. With exposure to global economies, customers' preferences are changing drastically and accordingly, organizations need to enhance their products / services. **P. T. Kale, S. S. Banwait and S. C. Laroiya (2010)**[50], In India ERP market is growing and ERP vendors have shifted their focus from the large industries to the SME segment, there are several issues to be resolved. Firstly, SMEs need to be made 'ERP aware'. Vendors need to micro vertically the ERP solution to better meet the requirements of SMEs. Since the financial resources of SMEs are limited, the cost of ERP system needs to be further reduced. SMEs on their part need to carefully evaluate their current IT systems and document it shortcomings while creating a wish list of what they want to achieve.

Levy et al, (2005)[51] Many new SMEs start each year, nearly 50% cease to exist in the first 3 years of business itself. Though it is assumed that all SMEs desire growth, only 40% survive beyond 10 years. Majority of the firms do not think of long-term business strategy but focus only on survival. They think of change only when the business begins to fail as a result of not keeping track of the changing market scenario. The firms who survive and grow are the ones who have the ability to take risks and respond to the changing circumstances. According to **Malhotra and Temponi, (2010)**[52] An ERP system, implemented across an organization can able to affect almost all of the business processes of that organization

Customization and Ease of integration are quite critical issues when implementing the ERP system in an organization. Since different organizations need different software, they need to adapt the available ERP in the market for their own use along with their previous software in their organization. Thus, the ERP modules should be integrated and provide seamless data flow among the other modules, increasing operational transparency. Furthermore, ERP should be available to exchange data with the current application. However, many SMEs either do not have sufficient resources or are not willing to commit resources due to the long implementation times and difficulties associated with ERP implementation .

(Cragg and Zinatelli, 1995[54]**; Nah and Lau, 2001**[53]**)** :There are a variety of "cost" factors that may escalate the initial budget. These include implementation assistance cost, cost of system integration, reengineering cost, cost of changing a companies' IT architecture to support ERP technology, etc. **(Shang and Seddon, 2002)**[55] Implementation describes how the new EPR system can be adapted and integrated with your current system as well as the time consuming during the implementation process, and it can customize the unique system in accordance with your business strategy. According to **Seddon, (2002)**[55] Depending on the implementation strategy a company adopts ERP projects are often long and intense .The literature on ERP implementation success and failure is inconclusive. While some analysts report positive impacts and outcomes of ERP application, others have revealed ERP failures. One of the reasons behind these different views lies in the multidimensionality of the concept of success and the difficulty of developing a single success and failure measurement. Based on review of both ERP and IS success and failure literature. **(Al-Mashari et al, 2003**[56]**; Bingi et al, 1999**[22]**)** two dimensions of ERP success and failure were identified. The success and the failure of ERP systems can be classified into two categories; the success and failure of ERP adoption (end user or customer point of view) and the success and failure of ERP implementation (consultant or vendor point of view). The ERP Implementation dimension looks at the success and failure of ERP implementation process. Implementing an ERP system often constitutes a company's largest-ever IS investment, and in many cases the largest-ever corporate project. **M.Ferranti (1998)**[57], recommend the following steps for the implementation of the ERP package

- Formation of implementation team
- Preparation of implementation plan
- Mapping of business process on to the package
- Gap analysis
- Customization
- Development of user-specific reports and transaction
- Uploading of data from existing systems
- Test runs
- User training
- Parallel run
- Concurrence from user on satisfactory working of the systems
- Migration to the new system
- User documentation support
- Post implementation support
- System monitoring and fine tuning

G. Westerman(1999)[58], have presented a discussion of the advantages and disadvantages of **phased** and **bigbang** implementation methodologies."Phased" and "big bang" are the two primary (and contrasting) approaches used to implement ERP systems.

Big – Bang Implementation: In a full big-bang implementation, an entire suite of ERP applications is implemented at all locations, at the same time. Using big bang, the system goes from being a test version to being the actual system used to capture transactions. This transformation takes place only in a matter of days and hence the name "big bang". The big bang approach usually employs a three-step process. In the first step, virtually all relevant processes and artifacts are chosen (or developed) and implemented in the software. In the second step, all modules are test individually and in the third step their interfaces with other modules.

Phased Implementation: A phased approach is one where modules are implemented one at a time or in a group of modules, often a single location at a time. Phased implementations are sequential implementations that consist of designing, developing, testing and installing different modules.

2.7 Critical Success Factors Affecting on ERP implementation in SME.

Critical Factors approach was first used by Rockhart, (1979) in IS (Information Systems) area. Several studies identified the critical factors needed to enable the project managers and management boards to improve their ERP implementation projects. Implementing successful ERP systems is investigated by many researchers. Their general focus was on identifying CSFs that need to exist in any organization to have successful ERP implementation. These factors have been tested in different organizations in many developed and developing countries by number of researchers (**Al-Mashari et al., 2003**[56]; **Bradford and Florin, 2003**[99]; **Holland and Light, 1999**[25]; **Mabert, at al 2003**[44]; **Parr and Shanks, 2000**[12]; **Somers and Nelson, 2003**[100]; **Umble et al., 2002**[71]; **Zhang et.al., 2002**[101]): It has been applied to many aspects of IS including project management, manufacturing systems implementation, reengineering, and, more recently, ERP systems implementation.

The adequacy of general – ERP implementations CSF in relation to Belgian SMEs-specific characteristics were examined in (**C. Doom, K. Milis, S. Poelmans, and E. Bloemen,, 2009**)[89]. The study discovered that most of ERP CSF apply to SMEs with some exceptions. Likewise, a study analyzed implementation success factors in small size firms and concluded that the CSF in literature are adequate when applied on small organizations (**A. Winkelmann and K. Klose,, 2008**)[102]. Another article presented an analysis of the CSF related to Chinese SMEs' characteristics (**Y. Xia, P. Lok, and S. Yang, 2009**)[90]. While top management support, ERP system quality, and knowledge sharing during implementations, were found key CSF in Thai SMEs (**A. Nattawee and R. Siriluck,, 2008**) [103], however, BPR was found to be a key factor of success (**Y. Xia, P. Lok, and S. Yang, 2009**)[90]. In (**A. Y. T. Sun, A. Yazdani, and J. D. Overend,, 2005**) [37], the authors developed a framework for ERP implementation CSF assessment in small manufacturing firms. Moreover, (**Loh et al., T. C. Loh and S. C. L. Koh,, 2004**)[104] used the Process Theory in order to identify the implementation critical elements through case studies in the UK. The study concluded that critical success factors, critical people and critical uncertainties contribute to the success or failure of ERP implementations in SMEs. **Reuther et al. (D. Reuther and G. Chattopadhyay, A. Marsh, 2000)** [105] carried out an analysis to determine the key success and failure factors of ERP implementations in Australian SMEs. Further, in **Snider et al. (B. Snider, G. J. C. d. Silveira, and J. Balakrishnan, 2009**)[106], they presented a detailed case analysis of successful and unsuccessful selecting appropriate ERP Systems, which match their process requirements. They argue that this method would decrease the risk of ERP and organizations misalignment.

One of the few ERP marketing studies has been done by (**V. Morabito, S. Pace, and P. Previtali,, 2005**)[107]. The research had a vendor-customer perspective. The paper construes that ERP suppliers' marketing abilities and customer reach strategies determine ERP diffusion and adoption success in SMEs, rather than SMEs' low demand or failure in the adoption process. The success of ERP implementation has variety of factors, that are considered to be critical and many researches are trying to list them. **Al-Mashari et al. (2003)**[1] suggests that *"clear vision and business director is fundamental for the success of ERP system implementation"*.

According to **Gupta (2000)**[108], the key to successful implementation of ERP is as follows:

- Commitment from top management;
- Form a task force with personnel from all functional areas to foster ties between project management and business units
- Take an assessment of hardware requirements;
- Step-by-step introduction rather than all at once;
- Start early planning on user training and support;
- Streamline decision making so that implementation work can move quickly;
- Be patient because ERP implementation takes time.

Mabert et al. (2003)[44] are summarizing CSFs from three case studies based on different organization implementing ERP systems. They found similarities between those organizations which implementation was successful. These are listed below:

- Senior executives were very involved throughout the project, from the outset to completion, and also established clear priorities.
- A cross-functional ERP Steering Committee with executive leadership was established to oversee the project. The Steering Committee was empowered to make key decisions, both during the planning and implementing stages.
- The implementation team spent extra time up front to define in great detail exactly how the implementation would be carried out.
- These companies laid out clear guidelines on performance measurements.
- Modifications to the ERP system code were kept to a minimum.
- Organizational change and training strategies were developed in advance and were continually updated during the implementation.

- Key technology issues, such as data integrity and technology infrastructure, were addressed early.
- Only minor re-engineering efforts were carried out up front.

Willcocks and Sykes (2000)[27] look at the CSFs from an IT point of view and defined 8 enabling factors:

- Senior-level sponsorship, championship, support and participation;
- Business themes, new business model and reengineering drives technology choice;
- "Dolphin" multifunctional teams, time box philosophy, regular business benefits;
- CIO as strategic business partner;
- Nine core IT capabilities retained/being developed in-house;
- In-house and in sourcing of technical expertise preferred;
- Supplier partnering—strong relationships and part of team; and

ERP perceived as business investment in R&D and business innovation rather than primarily as a cost efficiency issue.

Somers and Nelson (2001)[80] summarize a comprehensive list of 22 CSFs during ERP implementation. The list is based on factors that may affect the ERP implementation process and the probability of conversion success has been identified in the IT implementation, IT failures, and business process reengineering. Among the more important factors are:

- Top management support and involvement,
- The need for a project champion,
- User training,
- Technological competence,
- Process delineation,
- Project planning,
- Change management,
- Project management.

Bradford and Frorin (2003)[99] test those eight CSFs and they proven their significance for the success implementation.

In addition to those, the rest of 22 CSFs are:

1. Management of expectations
2. Vendor/customer partnerships
3. Use of vendors' development tools
4. Careful selection of the appropriate package
5. Steering committee
6. Use of consultants
7. Minimal customization
8. Data analysis and conversion
9. Defining the architecture
10. Dedicated resources
11. Clear goals and objectives
12. Interdepartmental communication
13. Interdepartmental cooperation
14. Ongoing vendor support

(Bancroft, 1996)[60] Within ERP implementation context, CSFs are defined as factors needed to ensure a successful ERP project, these factors include, but not limited to, clear objectives, user involvement, effective communications, change management, project team, project champion, consultants, architecture choices, minimal customization, excellent project management, top management support, data analysis and conversion, business process reengineering and user training and education. The findings shown by the these researchers are that the top management commitment and leadership, customer focus, information and analysis, training, supplier management, strategic planning, employee involvement, human resource management, process management, teamwork, product and service design, process control, benchmarking, continuous improvement, employee empowerment, quality assurance, social responsibility, and employee satisfaction were the most commonly extracted factors across these 76 studies. Al According to **Esteves and Bohórquez,(2007)**[59] Most of the research studies about ERP impact has been in the form of individual case studies, while experiences on the field of Small and Medium-sized Enterprises (SMEs) often fail in recognizing the economic and organizational impacts related to their ERP implementation and use. A theoretical framework has been identified and ranked for the critical success factors for the successful implementation of ERP for Indian SMEs.

Corcoran (1998)[61] advocates that ERP Planning and Implementation methodology consists of broadly the following steps:

- Identification of the needs for implementing an ERP package
- Evaluating the "as-is" situation of the business.
- Reengineering of the business process to achieve the desired result.
- Evaluation of the various ERP package.
- Finalizing of the ERP package.
- Installing the requisite hardware and network.
- Finalizing the implementation consultants.
- Implementation of the ERP package.

Duchessi, et al., (2009)[62] concludes that commitment from top management and adequate training is critical success factor for implementation. As per (**Dawson and Owens, (2008)**)[63] Top management advocacy, provision of adequate resources, commitment to the project, commitment of senior management with their own involvement and willingness to allocate valuable resources to the implementation effort. Major projects face increased external and internal risks when compared to large organizations. Externally, SMEs are more fragile than large companies and face greater difficulty in obtaining credit, such external risks can lead to project delays or even abandonment. According to (**Serafeimidis and Smithson, (2000)**) [64] Internally, SMEs may find it difficult to implement reengineering projects due to limited spare resources. **Zhang et al., (2002)**[65] Top management support in ERP implementation has two main aspects: providing leadership and providing the necessary resources. **Dezdar and Sulaiman(2009)**[66] Critical success factors (CSFs) are crucial to achieving the predetermined goals of an organization, and vital to the overall success of an ERP system implementation. The CSF approach facilitates the identification and prioritization of factors that could influence ERP implementation success. In terms of an ERP implementation, the CSFs are those conditions that must be met in order for the implementation process to happen successfully. Since 2005, many IS researchers have increased using CSFs to study ERP system implementations. Critical success factors for ERP projects have been studied from a number of different perspectives. Numerous authors have identified a variety of factors that can be considered to be critical to the success of an ERP implementation. According to Pearce **(2004)**[67], tactical factors are those that involve skillful methods and details. **Holland and Light (1999)**[31] Focused on tactical factors that can be applied to particular parts of the project. **Esteves-Sousa and Pastor-Collado (2000)**[68] also concluded that the CSFs model should have tactical perspectives. A recent comprehensive examination of the CSFs for ERP implementation which was carried out by **Finney and Corbett (2007)** identified CSFs based on the investigation of all CSFs in the literature and grouped them into strategic and tactical categories.

Nahetal.(2007)[69] believed that effective communication of requirements, direction, mission, plan, user input, feedback and changes is critical to all stages to ERP implementation. They stated that communication is essential for creating approval and widespread understanding and acceptance of ERP. Additionally, effective communication has a large impact on the success of change management efforts during a project.

Somers and Nelson (2004)[70] advised that strong communication throughout the various stages of the implementation is essential in allowing employees to understand that what is going on, why change is necessary, and how it will benefit the organization. **Nah et al. (2007)** [69] suggested that adequate training can increase success of ERP systems and lack of proper training can frustrate ERP users. Moreover, training decreases the level of resistance and increases ease of use, which in turn enhance success possibilities of ERP systems' usage. On the other hand, inadequate or lack of training has been one of the most significant reasons for failure of many ERP systems (**Somers and Nels on, 2004)**[70].

At last the summaries list of Factors affecting on the ERP system implementation get listed as follow, which carry four categories Managerial, Technical, Operational and Financial Critical Factors.

Critical Factors Affecting on ERP Implementation		
Types	**Success Factors**	**Failure Factors**
Managerial/ Organizational	1. Management commitment and leadership. 2. Teamwork and composition. 3. Business plan and vision. 4. Effective communication. 5. Project management. 6. Change management Programme 7. Strong executive sponsorship. 8. Focused project and scope management.	1. Problem in communication. 2. Organizational resistance. 3. Lack of organizational readiness for change. 4. Lack of training and education. 5. Problems relate to integration mechanism, job definition and allocation of responsibilities. 6. Problems related to commitment, support and leadership.

Critical Factors Affecting on ERP Implementation		
Types	**Success Factors**	**Failure Factors**
Managerial/ Organizational	9. User/ SME participation and engagement. 10. Process owner led user training. 11. Knowledge transfer. 12. Align the organization on the true destination. 13. Achieves balanced people, process, and technology change across all areas. 14. ERP must be driven by business case. 15. Active executive direction. 16. Focus on capabilities and benefits, not just going live. 17. Make ERP related decision quickly. 18. Organization commitment. 19. Sell, Sell and continue to sale the ERP to your stakeholder. 20. Build and leverage process enterprise. 21. Adequately resources your project (especially in the final areas). 22. Define metrics and manage them.	7. Problems related to championship and sponsorship. 8. Project size. 9. Lengthily implementation time. 10. High initial investment. 11. Unreasonable deadlines. 12. Insufficient findings. 13. Interface. 14. Organizational politics. 15. Scope creep. 16. Unexpected gaps. 17. Configuration difficulties 18. Failure of commodity evaluation of business process 19. User acceptance 20. Going live is not the end of the ERP journey 21. Companies should anticipate a temporary dip in performance after going live 22. ERP implement is at its core, people and project 23. Lack of top management commitment 24. Inadequate requirement definition 25. Inadequate resources

Critical Factors Affecting on ERP Implementation		
Types	**Success Factors**	**Failure Factors**
Managerial/ Organizational	23. Communicate and manage expectation at go alive. 24. Extend capabilities beyond the ERP foundations. 25. Encourage functional ownership of the project. 26. Develop dependency driven project schedule that can be tracked and managed to provide early alarming and help avoid crises. 27. Implement pre-project readiness assessment and overall project planning. 28. Implement aggressive project management process. 29. Create a project organization to provide planning and quick response to decision making and issues management. 30. Assign clear ownership of benefits.	

Critical Factors Affecting on ERP Implementation		
Types	**Success Factors**	**Failure Factors**
Operational	1. Change management Programme 2. BPR. 3. Performance evaluation and measurement. 4. Training and education 5. Approved solution design. 6. Documented user procedures. 7. Project planning. 8. Architectural design. 9. Transaction project roles to way of life. 10. Data requirement. 11. Apply planning and program management practices throughout the program life cycle. 12. Put the very best people on implementation team. 13. Phased approach. 14. Adequately resources your project (especially in the final areas). 15. Define metrics and manage them. 16. Make the best use of external consultant and experts.	1. Problems related to planning and project management. 2. Problems related to goals and measures. 3. Problems related to project resources. 4. Internal staff adequacy. 5. Staffing (includes turn over). 6. Top management support. 7. Consultants. 8. Discipline. 9. Program management. 10. Stage transition. 11. Benefit realization. 12. Managing risk of ERP projects. 13. Find potential failure points or risk. 14. Analyze potential failure points to determine damage they might do. 15. Assess the probability of failure occurring. 16. Based on first three factors prioritize the risks. 17. Mitigate risk through whatever action is necessary.

Critical Factors Affecting on ERP Implementation		
Types	**Success Factors**	**Failure Factors**
Operational	17. Teach the organization to use new capabilities. 18. Implementation review.	
Financial	1. Ensure the project has sufficient budget. 2. Controlled ERP Implantation Cost 3. Proper Planning and Execution Cost 4. Change in Infrastructure Cost 5. Reduced direct operating costs 6. Decreased information technology costs 7. Miscellaneous 8. Improved cash management	1. Ineffective project cost and time management 2. Market instability 3. Government financial policies 4. Poor Cash and fund flow 5. Un-Structured Financial management 6. Budgetary Overrun 7. Higher Implementation Cost as Compare for Traditional workflow 8. Improper training cost 9. Project Delay cost 10. Uncontrolled Maintenance Cost 11. Redesign cost 12. Ineffective cost control 13. Unavailability or instability of funding 14. Ignoring or underestimating hidden cost

Critical Factors Affecting on ERP Implementation		
Types	**Success Factors**	**Failure Factors**
Technical	1. Appropriate business legacy software 2. Software development, testing, and trouble shooting. 3. ERP architecture selection and system integration. 4. Approved solution design. 5. Targeted data migration strategy. 6. Through system testing. 7. Knowledge transfer. 8. Put the very best people on implementation team. 9. Phased approach. 10. Data conversion. 11. Create partnership better year software. 12. Avoid ERP customization 13. Adequate ERP version 14. Adequate infrastructures and interfaces 15. Adequate legacy systems knowledge	1. Improper ES integration. 2. Ineffective IT infrastructure planning. 3. Software functionality. 4. Technological obsolescence. 5. Application portfolio management. 6. Enhancement and upgrades. 7. A poor fit between the software and users and procedures 8. Unrealistic expectations of two benefits and the ROI(return on investment) 9. Poor ERP package selection 10. Extensive customization

References:

1. Al-Mashari, M., Al-Mudimigh, A., Zairi, M. (2003). "Enterprise resource planning: A taxonomy of critical factors", European Journal of Operational Research, Volume 146, Issue 2, 16 April 2003, pp. 352-364, ISSN 0377-2217

2. Stewart, G. and Rosemann, M. (2001) 'Industry-oriented design of ERP-related curriculum – an Australian initiative', Business Process Management Journal, Vol. 7, No. 3, pp.234–242.

3. D P Goyal "Enterprise Resoruce Planning: A Managerial Perspective", TMH , 2011

4. Mahadeo Jaiswal & Ganesh Vanapali "Enterprise Resource Planning" , MACMILLAN, 2011

5. Gable, G. and Stewart, G. (1999). "SAP R/3 implementation issues for small to medium enterprises," The Proceedings of 5th Americas Conference on Information Systems (AMCIS), Milwaukee, WI

6. W.-L. Shiau, P.-Y. Hsu, and J.-Z. Wang, "Development of measures to assess the ERP adoption of small and medium enterprises," Journal of Enterprise Information Management, vol. 22, 2009, pp. 99.

7. Chen, I. J., "Planning for ERP Systems: Analysis and Future Trend", Business Process Management Journal, 7(5), 374-386, 2001

8. Mabert, V.A., Soni, A., et al. (2001) 'Enterprise resource planning: measuring value', Production and Inventory Management Journal, Vol. 42, Nos. 3–4, pp.46–51.

9. Koh S. C. L. and Simpson Mike (2005), "Change and uncertainty in SME manufacturing environments using ERP". Journal of Manufacturing Technology Management, Volume 16/6, pp. 629-653

10. Leonard Simon, (1997), "Effective use of ERP: Making most of Enterprise resource Planning", chemical market report, Vol-251, Issue-19, PP-30.

11. Rick and Mullin, (1997), "ERP/Supply Chain software integration though i2 Technology ", Vol-159, Issue-25, pp 28-29

12. Parr, A. and Shanks, G. (2000) 'A model of ERP project implementation', Journal of Information Technology, Vol. 15, No. 4, pp.289–304.

13. Rao, S.S. (2000) 'Enterprise resource planning: business needs and technologies', Industrial Management & Data Systems, Vol. 100, No. 2, pp.81–88.
14. Grossman Theodre, Walsh James, "Avoiding the pitfalls of ERP system implementation", Information systems management, 2004
15. Peffers, Ken Charles E. Gangler and Tuure Tuunanen, "Extending Critical Success Factors Methodology to Facilitate Broadly Participative Information System Planning," Journal of Management Information Systems, summer 2003, vol. 20, Issue 1, pp. 51-85.
16. Mohammed H.A. Tafti, (2005) "Risks factors associated with offshore IT outsourcing", Industrial Management & Data Systems, Vol. 105 Iss: 5, pp.549 – 560
17. Jaiswal, M.P. and Kaushik, A. (2005) 'Realising enhanced value due to business network redesign through extended ERP systems: case study of HLLNet', Business Process Management Journal, Vol. 11, No. 2, pp.171–184.
18. S Dezdar, S Ainin, (2011), "ERP systems implementation success: A study on Iranian organizations", International Journal of Current Research and Review, Vol-3, Issue-5, pp-78-100
19. Finney, S. and Corbett, M. (2007), "ERP implementation: a compilation and analysis of critical success factors", Business Process Management Journal, Vol. 13 No. 3, pp. 329-47.
20. Eric T.G. Wang, Sheng-Pao Shih, James J. Jiang, Gary Klein, "The consistency among facilitating factors and ERP implementation success: A holistic view of fit." The Journal of Systems and Software 81 (2008) 1609–1621
21. S Dezdar, S Ainin, (2011), "Measures of success in projects implementing enterprise resource planning", International Journal of Business Performance Management, Vol-12, Issue-4, pp-334-353
22. Davenport, T.H. (1998). —Putting the Enterprise into the Enterprise System|, Harvard Business Review, July/August 1998, 76(4), pp. 121-131, 1999,
23. Melymuka K. (1998), "ERP is growing from being just an efficiency tool to one hat can also help a company grow", Computerworld, Sep-1998.

24. Bingi, P.; Sharma, M.K. and Godla, J. (1999), "Critical issues affecting an ERP implementation", Information Systems Management, Vol. 16 No. 3, pp. 7-14.

25. Holland C. and Light B. (1999) "A Critical Success Factors Model For ERPImplementation", IEEE Software, Vol. 16, No. 3, May/June, pp. 30-36.

26. Sumner, M. 'Critical success factors in enterprise wide information management systems projects', in Proceedings of the SIGCPR '99, 1999, New Orleans, LA, USA, 1999, pp. 297-303, 1999

27. Willcocks, L.P., Sykes, R. (2000) "Enterprise resource planning: the role of the CIO and it function in ERP". Commun, ACM, Issue 43, 4 April 2000, pp. 32-38.

28. Rosario, J.G.(2000) , " On the leading edge: Critical success factor in ERP implementation projects", Business world Philippines

29. Nah, F.F-H., Lau, J.L-S., et al. (2001b) 'Critical factors for successful implementation of enterprise systems', Business Process Management Journal, Vol. 7, No. 3, pp.285–296.

30. Bingi, P.; Sharma, M.K. and Godla, J. (1999), "Critical issues affecting an ERP implementation", Information Systems Management, Vol. 16 No. 3, pp. 7-14.

31. Holland C. and Light B. (1999) "A Critical Success Factors Model For ERPImplementation", IEEE Software, Vol. 16, No. 3, May/June, pp. 30-36.

32. Sumner, M. 'Critical success factors in enterprise wide information management systems projects', in Proceedings of the SIGCPR '99, 1999, New Orleans, LA, USA, 1999, pp.297-303, 1999

33. Ibrahim, A., and J. Goodwin. (1986). Perceived causes of success in small business. American Journal of Small Business, 11 (Fall), 41-50

34. Ghobadian, A.; Gallear, D.,(1996), Total Quality Management in SMEs, Omega, Volume 24, Number 1, 1 February 1996, pp. 83-106

35. Sumner, M. 'Critical success factors in enterprise wide information management systems projects', in Proceedings of the SIGCPR '99, 1999, New Orleans, LA, USA, 1999, pp.297-303,

36. Gunasekaran, A., Okko, P. and Martikainen, T. (1996), "Improving productivity and quality in small and medium enterprises: cases and analysis", International Small Business Journal, Vol. 15 No. 1, pp. 59-72.

37. Sun, A.Y.T., Yazdani, A., et al. (2005) 'Achievement assessment for Enterprise Resource Planning (ERP) system implementations based on Critical Success Factors (CSFs)', International Journal of Production Economics, Vol. 98, No. 2, pp.189–203.

38. Adam, F. and O'Doherty, P. (2000) 'Lessons from enterprise resource planning implementation in Ireland – towards smaller and shorter ERP projects', Journal of Information Technology, Vol. 15, No. 4, pp.305–316

39. Mabert, V.A., Ashok, S. and Venkataramanan, M.A. (2000), "Enterprise resource planning survey of US manufacturing firms", Production and Inventory Management Journal, Vol. 41 No. 2, pp. 528

40. Rodney McAdam, Renee Reid, (2001) "SME and large organisation perceptions of knowledge management: comparisons and contrasts", Journal of Knowledge Management, Vol. 5 Iss: 3, pp.231 – 241

41. J. R. Muscatello, M. H. Small, and I. J. Chen, "Implementing enterprise resource planning (ERP) systems in small and midsize manufacturing firms," International Journal of Operations and Production Management, vol. 23, 2003, pp. 850-871

42. S. Laukkanen, S. Sarpola, and P. Hallikainen, "Enterprise size matters: objectives and constraints of ERP adoption," Journal of Enterprise Information Management, vol. 20, 2007, pp. 319-334

43. Mabert, V. A., Soni, A., Venkataramanan, M. A. (2003) "Enterprise resource planning: Managing the implementation process", European Journal of Operational – Research, Volume 146, Issue 2, 16 April 2003, pp. 302-314, ISSN 0377-2217

44. Markus, M.L., Axline, S., Petrie, D. and Tanis, C. (2000), "Learning from adopters' experiences with ERP: problems encountered and success achieved", Journal of Information Technology, Vol. 15, pp. 24565

45. Buonanno, G., Faverio, P., et al. (2005) 'Factors affecting ERP system adoption: a comparative analysis between SMEs and large companies', Journal of Enterprise Information Management, Vol. 18, No. 4, pp.384–426

46. E-Commerce 2009, 5/E: Kenneth C. Laudon, New York University: Carol Guercio Traver

47. Parijat Upadhyay and Pranab K. Dan (2009), —ERP in Indian SME's: A Post Implementation Study of the Underlying Critical Success Factors|,

International Journal of Management Innovation System ISSN 1943-1384, Vol. 1, No. 2: E1

48. Rana Basu, Parijat Upadhyay, Manik C. Das, Pranab K. Dan, 2012, An approach to identify issues affecting ERP implementation in Indian SMEs, Journal of Industrial Engineering and Management, Vol 5, No 1.

49. P. T. Kale, S. S. Banwait and S. C. Laroiya (2007), —Enterprise Resource Planning Implementation in Indian SMEs: Issues and Challenges|, National Institute of Technical Teachers' Training and Research, www.csisigegov.org/critical_pdf/27_242-248.pdf

50. Levy Margi, Powell Philip, (2006), "Strategies for growth in SMEs: The role of Information and Information Systems", Information Processing and Management: an International Journal. Vol 42

51. Nah, F.F-H., Lau, J.L-S., et al. (2001b) 'Critical factors for successful implementation of enterprise systems', Business Process Management Journal, Vol. 7, No. 3, pp.285–296

52. Malhotra, R., and Temponi, C. (2010). Critical decisions for ERP integration: Small business issues. International Journal of Information Management, 30(1), 28-37

53. Cragg, P.B. and Zinatelli, N. (1995), "The evolution of information systems in small firms", Information & Management, Vol. 29, pp. 18

54. Bingi, P.; Sharma, M.K. and Godla, J. (1999), "Critical issues affecting an ERP implementation", Information Systems Management, Vol. 16 No. 3, pp. 7-14

55. Al-Mashari, M., Al-Mudimigh, A., et al. (2003) 'Enterprise resource planning: a taxonomy of critical factors', European Journal of Operational Research, Vol. 146, No. 2, pp.352–364

56. Shang, S. and Seddon, P. (2002). "Assessing and managing the benefits of enterprise systems: the business manager's perspective". Information Systems Journal, Vol. 12, No. 4, pp271-299.

57. Ferranti, M (1998), "Debunking ERP misconceptions", Infoworld, 17 August 1998, pp 46

58. George Westerman, 1999, "Tektronix, Inc.: Global ERP Implementation", Harvard Business School Pub. Corporation

59. J. Esteves and V. L. Bohorquez, "An Updated ERP Systems Annotated Bibliography: 2001 – 2005," Communications of the Association for Information Systems vol. 19, 2007, pp. 18

60. Bancroft, N. H. (1996) Implementing R/3. How to introduce a large system into a large organization. Manning/Prentice Hall.

61. Corcoran , (1998), "ERP is changing manufacturing Jobs", Infowords, July edd.

62. P. Duchessi, C.M. Schaninger, D.R. Hobbs, and L.P. Pentak, "Determinants of Success in Implementing Material Requirements Planning (MRP)," Journal of Manufacturing and Operations Management, Vol. 1, No. 2, 1988, pp. 263-302.

63. Dawson J and Owens J. 2008. 'Critical Success Factors in the Chartering Phase: A Case Study of an ERP Implementation'. International Journal of Enterprise Information Systems, 4(3): 9-24.

64. Serafeimidis, V., and Smithson, S. (2000) "Information Systems Evaluation in Practice: A Case Study of Organizational Change," Journal of Information Technology, Vol 15, No 2, pp 93-105.

65. Zhang L., Lee K.O.M., Zhang Z. and Banerjee P.(2002), —Critical Success Factors of Enterprise Resource Planning Systems Implementations Success in China|, IEEE Computer Society

66. Dezdar, S., and Sulaiman, A. (2009) Successful enterprise resource planning implementation: taxonomy of critical factors. Industrial Management & Data Systems 109(8): 1035-1052.

67. Pearce, F. (2004), Business Building and Promotion: Strategic and Tactical Planning, Pearman Cooperation Alliance, Houston, TX, June.

68. Esteves, J. and Pastor, J. (2001) 'Enterprise resource planning systems research: an annotated bibliography', Communications of the Association of Information Systems, Vol. 7, pp.1–52

69. Nah, F.F-H., Lau, J.L-S., et al. (2001b) 'Critical factors for successful implementation of enterprise systems', Business Process Management Journal, Vol. 7, No. 3, pp.285–296

70. Syed M. Ahmed, Irtishad Ahmad, Salman Azhar and Suneetha Mallikarjuna, (2007), "Implementation of Enterprise Resource Planning (ERP) Systems In The Construction Industry".pp1-8

71. Somers, T.M. and Nelson, K.G. (2004) 'A taxonomy of players and activities across the ERP project life cycle', Information and Management, Vol. 41, No. 3, pp.257–278

72. Fergal Carton and Frederic Adam, (2005)," Understanding the Impact of Enterprise Systems on Management Decision Making: An Agenda for Future Research", Electronic Journal Information Systems Evaluation Volume 13, Issue 1, PP – 99-106.

73. Elisabeth J. Umble, M.Michael Umble (2002):"Avoiding ERP implementation Failure", Industrial Management

74. W. H. IP, C. L. LAI and C. W. LAU, (2004) ,"A Web-based Training Model of Enterprise Resources Planning for the Manufacturing Industry", Int. J. Engng Ed. Vol. 20, No. 5, pp. 733-741

75. Olhager, J. and Selldin, E. (2003) 'Enterprise resource planning survey of Swedish manufacturing firms', European Journal of Operational Research, Vol. 146, No. 2, pp.365–373

76. Sarkis, J. and Sundarraj, R.P. (2003) 'Managing large-scale global enterprise resource planning systems: a cast study at Texas Instruments', International Journal of Information Management, Vol. 23, No. 5, pp.431–442

77. Al-Mashari, M., Al-Mudimigh, A., Zairi, M. (2003). "Enterprise resource planning: A taxonomy of critical factors", European Journal of Operational Research, Volume 146, Issue 2, 16 April 2003, pp. 352-364, ISSN 0377-2217

78. J. R. Muscatello, M. H. Small, and I. J. Chen, "Implementing enterprise resource planning (ERP) systems in small and midsize manufacturing firms," International Journal of Operations and Production Management, vol. 23, 2003, pp. 850-871

79. Edward A. Duplaga and Marzie Astani,(2003),"IMPLEMENTING ERP IN MANUFACTURING", INFORMATION SYSTEMS MANAGEMENT SUMMER, pp-68-75

80. S. Laukkanen, S. Sarpola, and P. Hallikainen, "ERP System Adoption – Does the Size Matter?," in Hawaii International Conference on System Sciences (HICSS) 2005, pp. 226b-226b

81.	Somers, T., Nelson, K. (2001) "The Impact of Critical Success Factors across the Stages of Enterprise Resource Planning Implementations", 34th Annual Hawaii International Conference on System Sciences (HICSS-34)-Volume 8, pp.8016

82.	V. A. Mabert, A. Soni, and M. A. Venkataramanan, "The impact of organization size on enterprise resource planning (ERP) implementations in the US manufacturing sector," Omega, vol. 31, 2003, pp. 235-246

83.	Mandal, P. and Gunasekaran, A. (2003) 'Issues in implementing ERP: a case study', European Journal of Operational Research, Vol. 146, No. 2, pp.274–283

84.	Nah, F. and Delgado, S. (2006) Critical Success Factors for ERP Implementation and Upgrade, Journal of Computer Information Systems, 46, 5, 99-113

85.	Christopher (1999): "Enterprise Resource Planning: A Business Approach to Systems Development", Proceedings of 32nd Hawaii International Conference on System Sciences

86.	Ross, Jeanne W., and Michael R. Vitale. "The ERP revolution: surviving vs. thriving." Information systems frontiers2.2 (2000): 233-241.

87.	G. Gable and G. Stewart, "SAP R/3 Implementation Issues for Small to Medium Enterprises," in Americas Conference on Information Systems (AMCIS), 1999

88.	F. Adam and P. O'Doherty, "Lessons from enterprise resource planning implementations in Ireland – towards smaller and shorter ERP projects," Journal of Information Technology, vol. 15, 2000, pp. 305-316

89.	H. Liang and Y. Xue, "Coping with ERP-related contextual issues in SMEs: a vendor's perspective," The Journal of Strategic Information Systems, vol. 13, 2004, pp. 399-415

90.	C. Doom, K. Milis, S. Poelmans, and E. Bloemen, "Critical success factors for ERP implementations in Belgian SMEs," Journal of Enterprise Information Management, vol. 23, 2009, pp. 378 – 406

91.	Y. Xia, P. Lok, and S. Yang, "The ERP implementation of SME in China," in 6th International Conference on Service Systems and Service Management, 2009, pp. 135-140

92. V. A. Mabert, A. Soni, and M. A. Venkataramanan, "The impact of organization size on enterprise resource planning (ERP) implementations in the US manufacturing sector," Omega, vol. 31, 2003, pp. 235-246

93. J.-H. Wu and Y.-M. Wang, "Enterprise resource planning experience in Taiwan: an empirical study comparative analysis," in Hawaii International Conference on System Sciences (HICSS), 2003, pp. 10

94. Nandhakumar, J., Rossi, M., et al. (2005) 'The dynamics of contextual forces of ERP implementation', Journal of Strategic Information Systems, Vol. 14, No. 2, pp.221–242

95. Laframboise, K. (2002). Business performance and enterprise resource planning. Proceedings of the Tenth European Conference on Information Systems (Wrycza S ed.), Gdansk, Poland.

96. Westrup, C. & Knight, F. (2000). Consultants and enterprise resource planning (ERP) systems. Proceedings of the Eighth European Conference on Information Systems (Hansen HR, Bichler M, Mahrer H eds.), Wien, Austria.

97. J Magnusson, A Nilsson, F Carlsson, (2004), "Forecasting ERP implementation success-Towards a grounded framework" – ECIS 2004 Proceedings.

98. Schubert, P. and Leimenstoll, U. "Personalization of e-Commerce Applications in SMEs: Conclusions from an Empirical Study in Switzerland", Journal of Electronic Commerce in Organizations, Volume 2, Number 3, 2004, pp. 21–39.

99. James T. Lindley, Sharon Topping, Lee T. Lindley, (2008) "The hidden financial costs of ERP software", Managerial Finance, Vol. 34 Iss: 2, pp.78–90

100. Bradford, M. and Florin, J. (2003) 'Examining the role of innovation diffusion factors on the implementation success of enterprise resource planning systems', International Journal of Accounting Information Systems, Vol. 4, No. 3, pp.205–225

101. Somers, T.M. and Nelson, K.G. (2004) 'A taxonomy of players and activities across the ERP project life cycle', Information and Management, Vol. 41, No. 3, pp.257–278

102. Zhang L., Lee K.O.M., Zhang Z. and Banerjee P.(2002), —Critical Success Factors of Enterprise Resource Planning Systems Implementations Success in China|, IEEE Computer Society

103. A. Winkelmann and K. Klose, "Experiences While Selecting, Adapting and Implementing ERP Systems in SMEs: A Case Study," in Americas Conference on Information Systems (AMCIS), 2008

104. A. Nattawee and R. Siriluck, "Developing ERP implementation success factors of Thai SMEs," in GMSARN International Conference on Sustainable Development: Issues and Prospects for the GMS 2008

105. T. C. Loh and S. C. L. Koh, "Critical elements for a successful enterprise resource planning implementation in small-and medium-sized enterprises," International Journal of Production Research, vol. 42, 2004, pp. 3433-3455

106. D. Reuther and G. Chattopadhyay, "Critical factors for ERP system selection and implementation projects within small to medium enterprises," in International Engineering Management Conference, Vol.2, pp. 851-855

107. B. Snider, G. J. C. d. Silveira, and J. Balakrishnan, "ERP implementation at SMEs: analysis of five Canadian cases," International Journal of Operations and Production Management, vol. 29, 2009, pp. 4-29

108. V. Morabito, S. Pace, and P. Previtali, "ERP Marketing and Italian SMEs," European Management Journal, vol. 23, 2005, pp. 590-598

109. Gupta, A. (2000) 'Enterprise resource planning: the emerging organizational value systems', Industrial Management & Data Systems, Vol. 100, No. 3, pp.114–118

Chapter 03

ERP System Fundamentals & Its Relevance with Manufacturing Units

3.1 ERP means:

In today's era is rapid development era where everyone looking for fast growth in their work and simultaneously the organization also want better utilization of resources. Every organization try to keep limited number of resource while running any project to control the cost of the project which will also help to increase their profitability. The resource utilization is one of the most difficult and challenging job for any organization and every organization try reduce the human dependency plus need as automated tool which help to increase the effectiveness in integrity between all different functional aspect of the organization and decrease the human efforts which might affect of accuracy and rapid response during dynamic situation during workflow. To face and fulfill all above aspect the organization require an integrated, automated, fast, feasible computerized tool which help in decision making, strategy planning, monitoring and controlling all the activities done during organization Works.

The above all aspects are having one common solution i.e. ERP. Enterprise Resource planning (ERP) is latest high-end solution, information has lent to business application. The ERP solution seek to streamline and integrate operation processes and information flows ion the company to synergize the resources of an organization namely men, material, money and machine through information.

ERP serves many industries and numerous functional areas in an integrated fashion, attempting to automate operations from supply chain management, inventory control, manufacturing scheduling and production, sales support, customer relationship management, financial and cost accounting, human resources and almost any other data oriented management process. ERP systems are designed to enhance organization's competitiveness by upgrading an organization's ability to generate timely and accurate information throughout the enterprise and its supply chain. A successful ERP system implementation can shorten production cycles, increases accuracy of demand for materials management & sourcing and leads to inventory reduction because of material management, etc. Moreover it can be used as a primary tool for re-engineering.

ERP Implementation process: – ERP implantation process have three main Phases, firstly Pre-implementation phase, secondly In-implementation phase and finally Post-implementation phase.

Every phase is unique but interdependent to each other, following table shows ERP implementation in very detail;

Phase	Pre-implementation phase	In-implementation phase	Post-implementation phase
Process	BPR + BE	Development Approach + SDLC	Monitoring + Maintenance
Activity	• Analysis • Business engineering • TQM • Business modeling	• Planning • Design • Implementation • Testing • Deployment • Training • Use	• Review • Monitor • Resolve • Control • Maintenance
Outcome	Ready to implement ERP	ERP is ready to use	ERP Results and Reviews

Figure 3.1 ERP implementation model [1].

In the above mention activity every phase has different sub-activities; in pre-implementation phase the organization doing Business Process Reengineering (BPR) in which analysis current business process to achieve dramatic improvement, in critical, contemporary measures of performance such as cost, quality, service and speed. Ultimately BPR decide the strength and weakness of the organization and give the result to management need some improvement in their old and traditional way of working. After getting idea from BPR the organization has to do Business Engineering (BE) where emerging two concept namely Information Technology and Business Process Engineering. Which help to maintain total quality management to maintain the quality in their existing working system and then the business management and modeling has to perform which gives an idea about different modules of organization and their internal relationship, where the organization get the different data models and information which gives the resource requirement and utilization needs through some automated tool i.e. ERP.

After analyze the need of ERP in organization In-implementation Phase, where actual Software development life cycle (SDLC) going to implement.ERP implementation is the special and sensitive process for organization, it brings together in one platform, different business functions, different personalities, procedure, ideology with an aim to pool knowledge base to effectively integrate and bring worthwhile and beneficial changes throughout the organization. In implementation phase first and most important process is analysis of the current state and working environment, information, need, resources, objective and goals of the organization. After analysis the design step going to implement where all the different functional and modular information gathered together logically. Next process is to development of software according to its design using some appropriate software tools e.g. SAP, BAAN, OracleSoft etc. by getting actual package development the most and crucial process is testing where checking whether the ERP is implemented according to its objective or not in different prospective like functional, managerial, operational etc. if everything goes as per plan then the deployment of the software package in organization for actual use. Before handover the ERP into the organizational people the ERP development team has to provide special training to give some motivation to the organizational employee to ERP specifications and the usability terminology. Finally the technical team at organizational side will use the ERP for which it actually gets implemented. The Post-implantation phase also continuous, dynamic and time consuming process in nature because none of the team member guaranty about the problems which may come after the ERP implementation. This phase reviews the ERP tool and monitor regularly, if any technical issue may arise then according to its nature the suitable resolving get done for maintaining continuous control over the ERP system.

ERP (Enterprise Resource Planning) is an industry term for the broad set of activities supported by multi-module application software that help a manufacturer or other business managers [2]. Originally, ERP packages were targeted at the manufacturing industry. ERP is a massive software engine that seeks to provide one seamless interface to all departments, systems and existing data within the organization. Enterprise Resource Planning systems are commercial software packages that enable integration of transaction-oriented data and business processes throughout the organization and perhaps eventually throughout the entire inter organizational supply chain [3]. A typical ERP system integrates all of a company's functions by allowing the modules to share and transfer information freely [4],[5].

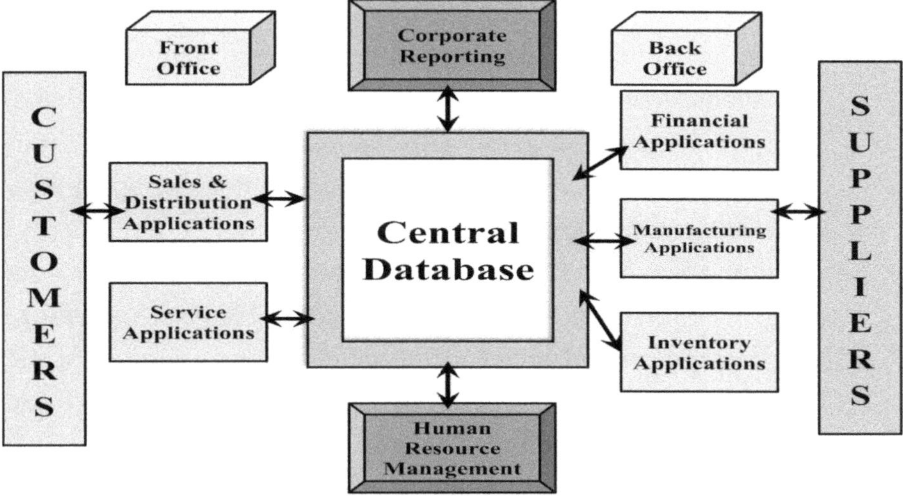

Figure 3.2 ERP System.(Source: Rashid, Hossain & Patrick 2002)

Year of Development	Evolution in ERP Version
2000s	Extended Enterprise Resource Planning
1990s	Enterprise Resource Planning (ERP)
1980s	Manufacturing Resource Planning (MRP II)
1970s	Material Requirement Planning (MRP)
1960s	Inventory Control Packages

Figure 3.3 Evolution of ERP Implantation.

(Source: ERP Demystified, Alexis Leon)

3.2 ERP Characteristics:

Any system has to possess few key characteristics to qualify for a true ERP solution. These features are:

- **Flexibility:** An ERP system should be flexible to respond to the changing needs of an enterprise. The client server technology enables ERP to run across various database back ends through Open Database Connectivity (ODBC).
- **Modular & Open:** ERP system has to have open system architecture. This means that any module can be interfaced

or detached whenever required without affecting the other modules. It should support multiple hardware platforms for the companies having heterogeneous collection of systems. It must support some third party add-ons also. ERP provides multi-platform, multi-facility, multi-mode manufacturing, multi-currency, multi-lingual facilities.

- **Comprehensive:** It should be able to support variety of organizational functions and must be suitable for a wide range of business organizations. It supports strategic and business planning activities, operational planning and execution activities, creation of Materials and Resources.

    ERP covering all functional areas like manufacturing, selling and distribution, payables, receivables, inventory, accounts, human resources, purchases etc.

- **Beyond The Company:** It should not be confined to the organizational boundaries, rather support the on-line connectivity to the other business entities of the organization. ERP allows automatic introduction of the latest technologies like Electronic Fund Transfer (EFT), Electronic Data Interchange (EDI), Internet, Intranet, Video conferencing, E-Commerce etc. ERP provides intelligent business tools like decision support system, Executive information system, Data mining and easy working systems to enable better decisions.

- **Best Business Practices:** It must have a collection of the best business processes applicable worldwide. An ERP package imposes its own logic on a company's strategy, culture and organization.

3.3 Need of ERP

- **Integrate financial information:** As the CEO tries to understand the company's overall performance, he may find many different versions of the truth. ERP creates a single version of the truth that cannot be questioned because everyone is using the same system.

- **Integrate customer order information:** ERP systems can become the place where the customer order lives from the time a customer service representative receives it until the loading dock ships the merchandise and finance sends an invoice. By having this information in one software system companies can keep track of orders more easily, and coordinate manufacturing, inventory and shipping among many different locations simultaneously.

- **Standardize and speed up manufacturing processes:** Manufacturing companies especially those with an appetite for mergers and acquisitions often find that multiple business units across the company make the same transaction / recording / report using different methods and computer systems. ERP systems come with standard methods for automating some of the steps of a manufacturing process.

- **Reduce inventory:** ERP helps the manufacturing process flow more smoothly, and it improves visibility of the order fulfillment process inside the company. That can lead to reduced inventories of the materials used to make products (work-in-progress inventory), and it can help users better plan deliveries to customers, reducing the finished goods inventory at the warehouses and shipping docks.

- **Standardize HR information:** Especially in companies with multiple business units, HR may not have a unified, simple method for tracking employees' time and communicating with them about benefits and services. ERP can fix that.

3.4 Benefits of ERP:

Following are some of the benefits they achieved by implementing the ERP packages;

- Gives Accounts Payable personnel increased control of invoicing and payment processing and thereby boosting their productivity and eliminating their reliance on computer personnel for these operations.

- Reduce paper documents by providing on-line formats for quickly entering and retrieving information.
- Permitting the posting daily instead of monthly, this improves the timeliness in information.
- Great accuracy in information with detailed content, better presentation for increase satisfactory for the auditors.
- More efficient cash collection, say, material reduction in delay in payments by customers.
- Enables quick response to change in business operations and market conditions.
- Improves supply-demand linkage with remote locations and branches in different countries.
- Improves International operations by supporting a variety of tax structures, invoicing schemes, multiple currencies, multiple period accounting and languages.
- Improves information access and management throughout the enterprise.

3.5 Business Process Re-engineering

As Figure 1.1 shows the ERP implementation process having three phase during its implementation Pre-Implementation, In-Implementation and Post-Implementation and BPR is the process comes in picture during the very first phase of ERP implantation. Business Process Reengineering (BPR) is an organizational method demanding radical redesign of business processes in order to achieve efficiency, better quality and more competitive production (Hammer and Champy, 1993).

3.5.1 BPR Process Overview.

Michael Hammer is the pioneer of the concept called business process reengineering in the 1990. They define the BPR as "the fundamental rethinking and radical redesigning of business process to achieve dramatic improvement in critical contemporary measures of performance, such as cost, quality, services, and speed". Homeas H. Davenpoirt is the American academician and well known author in area of business strategy defines the BPR terms as "encompasses the envisioning of new work strategies, the actual process design activity, and the implementation of the changes in all its complex technological, human, and organizational diminutions". BPR gives the idea about the current working environment and business process, on the bases of this information the organization can take the decision to redesign the business process according to the new plans and objectives to reach the new milestones in their business.

3.5.2 BPR Implantation Model.

The execution of the BPR is quite similar to the traditional lifecycle of the software development and we can find following step in the BPR process;

Step 01	• Planning for BPR
Step 02	• Data Collection and Analysis
Step 03	• Design the BPR Process
Step 04	• Implenment the BPR Process
Step 05	• Test BPR Progress

Figure 3.4 BPR Implementation Model

(Source: Amar R. Mudiraj, 2014) [6]

- **Planning for BPR**

  Top level management creates their mission and vision in such level, so they going for such huge and long term costly process like BPR. Every organization has to think differently and take the decision for implementing ERP in their organization. After finalizing the Top level management for ERP implementation, they plan for the BPR process to indentifying the current business process and loopholes in the current working style. During the planning phase the organizational top level management has to think about the BPR as positive way. Organization has to consider their vision and mission in-front of their aim to plan for the BPR

- **Data Collection and Analysis**

  After plan the BPR process the organization start to collect the data from the different resources like external and internal resources, which require clarifying current scenario of the business process. Top level vision and mission, protocol of the organization, current technology, problem and treats faced during the current business process, risk management in the business process, cost and time constraint in traditional business process etc. after collecting all the data from the different resources the BPR team will identifying the GAP of existing process and the factors which are affecting on the current business process and their impact level on the business.

- **Design the BPR Process**

  Now the organization is ready with all the detail information about the factors, methodology of traditional business process. In the design the BPR process the BPR team will create step by step approaches for reaching their aim. Development team will distribute the whole task among the all team member of BPR. While design the BPR process the team will always have many alternative which help to implement team to use in the different scenario and situation. Most suitable alternative will get select by the team member, which gives them more potential and positive answer of their question which the team planned to find in the BPR process.

- **Implements BPR Process.**

  The implementation phase is where reengineering efforts meet the most resistance and hence it is by far the most difficult one[7]. Here the planned new business process will meet the traditional business process. When the organization implements the BPR process, the time and cost is consider at very high priority level. While implementing the BPR process the two basic strategies are generally used. Firstly, implement complete BPR at same time. Secondly, implement partially i.e. implement phased approach (Alexis leon, 2008). Implementation phase requires continuous monitoring for identifying the structural and behavioral changes in the existing process and also the people who are get affected by the new BPR process directly or in-directly.

- **Test BPR Progress**

  While finalized the BPR process execution, the organization has to take the better control over the process by continuous monitoring the progress of the new business process. Every testing needs some of benchmarks and we expect that, the new business process will reach the goals set by the organization or not. The testing of BPR progress is validates on the bases of time and cost factors. While testing the progress we have to monitor the outcome of the process and consistency in the outcome. BPR is process not one sitting process, so it requires continuous monitoring to analyzing the outcomes. As the process gives the outcomes as per the plan then it acceptable, but if it is not upto the mark then organization has to try some other alternatives which they have planned during the implementation phase.

3.5.3 Factors Affecting on BPR Process

Now in this section we are tries to analyze the factors which are affecting on the BPR process and all the factors also has different aspects of the organization like managerial, operational, financial and technical.

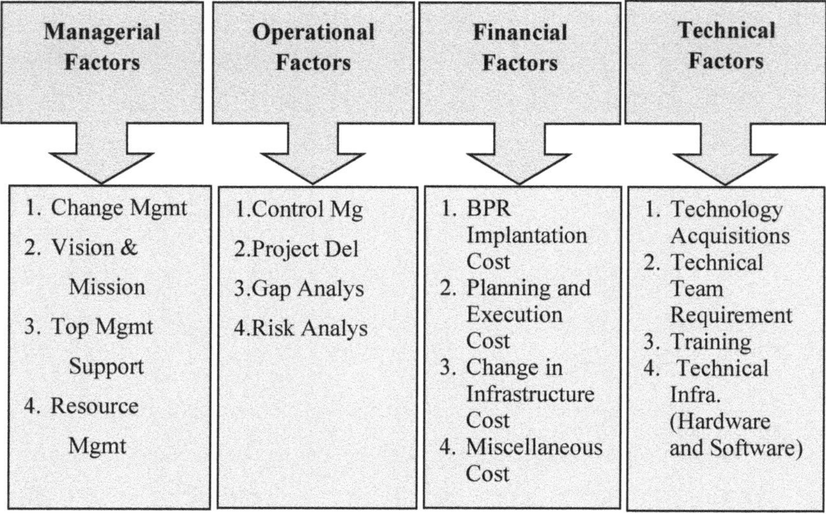

Figure 3.5 Factors Affecting on BPR Process

(Source: Amar R. Mudiraj, 2014).[6]

- **Managerial Factors:**

  These factors are related with the Top level management like the managers, board members etc. As they have the vision and mission in their mind, they plays very vital and un-avoidable role in the BPR process. Chang management means the organization is ready to accept the change in the existing working style. They also keep the bright and clear vision & mission to accept the new changes in the organization. While performing the same, the Top level management support requires by the development team. Every process require ample amount of resource to get into the reality and if the given resources are limited, it has to get utilize in such proper manner that the wastage or idealism of the resources will not happen during the BPR implementation.

- **Operational Factors:**

  During the implementation of the BPR process the better control over the operational activity is more important. By better control over the operational activity we can identify and analyze the different constraints like time, cost, and resources and also change in behavioral and structural changes in the BPR process implementation. While considering the better monitoring and control over the BPR process if any gap get indentifying in the process, so immediate action has to take to avoid any serious consequences get occurred because of gap. Risk analysis play a very vital role in the BPR process by which we can identify the internal and external risk which can affect badly on the process.

- **Financial Factors:**

  It's a fact that, to get more money you need more money. Finance is the factor which has more closed link with the business as compare to any other factors. While considering the financial factors, we mostly concentrate on overall BPR implementation cost. As the BPR process is very time consuming process, it requires more resources and for the resources you require more finance. Other than above, planning and execution cost also play the important role in the financial factors category, where resources like planning and execution time, people involve in the team require more finance. With the same costing factors the business process reengineering have to consider infrastructure cost where the organization might be require more and advance infrastructure to establish and implement new BPR process. Finally some Miscellaneous cost which need on the basis of external bodies of the organization like trend union, government financial policy, stock market also affect on the BPR process during its execution and implementation.

- **Technical Factors:**

  One of the most important and critical factor during the BPR process implementation is technical factors in other word IT factors. First and most important factor is the organizational acquisition for the new technology, which it takes long time and if there is time taken activity then the cost of the process get increase. To implement, monitor and control the BPR process we must have well qualified, technically sound and highly experienced team members. After implementation people who are going to work on the new process they must be familiar of the new technology and working environment so they have to get trained before going on actual work. In this session lots of efforts has to take by the technical team of BPR process. Technical infrastructure for BPR process also plays the very crucial and vital role, where the organization has to setup the new hardware and software for the new business process. The installation, backup, controlling and monitoring the equipment, analyzing integrity and consistency in the IT infrastructural components has to get maintain and monitor to avoid future problem.

3.6 Risk Management in ERP implementation

3.6.1 Introduction

The notions of Risk replicate the variation in the allocation of potential outcomes, their like hoods and their biased values (Arrow, 1965). Risk is used as a synonym for potential troubles in the project linked with the ambiguity of the possible outcomes. The ERP consists of strongly connected interdependencies of business processes, software systems, and process reengineering (Wright and Wright, 2001; Xu et al., 2002), that present exceptional risk things get created with software systems and its broad applications.

ERP systems provide significant benefits, and companies adopted them with the goal of replacing inefficient stand-alone legacy systems, increasing communications between business functions, increasing information processing efficiencies, improving customer relations, and improving overall decision making[8]. The benefits from ERP comprise a packed set of statement and tools as apparatus across the organization with complete company using the same set of records. The coverage of benefits depends on how far across an organization it is taken and whether companies continue to upgrade their systems. ERP make stronger to the companies by providing a backbone for construction of enterprise-wide answer like sophisticated scheduling and customer association and administration. ERP also provides data uniformity and a universal view of data.

3.6.2 Risk Management

The organization of risk is construed as mastering the surroundings and making belongings happen in the designed manner. Managers need to enumerate all the prospect of the promising end result, and appraise the benefit or the loss of that alternative in numbers. Then, they should choose the path that directs to the best estimated value. However theorists see that, it is never possible to have full amount control over risk. Top Level Managers and decision-makers recognize and arrangement with risk every day. For them, risk is the whole things that can make a project interruption or some time fail. Their achievement is connected with the success of strong-minded goals, within the accurate timeframe and resources. Consequently managers need a tool to investigate the risk in a project and have technique to deal with it.

3.6.3 Risk Management Cycle

- **Indentify the risk**

  Identifying and listing the threats, hazards, problems, and other negative issues that may affect the system; List out the list of the risk with their sources of information.

- **Analysis the risk**

  Qualitative risk analysis: documenting the characteristics of the risks, analyzing their effects on the system, and understanding their relationships;

  Quantitative risk assessment: estimating the probability of occurrence of the risks, and numerically assessing their impact on the system;

- **Design the Solution on risk**

  Planning and developing options and actions to prevent or reduce the negative impact of risks on the system, and enhance their positive impacts.

  Keep multiple options available for keep ready for any other alternative situation comes in the frame.

- **Deploy and Test the solution on risk**

  Implement the Possible countermeasure to avoid the risk.

  Test and analyze the impact level of the solution on the risk for which the solutions are get design and deploy on the organization.

- **Monitor and Control the risk**

  Risk management is the on-going process so it is necessary for the mangers and decision makers to keep the eyes on the behavior of the ERP systems.

  It is not possible for anyone to have complete control over the risk so, it is better to have optimal control over the risks to reduce the impact of them on ERP systems.

Figure 3.6 Risk Managmenet Cycle.

(Source: Dr. R.S. Wanare, A. R. Mudiraj, 2014)[12]

3.6.4 Potential Risks in ERP Implementation

- **Management Risk**

  Ineffective project management techniques and practices

  Bad managerial conduct

  Inadequate change management

  Poor leadership

  Inadequate Strategy management

- **Technology Risk**

  Technical barrier

  Inadequate IT system capability

  Inadequate IT system maintenance and upgrading

  Insufficient legacy system management

  Lack of information distribution or incorporation with non-ERP systems

- **Operational Risk**

  Inadequate BPR

  Inadequate guidance and training

  Ineffective communication system

  Ineffective consulting services

  Inadequate IT purveyor dependability and performance

- **Financial Risk**

  Ineffective project cost and time management

  Market instability

  Government financial policies

  Cash and fund flow

- **Other Risk**

  Ineffective strategic belief and strategic preparation

  Inadequate ERP choice

  Cultural and environmental issues

  Legal and regulatory risks

  Multi-site issues

3.7 Risk Treatment or Countermeasure process on Risk factors in ERP Implementation

A risk treatment is mandatorily a part of a successful risk managing plan. The plan here means how you react to the reported probable risks. It details on approaches on how to attempt with the various risks – low or high, satisfactory or undesirable. The plan also summarizes the responsibility and tasks of the team members. Risk treatment also known as risk control system, is that part of the risk management where conclusion are prepared regarding how to deal with risks either in the external or internal surroundings. Ahead of we go aboard on risk treatment there is something called as risk reply preparation that desires to be taken care of. A successful risk management preparation may negotiate through following checklist:

- **Construct a List:**
  Before starting or make a decision on anything else it is essential to construct a list of potential risks. Even the minutest details need to be taken care of. Something that shows a miniature hazard now may change into a potential risk in the near prospect.
- **Prioritize the Risks:**
  Arrange the risk in order of priority. Those that need to be deal with first are listed first. Risks are prioritized on the origin of scale of blow and the probability of happening.
- **Developing and Action Plan:**
  Plans are intended to reduce the collision of the risk and to check the occurrence. In addition, an action plan in developed against each risk i.e. in occasion of incidence how do we react to the risk, who all will be accountable and what are the eventuality.
- **HR Deployment:**
  Now people are deputed at precise points with precise roles. They work in cycle with the whole team and are particularly organized to assume designed procedures in case the predictable risks come correct.

- **Announcement:**
Finally, announcement of the plan to stakeholders (both internal and external becomes necessary). Present the plan to those who are supposed to make key involvements.

- **Risk Reply Preparation**
Risks Reply Preparation no hesitation is an vital phase of risk treatment. The preparation covers converse and appraise inputs like risk register, risk profiles and cause control matrix. Strategies are devising and documented in this stage. The subsequent four various strategies are discussed upon.

- **Avoidance of Risk:**
Risk avoidance requires identification of the risks first and foremost. This can be achieved through previous project experiences and histories. An analysis is then made upon those that have a tendency to arise upfront at project initiation. Then finally a course of action is arrived upon after assessing the relative impact of the risks.

- **Conveying to Risk:**
Risk conveying is one of the superior means to reduce the collision of the risk. In project management as in finance a risk is frequently convey to a third party. It only means the collision of risk is diluted to a degree that event or project for that issue does not undergo a body blow.

- **Justifying Risk:**
Risk Justification is a organize procedure that basically stops a risk sooner than it starts building an impact and transport it to a tolerable level. Often a contingency plan is put in place to prevent the risk.

- **Tolerating Risk:**
Finally, there are certain risks that are manifest. This strategy is the best when the risk is small. But there has to be an owed preparation for the similar such as formative when the project

will be showing to the risk and producing a small modification consequently. A risk that is tolerable can be measured reactive since no act at all is taken upon the same.

As a result of the risk reply preparation a variety of risks and the equivalent strategies are acknowledged. A risk record is ready that contains all details time to time as their occurrence, priority and the people concerned in management the risk. The risks have already classified as either internal or external.

3.8 SWOT Analysis need to apply while ERP implementation.

3.8.1 Introduction to SWOT Analysis:

The SWOT Analysis the business tool used to highlight the different factors affecting on the business process which the organization plan to design and implement for achieve the mission and vision of the organization. The SWOT analysis firstly describe by the American business and management consultant Albert S. Humphrey in the 1960 and 1970. The SWOT stands for **S**trengths, **W**eaknesses, **O**pportunities, and Threats. The tool identifies the internal and external key factor which seems to be very crucial and important to achieve the organizational goals and objectives. Any organization which want to implement ERP the organization look for the factors which effecting on this process to control and mange the problems which comes during the ERP implementation.

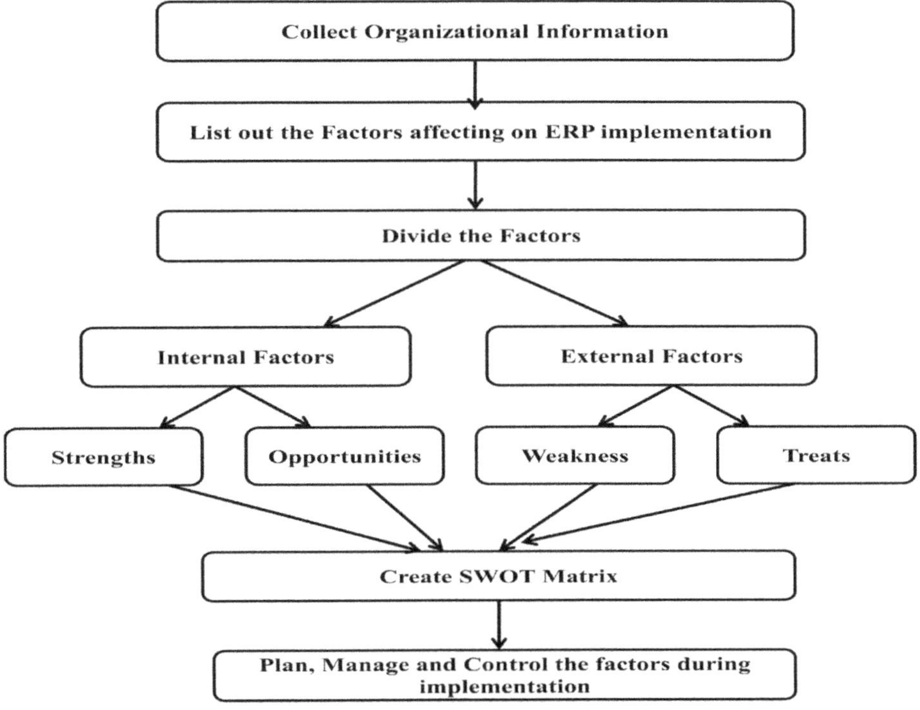

Figure 3.7 SWOT Analysis Process.

(Source: Dr. R. S. Wanare, A. R. Mudiraj, 2014)[10]

Which shows the process gets started with the Top level management and they ready to implement the ERP in their organization. Ones they decided they are call the meeting with the all concern people who have direct and indirect influence on ERP implementation from different level of organization like Board Members, Mangers, Dept Heads, Technical Staff, Supervisors etc. The meeting gives the idea about the vision and mission of the organization and the objective which the organization plans to achieve with ERP implementation. The meeting also clarifies the role of individual and groups in implementation process.

Ones everyone gets the clear idea about their role in the process, the top management start to collect the information about the current status of the internal and external environment of the organization. On base of this information, organization starts to make a list of factors which will create the influence on the ERP implementation.

Ones the list get finalize about the factors affecting on ERP implementation, the organization starts to divide the factor divide them into two major categories internal factors and External Factors. Internal Factors which a can controllable and inside the organization environment. External Factors are those factors which have the influence on the organization from the outside world, which are mostly not under control of the organization.

Further the internal factors are divided into two sub categories Strengths & Weaknesses of the organization. The External Factors are gets divided in Opportunities and Threats.

The next step in the SWOT analysis will be creating the SWOT matrix which consisting the list of factors which comes under the Strengths, Weaknesses, Opportunities and Threats of the organization.

The last step to SWOT analysis will be top level management analyze the strengths of the organization and keep them as weapon for achieve the target. Similarly organization focuses on the weaknesses on the organization which they have to control and cover-up during the ERP implementation. With the same top level management look for the opportunities in the outside world to grab with the help of their strengths during the ERP implementation. During the analysis and grabbing the opportunities the tangible and intangible threats creates the hurdles in the ERP Implementation which has to get manage and control during the execution of ERP implementation process.

3.8.2 SWOT Analysis Process:

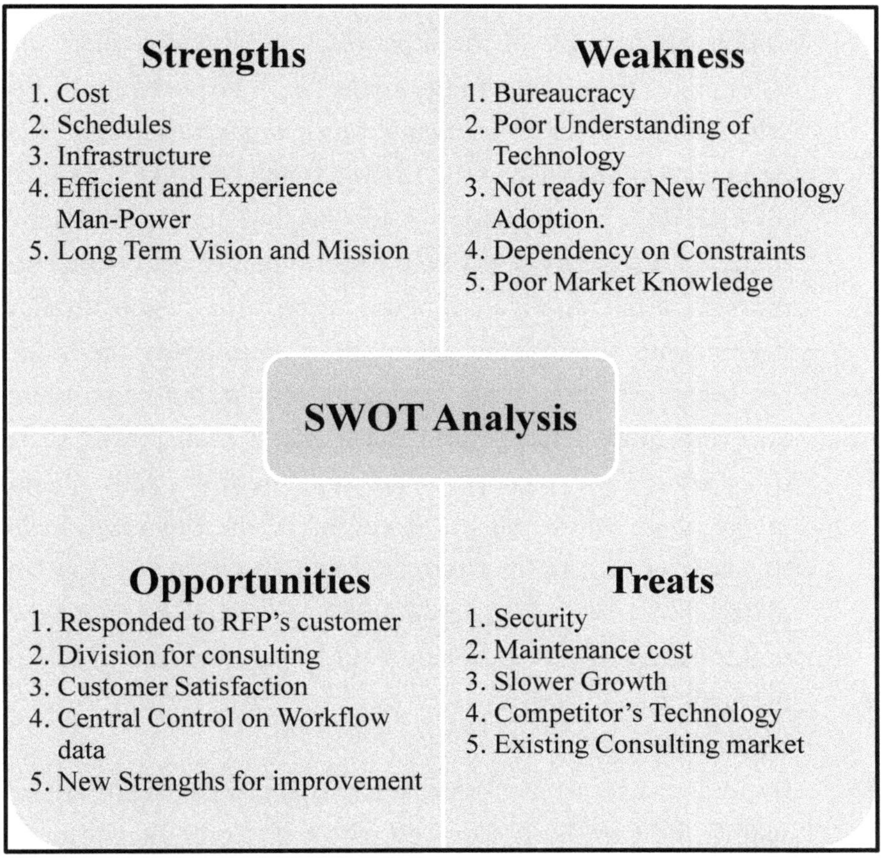

Strengths

1. Cost
2. Schedules
3. Infrastructure
4. Efficient and Experience Man-Power
5. Long Term Vision and Mission

Weakness

1. Bureaucracy
2. Poor Understanding of Technology
3. Not ready for New Technology Adoption.
4. Dependency on Constraints
5. Poor Market Knowledge

SWOT Analysis

Opportunities

1. Responded to RFP's customer
2. Division for consulting
3. Customer Satisfaction
4. Central Control on Workflow data
5. New Strengths for improvement

Treats

1. Security
2. Maintenance cost
3. Slower Growth
4. Competitor's Technology
5. Existing Consulting market

Figure 3.8 SWOT Matrixes for ERP Implementation.
(Source: Dr. R. S Wanare, A. R. Mudiraj, 2014) [10]

- **Strengths:**

  It stands as a characteristics or factors that give an edge for the company over its competitors, which give the advantages over others in the market. The Strengths factors are the factors depends upon the organization can go for ERP Implementation some of the factors are listed in the matrix like Cost, Schedule, Infrastructure, efficient and experiences manpower and last long-term mission & vision. The organization having strong financial hand can go for any new change in the organization and as, ERP needs lots of money so cost can be one of the important Strength of the organization. ERP implementation is long and time consuming process so, it required more time schedule for better implementation in organization and if the organization has the enough time so it will be more beneficiary for ERP. If the organization already has the better infrastructure in hand it makes more easily to ERP implementation otherwise more time take to create a new setup for the new technology deployment. Most of the organization considering the human resources are their main strengths and if the organization have the more efficient and experienced man power so the thing are get easily adopted and implement perfectly in most of the cases. Above all the strengths of the organization has the clear, advances, long-term mission and vision in Top level management the organization will always stand as supporting poll for the ERP development team as parental tree to achieve the goals and objective.

- **Weaknesses:**
  It stands as characteristics or factors that can be harmful if used against the firm by its competitors or it can be disadvantages relative to internal environment of the organization. During the ERP implementation the role and support of Top level management plays a vital role and if decision making is having any Bureaucratic nature of the Top level management during the implementation the people on other level of organization may not have faith on the Top level and it may affect very badly on the ERP implementation. Some time all the people of the organization may not technically sound as compare to the ERP development team and if the people who are having the direct operative position on ERP system then they must understand the technology. If they failed in understand the technology so it

will be one of the weakest thing for the organization. Some time the people of the organization not in position to change their traditional working environment and they are not in position to acquire the new technology in their working mode, some time can be more dangerous for the organization to acquire the new technology. While end of ERP implementation most of the organization hired the consultants for implementation and deployment of the ERP and after finishing the task the consultant are leave the organization. Here the problem arises in the regards of maintenances of the ERP and if we have no group of people who have the enough knowledge of ERP technology deeply so, again the consultation process get started and it increase the cost of process. Most of the organization fails to analyze the need of market and customer requirement and by poor knowledge of the market the ERP implementation may get failed.

- **Opportunities:**
It stands as characteristics or favorable situations which can bring a competitive advantage in the market. The organizations that always looking for opportunities to achieve an objective will never face the failure in market. Similarly the organizations that planning for ERP implementation need to find the opportunities in the market for the ERP implemented technology adopted organization. While considering the opportunities in market for organization the first element is customer and ERP will create the rapid and corrective responds to the Request for Proposals (RFP's) of customer. The next opportunities can be possible by ERP in organization is, it can create the one of the consultant division in the market for the ERP implementation for other non-ERP implemented organization. With the help of Rapid responds to the RFP's of customers, the ERP creates the opportunities to make our

customer satisfied at certain level. With the help of ERP we can have the idea about how and what data flowing among the different processing activities in organization, which keeps top level management updated in the regards of organizational information. The ERP also gives the better understanding of the current organizational workflow and fund-flow which help the organization to change its tactical decisions by creating new strategies for the improvements.

- **Threats:**

    It stands as characteristics or un-favorable situations which can negatively affect the business or cause trouble for organization. While considering the Threats parameter in the ERP implementation the very first factor comes in mind is security for providing the data which get travel from the different individuals, divisions, departments, offices and plant, some time at same location or different geographical location which need more security. One of the most costly threats for the ERP implementation is Maintenance Cost of ERP system which requires continuous monitoring, time and people in the process. Some time slow growth of the organization also plays the serious cause on the process where the organizational growth is not upto the mark as per decided by the Top level management during the ERP implementation. Competitor is the most and biggest threat for any organization and if the competitor is more advance in technology as compare to our technology then, there is nothing worst that it. After completing ERP implementation some people from the organization must have the technically enough to solve the problem may face in coming time, which can reduce the dependency on the ERP development consultant which are outsiders for the organization and it will defiantly reduce the cost of maintenance.

3.9 Security Issues in ERP implementation

3.9.1 Organizational Environment:

Any organization always has the two environments Internal and External Environment. Internal Environment comes with the favorable situation and conditions, where the employees of the organization, Top Level management, Board Members, etc. External Environment is can be not favorable all the time and the organization may not control over this environment which includes Competitors, Customers, Hackers, Government, Society etc. Organization plans to control more on the external environment with the help of internal environment. Many organizations consider as internal environment as pre-determined factors of them and bases of these factors the organization always plan to overcome the un-favorable factors affect on the ERP implementation.

3.9.2 People in ERP Implementation:

Any organization which implementing the ERP must have Two basic levels of user, first is Development Team which can be third party people who implementing and maintaining the ERP System. This level includes the Development team members, organizational staff like senior manager, IT administrator, Auditors etc. Second level of users is, who having direct interaction with the ERP system. It includes data operator, supervisors, and different admin, Head of the Departments and all other employees who are operating the ERP system for different purpose. All the ERP development is get developed by considering these two levels of the users. But now days, since last decade the ERP users are get changed; now we have two more levels of the users with above mention level like Other User which can be Customer, Suppliers etc. The fourth and Last level of users for ERP systems are the hackers, who going the use the ERP system for accessing the data or information of the organization for which they are not having any privileges to get it. The paper will more talk about the fourth level of the user and how to control or solves the problem created by the hacker on the ERP systems.

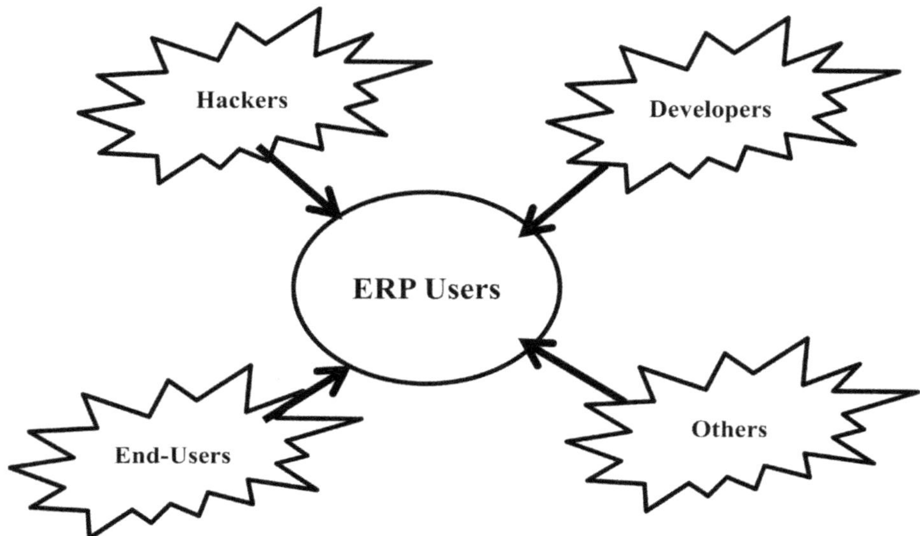

Figure 3.9 ERP Users.

(Source: Dr. R. S. Wanare, A. R. Mudiraj, 2014)[9]

3.9.3 Security in ERP Implementation:

While considering the different security issues in ERP systems, many miss-conceptions are in the mind of organization in the regards of ERP security like, ERP security is not much important as the application is within the organization and so we might not have any outsider entry, which might comes into the system and make the harm to the system. Another consideration by the organization is, default protection mechanisms are enough for the data security in ERP systems and because of it the organization not much more bothers about ERP security constraints. With the same miss-conception the organization also considering the efforts for ERP system security require additional resources like man, money, time and space which can disturb their regular workflow. The above mention some basic myths of the organization are created huge opportunities for the outsiders, hackers like people to get the easy access to the data of organization. By considering the discussion of this session we can consider the organizational approach to the ERP security and on the bases of this, we have some general and common problem faced by many organization that implemented ERP in their business are listed in the next session.

3.9.4 Security Issues in ERP Implementation:

While continuing the above discussion, some of the common security issues in ERP implementation are as follow;

- **Complexity of ERP System:**
  ERP is integrated application of various module and single person can have many roles to play in organization with different transaction require different privileges on various data on ERP system so to maintain the each users transaction secrecy the ERP has huge complexity into it. This complexity creates main hurdles in security of the ERP.

- **Lack of attention towards the ERP security:**
  Many organizations having the problem with security constraints and this creates the problem in security of ERP systems. Many organization considering the ERP security requires more resources and engaging the resources for the task which might comes ones in a month or even a year is the bad investment of the resources and so they are less bother about the ERP Security.

- **ERP Customization:**
  Not all organization having the same and standard versions of ERP Systems in the business. According to the requirement the organization customize of the ERP systems can be develop by the developers and so no standard countermeasures or preventive mechanisms able to create by the ERP developer for the organization.

- **Lack of Experienced and Expert Man Power:**
  The organization requires experienced and expert manpower that can justify the importance of ERP security to organizational people and try to take some preventive plans against the threats. But, because of less botheration about the security constraints the organization not having such team who can have and consider the security issues as such an important aspect in ERP system.

- **Security Policies and Administration:**
  Many organizations are not even considering the policies in the regards of ERP security. There are many international standards are available in the market, who have their policies in the regards of data and information security like King-II, CobiT, ITIL, ISO etc. But organization requires additional efforts for manage and maintain such security policies and administration in organization.

- **ERP is within a organization:**
  Organizations who implemented the ERP, they are considering the application is going to used within an organization only and so no outsider is going to allow and no outsiders having the interest in their data. If ERP systems are not get connected to outside world or internet then there will be no security issues will land in the system, this is general miss-conception comes in many organization's mind.

- **Lack of Interest in Updating ERP System:**
  Most of the ERP system user sets the day-to-day working environment on the ERP system and having the habitual of the same working style every day. Updating single patch in the ERP system can change their customize setup into default setup and that may disturb their regular work. This common fear keep in mind many people are not updating the ERP systems regularly and this creates the best platform for the hackers to attack on the ERP systems.

- **Miss-Communications among the Users of ERP system:**
  Many user of ERP system are less bother about the system security and they might be considering this issue very lightly. Keeping this same mindset they can forward this massage to all other user of the ERP systems and this creates the lack of interest in the ERP user's team in the regards of ERP security.

3.9.5 Solutions on ERP Implementations Security Issues:

By considering the above mention security issue in Fifth section, some of the countermeasures are suggest overcoming these problems in the regards of ERP Security.

- **Segregation of Duties (SoD) Controls:**
  SoD means splits the business operations among the individuals which give better monitoring and control over the business process and organizational data.
- **Supports and keep updated with ERP Development Team:**
  "Developer of the system can better secure the system" by considering the statement organization must be updated and take the regular support from the ERP development team in the regards of ERP security.
- **Better Security Policies making and Awareness among the stakeholders:**
  The policies in the regards of security must be secure, as per the standards which provided by the various international standards. Also the organization must keep aware to all the stakeholder of the ERP system about their security policies and their objectives.
- **Keep update and aware the user of ERP system about the Importance of Data and Information:**
  The organization has to clarify the importance of the organizational information and data to the all users of the

systems. All the user must updated with different security issues and policies developed by the organization time to time.

- **Be Updated regularly the ERP Systems by latest patches:** The regular updating provided by the vendors or developers are suppose to get accept and deploy by the organization time to time and the technical heads must keep this step as mandatory for all the system under the supervision of heads.

- **Develop The Auditing Mechanism For The ERP Security:** Many organizations forget to keep the records of auditing of the ERP systems and this can be possible by using automated tools which are available in the market as open-sources or commercially also.

- **Keep Regular Backup and Restoring Points in the ERP System:** By keeping the regular data and process backup the organization can secure most of the operation by unexpected security threats.

- **Make Good Monitoring and Controlling Mechanism for ERP security:** The creation of better mechanism to just monitor day-to-day activities of the ERP system and user the organization can better control over the problems at very beginning level and try to solve the problem before it affect the ERP security systems badly.

3.10 ERP Implementation Strategies

While Choosing the ERP system implementation, you should be thinking about it proactively when evaluating systems, you should raise the topic with prospective vendors and even ask for examples of their customers' strategies. There are hundreds of articles on "best practices" for implementing ERP software, but understanding each strategy and choosing the best option is difficult. So, the study set out to consolidate the information in a single guide. Our aim is to give you enough information – and the most important pieces – to choose the best implementation process for your organization. The chapter tries to cover the three most widely discussed ERP implementation strategies:

- **Big bang – Implementation happens in a single instance. All users move to the new system on a given date.**
- **Phased rollout – Changeover occurs in phases over an extended period of time. Users move onto new system in a series of steps.**
- **Parallel adoption – Both the legacy and new ERP system run at the same time. Users learn the new system while working on the old.**

Recently a survey hosted to find out which ERP implementation strategies are the most popular and most successful. With the help of Twitter and our favorite industry bloggers, the received 45 responses from organizations that have been involved in an implementation. Survey was brief and informal with just four simple questions:

"Which implementation strategy did your organization choose?, Big bang, phased rollout, parallel adoption, combo of big bang and phased rollout, or other."

If respondent selected other, please describe the strategy they choose.

Was the implementation a success?

If respondent selected no, please explain why.

When it comes to ERP implementations, these questions skim the surface. author understand a myriad of questions and answers would be required to learn when it's appropriate to choose a certain strategy. Additionally, they also realize reporting the "most successful strategy" would be erroneous. While one strategy may work for a majority of companies, it may not be the best strategy for your organization. Nevertheless, our survey did uncover some interesting data. Here are the results: Eighty-nine percent of respondents followed "big bang," "phased rollout" or a combination of the two strategies.

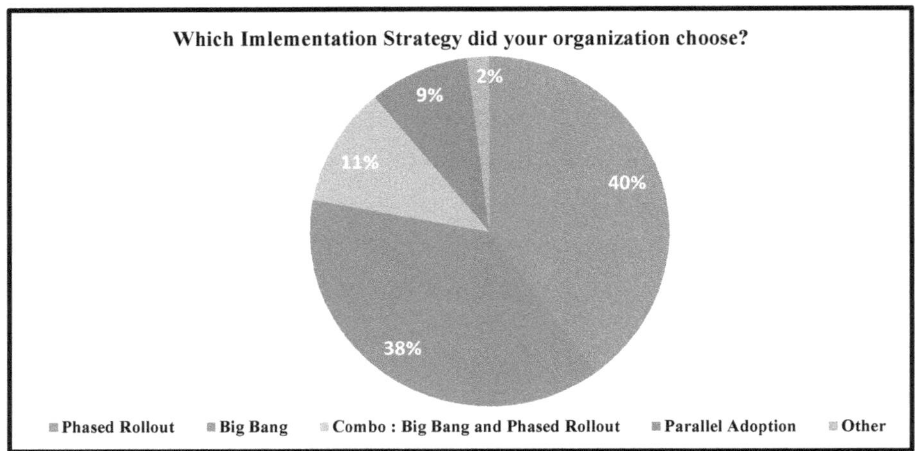

Figure 3.10 Which ERP Implementation Strategy Chosen (Percentile)

(Source: Insight Consulting Partner's, 2013)

The number of phased rollout users compared to big bang was split nearly evenly; parallel adoption trailed far behind with only four users; "other" came in last. The "other" respondent left us the following explanation for his strategy:

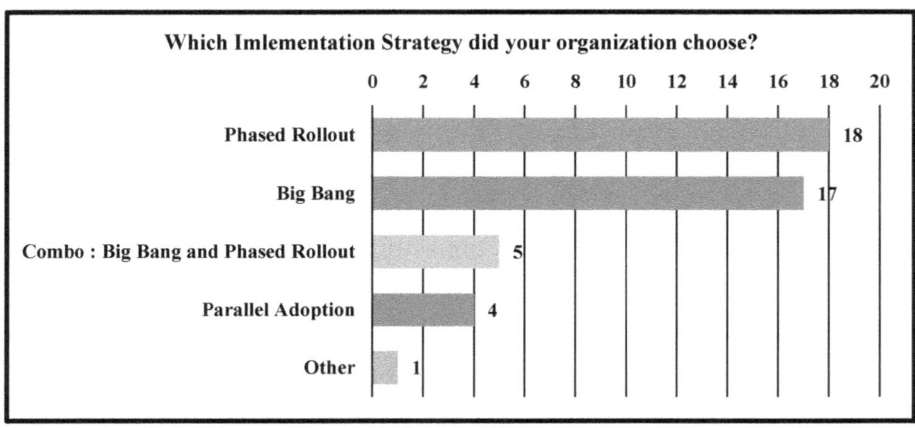

Figure 3.11 Which ERP Implementation Strategy Chosen

(Source: Insight Consulting Partner's, 2013)

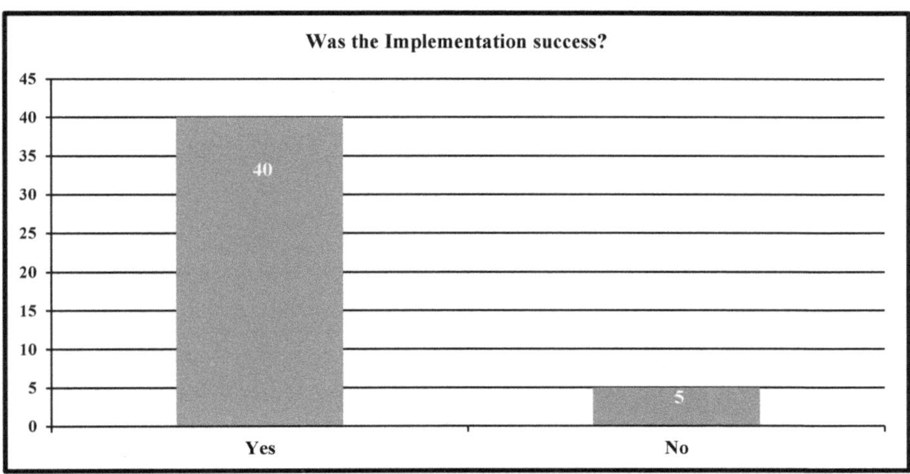

Figure 3.12 Success Ratio of ERP Implementation Strategy

(Source: Insight Consulting Partner's, 2013).

3.10.1 Big Bang

Just as the name implies, a big bang ERP implementation happens in a single, major event. All modules are installed across the entire organization all at once, more or less. Of course the changeover from the legacy system doesn't happen without proper planning. There are many pre-implementation activities that need to be carried out prior to the big bang.

After the planning activities have been successfully executed, the old system will be turned off, and the new system will be launched. At this point there is no turning back. However, there should be fall-back scenarios prepared just in case the initial changeover is a failure.

The big bang implementation strategy has supporters on both sides of the fence. The most common criticism is the risk factor; there are a number of things that could go wrong in an instant changeover. However, the implementation is quick and less costly than a long, drawn-out phased approach.

Here is a list of other benefits and drawbacks of big bang implementation:

Advantages	Disadvantages
Implementation time is shorter	Difficulties are more pronounced
Implementation difficulties and "pains" are condensed	Details may be overlooked in the rush to change
Costs are much lower than a long, drawn-out implementation	Employees have less time to learn the new system
Employees only need to be trained on the new system, not for the changeover period	Full end-to-end system testing is tough to carry our prior to implementation
Implementation happens on a single date and everyone knows the date	Fall-back scenarios are more difficult than originally perceived

Figure 3.13 Advantage and Disadvantages of Big Bang Strategy.

Eason, author of "Information Technology and Organizational Change" and one of the original authorities on implementation strategies, describes an "initial dip phenomenon" which happens shortly after an implementation. This catch-up period happens because users are struggling with the new system and organizational performance temporarily declines as a result.

3.10.2 Phased Rollout

In keeping with the theme of cosmological evolution, phased rollout would be analogous to the Steady State theory: instead of an implementation happening in a single instance, small changes occur over time. An organization moves off the legacy system and onto the new ERP system in a series of predetermined steps. This can be achieved in several different ways. Here are three well-known techniques:

Phased rollout by module – This is the most common phased rollout strategy. ERP modules are implemented one at a time. Typically you begin with core business functions – those necessary for daily operations – then add in more modules and functionality with each phase. However, some experts suggest starting with easy modules like general ledger, or beginning with the less mission-critical modules.

Phased rollout by business unit – Under this approach implementation is carried out in one or more business units or departments at a time. For example, you begin with implementing the new ERP system in human resources, then move to accounting. Some organizations may put together an implementation project team that travels between each department during implementation phases. As the team gains more experience with each implementation, subsequent phases become more efficient.

Phased rollout by geography – For organizations with multiple locations, a phased rollout by geography is a frequent approach. The new ERP system is introduced at one or more company locations at a time. This is also referred to as the "pilot adoption method." It's common for large organizations that have multiple locations or independent departments.

Of course there are hundreds of options, including many variations and combinations of these three. Just like big bang, a phased rollout strategy has advantages and disadvantages.

This following listed several common viewpoints:

Advantages	Disadvantages
Companies gain knowledge and experience during the initial implementation phase that can be applied to subsequent phases	Not as focused and urgent as big bang
Possible to introduce modules while programming future modules	Involves continuous change over an extended period of time
With conversion occurring in parts, time is available for adjustments	Each modules relies on information from other modules, so there could be critical information missing
There is no catch-up period, employees learn as they go	Several adjustments are needed

Advantages	Disadvantages
More time for users to adapt to the new system	Duration of the project is much longer than big bang
Technical staff can focus on one part of the system or a select group of users at one time	A fall-back to the old system becomes more difficult with each phase
Project members may develop unique implementation skills that they can be positioned for in later rollouts	Temporary bridges must be created between legacy system and new system

Figure 3.14 Advantages and Disadvantages of Phased Strategy.

3.10.3 Parallel Adoption

The third generic – though less talked about – ERP implementation plan is the "parallel adoption" approach. This has also been referred to as "parallel conversion," "parallel running," or "parallel cutover." Parallel adoption is thought to be the least risky implementation process. It includes running both the old and new ERP system at the same time. These way users can learn the new system while performing regular work activities on the old system. After requirements for the new system are met, then the legacy system is decommissioned.

Parallel adoption can be considered the middle road between big bang and phased adoption. For example, the pace of the changeover is slower than big bang, but faster than phased adoption. Similarly, user adaptation is easier than big bang, but more difficult than phased adoption.

The major trade-off is cost. Parallel adoption is the most expensive implementation method. Additionally, having employees enter data in both systems is not efficient. However, if the extra costs are less than costs incurred after a backfired big bang adoption, then it's a reasonable plan. Still, organizations cannot predict cost overruns of big bang, so parallel adoption has become decreasingly popular because of *perceived* high costs.

3.10.4 Which ERP Implementation Strategy is Best for Your Business?

There certainly is no one-size-fits-all when it comes to implementing an ERP system. Every company has unique goals, and an implementation requires careful planning and analysis. Some companies may choose a combination of strategies, like a mini big bang mixed with phased rollouts (i.e. "big bang" the important modules, then add in the peripheral modules later). Others may choose to implement a mid-market ERP system (e.g. Microsoft Dynamics, EPCOR) at the plant-level, while keeping a major ERP system (e.g. SAP, Oracle running at headquarters). And at times, the best implementation strategy will be obvious.

3.11 Indian Manufacturing Scenario

The Prime Minister of India, Mr Narendra Modi, has launched the 'Make in India' initiative to place India on the world map as a manufacturing hub and give global recognition to the Indian economy. The Government of India has set an ambitious target of increasing the contribution of manufacturing output to 25 per cent of Gross Domestic Product (GDP) by 2025, from 16 per cent currently.

Market Size

India's manufacturing sector could touch US\$ 1 trillion by 2025. There is potential for the sector to account for 25-30 per cent of the country's GDP and create up to 90 million domestic jobs by 2025.iBusiness conditions in the Indian manufacturing sector continue to remain positive. In August 2015, the seasonally adjusted Nikkei India Manufacturing Purchasing Managers' Index (PMI) stood at 52.3, thanks to a sharp increase in buying levels coupled with a record drop in stocks of finished goods. The composite PMI that combines both services and manufacturing sectors was at a five month high of 52.6 points in August 2015.

Investments

In a major boost to the 'Make in India' initiative, the Government of India has received investment proposals of over Rs 1,10,000 Crores (US$ 16.56 billion) in the last 12 months from various companies including Airbus, Phillips, Thomson, Samsung, LG and Flextronics among others.

Government Initiatives

In a bid to push the 'Make in India' initiative to the global level, Mr Narendra Modi, Prime Minister of India, pitched India as a manufacturing destination at the World International Fair in Germany's Hannover earlier this year. Mr Modi showcased India as a business friendly destination to attract foreign businesses to invest and manufacture in the country. The Government of India has taken several initiatives to promote a healthy environment for the growth of manufacturing sector in the country. Some of the notable initiatives and developments are:

- The Government of India has asked New Delhi's envoys in over 160 countries to focus on economic diplomacy to help government attract investment and transform the 'Make in India' campaign a success to boost growth during the annual heads of missions conference. Prime Minister, Mr Modi has also utilized the opportunity to brief New Delhi's envoys about the Government's Foreign Policy priority and immediate focus on restoring confidence of foreign investors and augmenting foreign capital inflow to increase growth in manufacturing sector.

- The Government of Uttar Pradesh (UP) has secured investment deals valued at Rs 5,000 crore (US$ 752.58 million) for setting up mobile manufacturing units in the state.

- The Government of Maharashtra has cleared land allotment for 130 industrial units across the state with an investment of Rs 6,266 crore (US$ 943.13 million)

- Dr Jitendra Singh, Union Minister of State (Independent Charge) of the Ministry of Development of North Eastern Region (DoNER), MoS PMO, Personnel, Public Grievances & Pensions, Atomic Energy and Space, Government of India, has announced the 'Make in Northeast' initiative beginning with a comprehensive tourism plan for the region.

- Government of India has planned to invest US$ 10 billion in two semiconductor plants in order to facilitate electronics manufacturing in the country.

- Entrepreneurs of small-scale businesses in India will soon be able to avail loans under Pradhan Mantri MUDRA Yojana (PMMY). The three products available under the PMMY include: Shishu – covering loans up to Rs 50,000 (US$ 752), Kishor – covering loans between Rs 50,000 (US$ 752) to Rs 0.5 million (US$ 7,520), and Tarun – covering loans between Rs 0.5 million (US$ 7,520) and Rs 1 million (US$ 15,052).

The contribution of India's manufacturing sector has remained stagnant in the past few years. Slowing external and domestic demand has caused the manufacturing sector to move at a slower pace than the overall economy for some time now however, the government's national manufacturing policy (NMP) aims to boost growth and ramp up its share in the country's GDP to 25% and create 100 million jobs by 2022.

India's rising demand, opportunities for organizations to invest and grow, favorable policies, and the tendency to establish low-cost plants by MNC's are few of the reasons that would lead the sector to achieve higher growth.

Figure 3.15 Manufacturing Goods Exports in India in 2007-2013

(Source: RBI, Indian Express, Business Lines, Aranca Analysis)

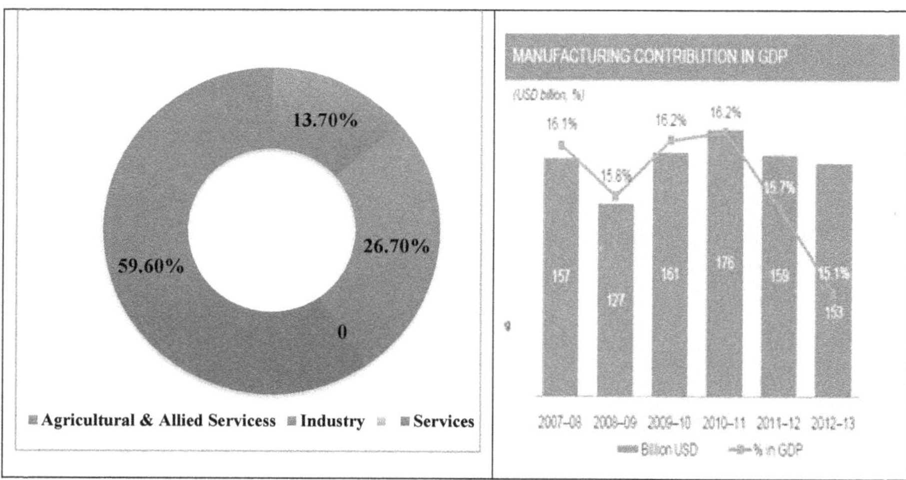

Figure 3.16 Sectorial Composisiton of GDP and Manufacturing Contribution in GDP in 2013 for India

(Source: RBI)

Road Ahead

The Government of India has an ambitious plan to locally manufacture as many as 181 products. The move could help infrastructure sectors such as power, oil and gas, and automobile manufacturing that require large capital expenditure and revive the Rs 1,85,000 crore (US$ 27.85 billion) Indian capital goods business.

India is an attractive hub for foreign investments in the manufacturing sector. Several mobile phone, luxury and automobile brands, among others, have set up or are looking to establish their manufacturing bases in the country. With impetus on developing industrial corridors and smart cities, the government aims to ensure holistic development of the nation. The corridors would further assist in integrating, monitoring and developing a conductive environment for the industrial development and will promote advance practices in manufacturing.

INDIAN MANUFACTURING SECTOR Vs. PEER COUNTRIES			
Countries	Countries Manufacturing Competitiveness Index Score-2013 (10=High, 1=Low)	Labor Cost (USD/Hr)- 2011	High-Technology Exports * – 2011 (% of Manufacturing Exports)
China	10	2.8	25.8
Germany	7.98	46.4	15
US	7.84	35.4	18.1
India	7.65	0.9	6.9
South Korea	7.59	17.7	25.7
Taiwan	7.57	9.2	NA
Canada	7.24	38.3	13.4
Brazil	7.13	12	9.7
Singapore	6.64	21.9	45.2
Japan	6.6	35.4	17.5
Thailand	6.21	NA	20.7
Note *: High-Technology exports are products with high R & D Intensity, such as in aerospace, computers, Pharmaceutical, Scientific instruments and electrical machinery.			

Figure 3.17 Indian Manufacturing Sector VS Peer Countries
(Source: Dloitte, World Bank and CII)

Domestic Demand: Rising demand, together with the multinationals' desire to diversify their production to include low cost plants could help India's manufacturing sector to grow six fold by 2025, to USD 1 trillion, while creating more than 100 million jobs.

China's Competitiveness Declines: As China's competitiveness declines, due to Yuan appreciation and wage inflation, and a drop in investment as a percentage of GDP is observed, it is expected that growth in China's manufacturing sector is unlikely to continue. There seems to be a clear opportunity for developing countries like India to fill this gap and become a global manufacturing hub.

Hi-tech Exports: Hi-tech exports from India have been witnessing a CAGR of 26% during 2007-11, with exports touching USD20.9 billion, a significant increase from USD 8.1 billion in 2007. Hi-tech exports are expected to boost the country's manufacturing sector.

3.12 Maharashtra Manufacturing Scenario.

Maharashtra is the second largest State in India in terms of population and 3rd largest as per geographical area (3.08 lakh sq.km) of the country. The state has actual population of 112,373,972 (as per 2011 Census (Provisional) which is 9.29 percent share of total population of India. It is bounded by Arabian Sea in the West, Gujarat in the North West and Madhya Pradesh in the North, Andhra Pradesh in the South-East and Karnataka and Goa in the South. The Konkan Coastal stretches about 720 kms long in the West and the Sahyadri ranges paralleled to the sea coast at about 80 Kms wide in the East. To the coast of the Sahyadri stretches a vast plateau. This plateau is drained by the three great rivers Godavari, Bhima and Krishna, which rise in the Sahyadri and flow eastward across Indian Peninsula into the Bay of Bengal.

Maharashtra is the most industrialized state in India and has maintained the leading position in the industrial sector in the country. The state is equally a frontrunner in small scale industries and boasts of the largest number of special export promotion zones.

Maharashtra accounts for approximately 35.1 per cent of the country's automobile output by value. Pune is the largest auto hub of India, with over 4,000 manufacturing units just in the Pimpri-Chinchwad region. The state also has the largest base of local original equipment manufacturers (OEMs).

The State has 35 districts which are divided into six revenue divisions' viz. Konkan, Pune, Nasik, Aurangabad, Amravati and Nagpur for administrative purposes. The State has a long tradition of having statutory bodies for planning at the district. For local self-governance in rural areas, there are 33 Zillah Parishads, 351 Panchayat Samitis and 27,906 Gram Panchayats. The urban areas are governed through 26 Municipal Corporations, 219 Municipal Councils, 7 Nagar Panchayats and 7 Cantonment Boards.

Mumbai, the capital of Maharashtra and the financial capital of India, houses the headquarters of most of the major corporate & financial institutions. India's main stock exchanges & capital market and commodity exchanges are located in Mumbai.

Maharashtra is one of the largest and richest states in India Maharashtra are third most urbanized state with urban population of 45% of whole population. Maharashtra has been in the forefront of economic development and is the economic power house of the country. With its proactive policies, the State continues to occupy the dominant position amongst the industrially advanced States in India. Maharashtra has been in the forefront in sustaining industrial growth and in creating environment conductive to industrial development. Investment – friendly industrial policies, excellent infrastructure and a strong and productive human resource base have made it a favored destination for manufacturing, export and financial service sectors.

Micro, Small and Medium Enterprises sector occupies an important position in the State's industrial economy and continues to contribute to industrial production, export, creation of employment opportunities, etc.

The Development Commissioner (MSME), Govt. of India, New Delhi formulates the policy governing the MSME in the country and chalk out schemes and programmes for development of the MSME sector as per the provisions in the MSMED Act. In accordance with the provision of Micro, Small & Medium Enterprises Development (MSMED) Act, 2006 the Micro, Small and Medium Enterprises (MSME) are classified in two Classes:

1. **Manufacturing Enterprises**

   The enterprises engaged in the manufacture or production of goods pertaining to any industry specified in the first schedule to the industries (Development and regulation) Act, 1951) or employing plant and machinery in the process of value addition to the final product having a distinct name or character or use. The Manufacturing Enterprises are defined in terms of investment in Plant & Machinery.

2. **Service Enterprises:**

   The enterprises engaged in providing or rendering of services and are defined in terms of investment in equipment. The enterprise belongs to Medium scale enterprise, if investment in plant and machinery is more than five crore rupees but does not exceed ten crore rupees;

Definitions of Micro, Small and Medium Enterprises in manufacturing and service sector are as follows: –

Category	Manufacturing	Service Sector
	Investment in Plant & Machinery (Excluding Land & Building)	Investment in Plant & Machinery (Excluding Land & Building)
Micro	Upto Rs. 25 Lakhs	Upto Rs. 10 Lakhs
Small	Above Rs. 25 Lakhs upto Rs. 5 Crore	Above Rs. 10 Lakhs upto Rs. 2 Crore
Medium	Above Rs. 5 Crore upto Rs. 10 Crores	Above Rs. 2 Crore upto Rs. 5 Crores

Figure 3.18 Definitions of Micro, Small and Medium Scale Manufacturing and Service Industries in India

(Source: MSME-2014)

Number of EM-II Fields Pertaining to				
Year	Micro	Small	Medium	Total
2007-08	1,53,110	16,730	467	1,70,307
2008-09	1,70,262	18,792	702	1,89,756
2009-10	1,85,180	23,870	1,409	2,10,459
2010-11	2,05,112	29,125	1,263	2,35,500
2011-12	2,42,539	34,225	2,949	2,79,713
2012-13	2,75,867	41,502	5,449	3,22,818
2013-14	2,96,526	59,127	7,338	3,62,991
2014-15	3,46,206	70,933	8,219	4,25,358

Figure 3.19 Growth in Number of Micro, Small and Medium Scale Manufacturing and Service Industries in India

(Source: MSME-2014)

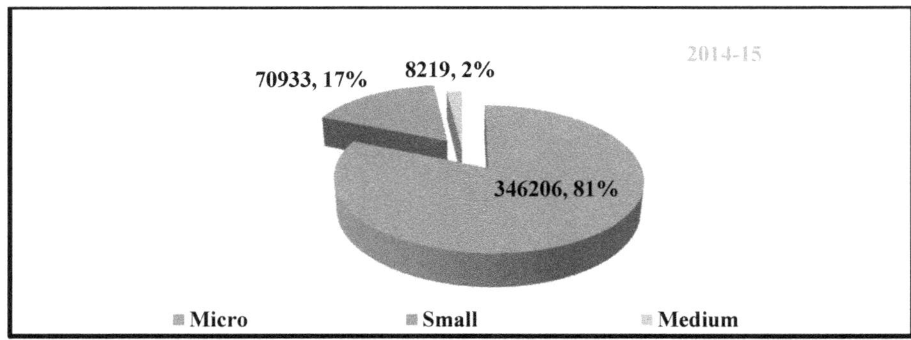

Figure 3.20 Number with Percentage of Micro, Small and Medium Scale Manufacturing and Service Industries in India

(Source: MSME-June 2015)

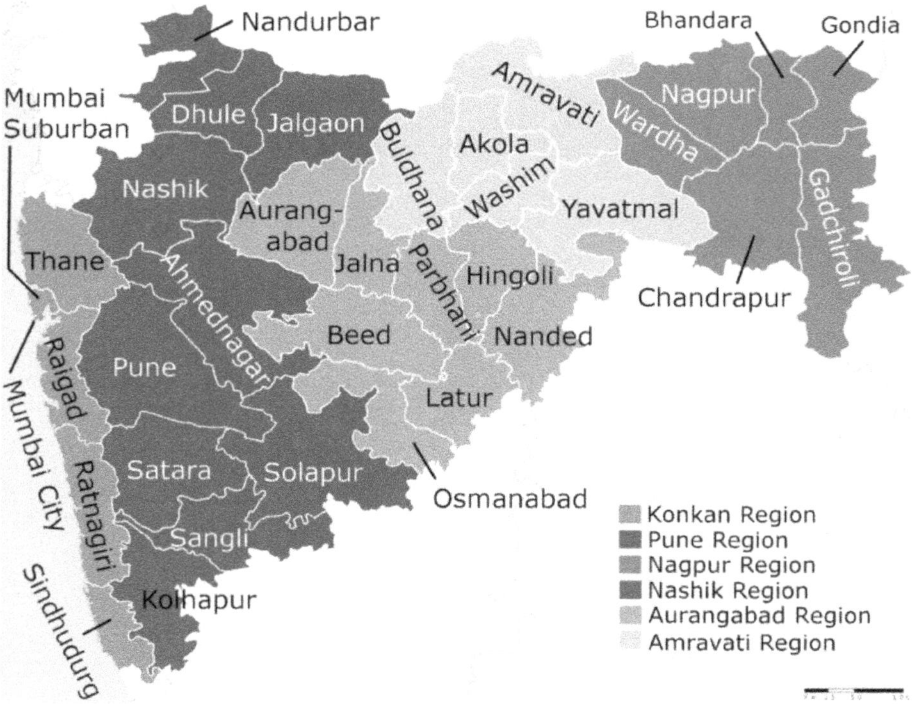

Figure 3.21 Maharashtra State Map with Industrial Zone

(Source: www.mapsofindia.com)

Maharashtra's gross state domestic product (GSDP) accounted for 12.98 per cent of India's gross domestic product (GDP) in 2014-15, the highest among all states. The GSDP grew at a CAGR of around 11.1 per cent between 2004-05 and 2014-15 to reach US$ 264.8 billion. Total FDI in the state stood at US$ 73.12 billion from April 2000 to May 2015, the highest among all states in India. Maharashtra's exports totaled US$ 73.9 billion in 2014-15.

The resources, policy incentives, infrastructure and climate support investments in the state. Maharashtra Agro Industries Development Corporation, founded in 1965, is responsible for development of agro-based units in the state. MIDC is responsible for the development of industrial infrastructure. Maharashtra Small Scale Industries Development Corporation was formed in 1962 to provide new orientation and strength to the development of small-scale industries in the state. Its main objective is to aid, counsel, assist, finance, protect and promote interests of small industries. The Government of Maharashtra is promoting the development of several Special Economic Zones (SEZs) across Maharashtra for sectors such as IT/ITeS, pharmaceuticals, biotechnology, textile, automotive & auto components, gems & jewellery and food processing. As of 2014 – 15, the state as 9 operational SEZs, out of which majority are contributed by engineering and electronics segment.

Establishment of MSME Units			
Year	MSME Units	Investment (US $ Million)	Employment (Lakh)
2007-08	10244	566.4	1.39
2008-09	11682	714.1	1.71
2009-10	11896	638.5	1.51
2010-11	14496	1219.4	1.87
2011-12	15606	947.7	2.07
2012-13	16136	1004.4	2.06
2013-14	19814	1054.7	2.48
2014-15**	24894	888.4	2.92

Figure 3.22 Establishment of MSME Units from 2007-2014 in Maharashtra (Source: Directorate on Industries, GoM).

Key Industries in Maharashtra

- Pharmaceuticals
- Biotechnology
- IT and ITeS
- Electronics
- Engineering
- Auto & auto components
- Oil & gas
- Food & agro processing
- Gems and jewellery
- Banking, financial services and insurance (BFSI)
- Textiles

3.13 ERP for Manufacturing Industries

In today's world it has become a task for any manufacturer to survive in the rising competition as he needs to take care of lot of things and processes which are cost incurring and have direct effect on manpower, material, resource, supplier, power and on the other hand, to be a success full manufacturer in today's competitive environment a manufacturer should have a good hold on all internal & external aspects related to manufacturing process such as labor, raw material, machinery, maintenance, supplier, contractor etc.

There are lots of questions which arise in mind of a manufacturer like how to maintain a good relationship with supplier, how to increase productivity, how to maintain quality, how to meet the customer satisfaction level, how to reduce the workforce, how to keep a track on inventory, how to maintain reports related to finance, stocks, how can we track resource, power, material, shifts, break down which we utilize for manufacturing the product, how to check the rejected material machine wise & mostly the difficulty is of human errors as we all know in case of manual intervention always there are chances of discrepancy in reports & which effect things very badly.

In the early days of its inception, ERP software was originally developed to meet the unique requirements of manufacturing organizations. Although modern ERP systems are able to accommodate the functionality required of most industries, manufacturing organizations are still unique in their implementation approach an in the challenges they face. Because of the complexity of manufacturing processes and the way these processes interact, manufacturing ERP implementations often cost more than implementations across all industries and often account for a greater percentage of organizations' annual revenues. Many manufacturing firms customize their ERP software in order to meet unique business requirements and this customization pushes implementation costs higher. In recent years, the manufacturing industry has evolved. Our last manufacturing report identified a number of industry trends that have recently been turned upside down.

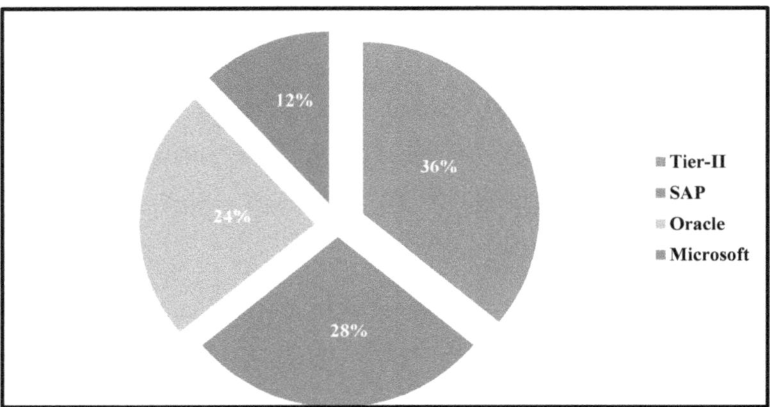

Figure 3.23 ERP Venders Share in Manufacturing Industries

(Source: 2014 Manufacturing ERP Reports)

SAP holds approximately 17% percent of the manufacturing ERP market. Oracle and Microsoft follow with about 14% percent and 7% percent respectively and Tier II solutions account for about 21% percent of the manufacturing ERP market.

The graph on the following page shows a more detailed breakdown of the top ERP vendors by market share for the manufacturing industry versus all industries.

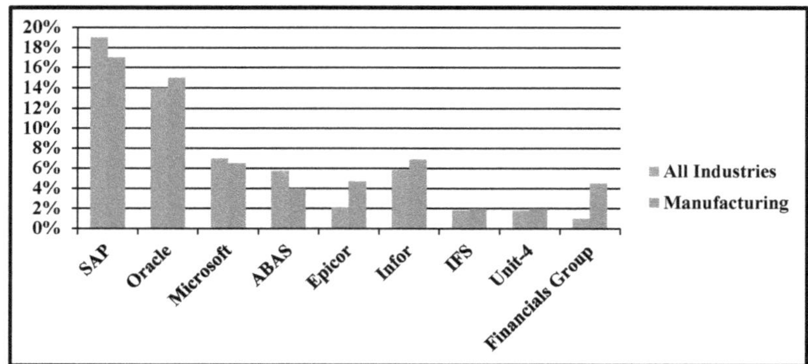

Figure 3.24 Top ERP Vender's market Share for Manufacturing Industries with other Industries

(Source: 2014 Manufacturing ERP Report).

Vendor market shares for the manufacturing industry are very similar to vendor market shares for all industries as a whole. The main difference lies in the prominence of Tier II vendors in the manufacturing industry where vendors such as Infor 7%, EPCOR 5% and ABAS 5% have higher market shares than they do in other non-manufacturing industries

3.14 ERP for Medium Scale Manufacturing Industries in Maharashtra State

As the Maharashtra state is growing face of the Indian manufacturing industrial, the manufacturing industries in the state need to upgrade their technical advancement to their business process and the objective can achieve via ERP implementation in their industry.

With the same objective and face today's era of hi-tech environment for business process many medium scale manufacturing units planning to adopt ERP system. The study proves that out of 792 medium scale manufacturing units in the Maharashtra state 249 MSMU have developed and successfully implemented ERP into their firm. The details of all medium scale manufacturing units who used ERP system in their MSMU are discussed in the chapter 4, (data analysis and interpretation).

The study discussed about thee 31% of total MSMU in Maharashtra state have implemented ERP system in their firm and still 69% organization need are in process or not yet started or think about ERP implementations and its benefits to their business process improvement.

Sr. No	Name of Industrial Zone	Total No of Medium Scale Manufacturing Units	Manufacturing Units Who Using ERP	Percentage
1	Pune Div	122	44	36.07%
2	Nasik Div	114	30	26.32%
3	Mumbai Div	245	84	34.29%
4	Aurangabad Div	143	33	23.08%
5	Nagpur Div	109	35	32.12%
6	Amravati Div	59	23	38.99%
Total Manufacturing Units		**792**	**249**	**31.44%**
Percentage of Sample for Responses		**100%**	**32%**	**32%**

Table 3.1 Number of MSMU (Zone wise) present in Maharashtra with MSMU who using ERP system in their Unit

(Source: MSME-2014, GoM and Primary Data)

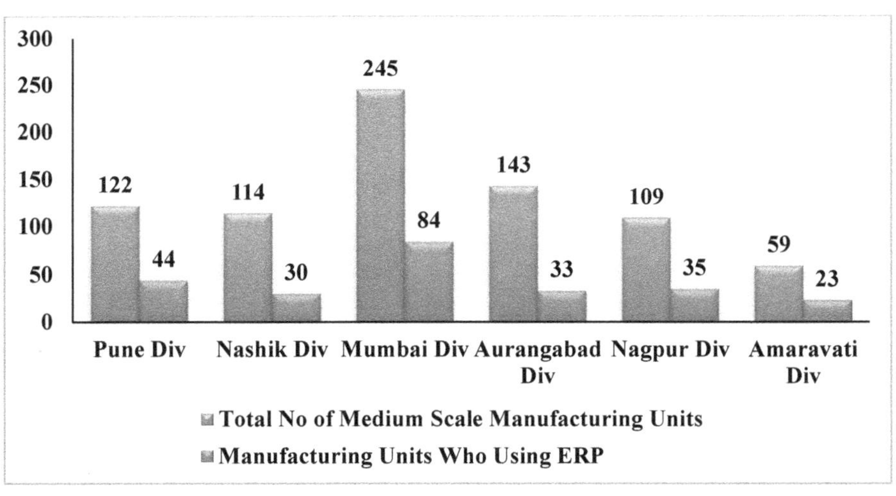

Figure 3.25 No. Of MSMU (Zone wise) present in Maharashtra Vs MSMU who using ERP system in their Unit

(Source: MSME-2014, GoM and Primary Data)

References

1. Prof. Amar R. Mudiraj (2013), "ERP: An Effective Resource Utilization Tool For Organization", Ijmbs, Vol. 04, Pp 68-73

2. Vinod Kumar Garg & N.K.Venkitakrishnan "Enterprise Resource Planning", Prentice –Hall of India, 2003

3. Chen, I. J., "Planning for ERP Systems: Analysis and Future Trend", Business Process Management Journal, 7(5), 374-386, 2001

4. Hicks, D. A., & Stecke, K. E., "The ERP Maze: Enterprise Resource Planning and other Production and Inventory Control Software", IIE Solutions, 27(8), 12-16, 1995.

5. Markus M. L., & Tanis, "The Enterprise Systems Experience-From Adoption to Success", In R. W. Zmud (Ed.), Framing the Domains of IT, 2000 Management: Projecting the Future – through the past, pp 173-209, Cincinnati, OH: Pinnaflex

6. Prof. Amar R. Mudiraj,, (2014), "BPR: The first step for ERP Implementation.", International Research Journal of Commerce, Business and Social Sciences (IRJCBSS), Vol. II, Issue 12 (III), March 2014, PP 1-4

7. Furey, Timothy.R., (1993), A Six Step Guide To Process Reengineering., Planning Review 21 (2), Pp 20-23

8. S.J. Cereola, "The performance effects of latent Risk on assimilation of commercial open-source ERP software on small-medium enterprises", Virginia Commonwealth University, Richmond, Virginia, September 2006.

9. Dr. Ramdas S. Wanare, Amar R. Mudiraj, (2014), "Security Issue and their Countermeasures in ERP Implementation "International Journal of Management and Social Sciences Research (IJMSSR), Volume 3, No. 6, June 2014, pp 13-16.

10. Dr. Ramdas S. Wanare, Amar R. Mudiraj, (2014), "Study the Importance of SWOT Analysis on ERP Implementation", International Journal of Management and Social Sciences Research (IJMSSR), Volume 3, No. 6, June 2014, pp 13-16.

11. Dr. Ramdas S. Wanare, Amar R. Mudiraj, (2014), "Study on Business Process Reengineering(BPR) and its importance in ERP Implementation

"International Journal of Research in Computer and Communication Technology, Vol 3, Issue 7, pp 715-719

12. Dr. Ramdas S. Wanare, Amar R. Mudiraj, (2014), "Risk Management in ERP Implementation", International Journal of Research in Computer and Communication Technology, Vol 3, Issue 7, pp 767-770.

13. Yasar F. Jarrar, 'Abdullah Al-Mudimigh' And Mohamed Zairi(2009) "ERP Implementation Critical Success Factors – The Role And Impact Of Business Process Management" Icmlt Pp 122-127.

14. EricY.Cheng, Ying JenWang,(2006),"Business Process Reengineering And ERP Systems Benefits", 11th Annual Conference Of Asia Pacific Decision Sciences Institute PP. 201-213.

15. David Williamson, Peter Cooke, Wyn Jenkins, and Keith Michael Moreton (2003) "Strategic Management and Business Analysis", Butterworth and Heinemann publications, Great Britain.

16. Furey, Timothy.R., (1993), A Six Step Guide To Process Reengineering., Planning Review 21 (2), Pp 20-23

17. Markus M. L., & Tanis, "The Enterprise Systems Experience-From Adoption to Success", In R. W .Zmud (Ed.), Framing the Domains of IT, 2000 Management: Projecting the Future – through the past, pp 173-209, Cincinnati, OH: Pinnaflex

18. Shankar Ravi and S.Jaiswal, "Enterprise Resource planning", Galgotia Publications, 1999

19. Sharma Dhiraj, "Foundation of Information Technology", p399, 2009

20. Vinod Kumar Garg & N.K.Venkitakrishnan "Enterprise Resource Planning", Prentice – Hall of India, 2003

21. G.S.Vijaya, Utpal Baul & Hari Haran, "Enterprise Resource Planning (ERP) – an innovativeKey for the Success of an Organization" Interscience Management Review (IMR), ISSN: 2231-1513, Volume-2, Issue – 3, 2012

22. Andreson, V. (2004), Research methods in Human Resource Management, Chartered Institute of Personnel Development, London; pp. 10-164.

23. Shivani Goal, Ravi Kiran, Deepak Garg', (2012) " Vulnerability Management for an ERP System" International Journal of Computer Application, Vol-53-No.4 Sep-2012, PP 19-22

24. Santosh K. Panday,(2009),"Major Challenges in Auditing ERP Security", BOS, ICAI.

25. Marnewick C. and Labuschagne L. (2006), "Security Framework for an ERP Systems"

26. Varang Acharya, Sweta Jethava and Adarsh Patel (2013), "Case Study of Database Security in Campus ERP System", International Journal of Computer Application, Vol-79, Oct-2013 PP 1-4.

27. Mariano Nunez (2012), "Cyber Attacks & SAP Systems", Onapsis Inc. Securing Business Essentials, Black-Hat Europe.

28. Blosch, M. & Hunter, R. (2004). "Sarbanes-Oxley: an external look at internal controls", Gartner. August.

29. Khosrowpour, Mehdi, ed. (2006) "Emerging Trends and Challenges in Information Technology Management" 2006 Information Resources Management Association International Conference, Washington, DC, USA, May 21-24, 2006. Vol. 1.

30. Manmeet Singh Hora (2012) "Predicting the future of ERP – A SWOT Analysis"

31. Yasar F. Jarrar ', Abdullah Al-Mudimigh 'And Mohamed Zairi(2009) " Erp Implementation Critcal Success Factors – The Role And Impact Of Business Process Management" Icmlt Pp 122-127

32. EricY.Cheng, Ying JenWang, (2006), "Business Process Reengineering And Erp Systems Benefits", 11th Annual Conference Of Asia Pacific Decision Sciences Institute PP. 201-213

33. David Williamson, Peter Cooke, Wyn Jenkins, and Keith Michael Moreton (2003) "Strategic Management and Business Analysis", Butterworth and Heinemann publications, Great Britain.

34. Barthorpe, S., Chien, H-J., et al. (2004) 'A survey of the potential for Enterprise Resource Planning (ERP) in improving the effectiveness of construction management in the UK construction industry', International Journal of Computer Applications in Technology, Vol. 20, Nos. 1–3, pp.120–128.

35. Beard, J.W. and Sumner, M. (2004) 'Seeking strategic advantage in the post-net era: viewing ERP systems from the resource-based perspective', Journal of Strategic Information Systems, Vol. 13, No. 2, pp.129–150.

36. Becerra-Fernandez, I., Murphy, K.E., et al. (2000) 'Integrating ERP in the business school curriculum', Communications of the ACM, Vol. 43, No. 4, pp.39–41.

37. Benders, J., Batenburg, R., et al. (2006) 'Sticking to standards; technical and other isomorphic pressures in deploying ERP-systems', Information and Management, Vol. 43, No. 2, pp.194–203.

38. Bendoly, E. (2003) 'Theory and support for process frameworks of knowledge discovery and data mining from ERP systems', Information and Management, Vol. 40, No. 7, pp.639–647.

39. Bendoly, E. and Jacobs, F.R. (2004) 'ERP architectural/operational alignment for order-processing performance', International Journal of Operations & Production Management, Vol. 24, No. 1, pp.99–117.

40. Chand, D., Hachey, G., et al. (2005) 'A balanced scorecard based framework for assessing the strategic impacts of ERP systems', Computers in Industry, Vol. 56, No. 6, pp.558–572.

41. Chen, I.J. (2001) 'Planning for ERP systems: analysis and future trend', Business Process Management Journal, Vol. 7, No. 5, pp.374–386.

42. Chen, R-S., Chen, C.C., et al. (2003) 'A web-based ERP data mining system for decision making', International Journal of Computer Applications in Technology, Vol. 17, No. 3, pp.156–169.

43. Choi, B.K. and Kim, B.H. (2002) 'MES (Manufacturing Execution System) architecture for FMS compatible to ERP (Enterprise Planning System)', International Journal of Computer Integrated Manufacturing, Vol. 15, No. 3, pp.274–284.

44. Chou, D.C., Tripuramallu, H.B., et al. (2005) 'BI and ERP integration', Information Management & Computer Security, Vol. 13, No. 5, pp.340–349.

45. Chung, S.H. and Snyder, C.A. (2000) 'ERP adoption: a technological evolution approach', International Journal of Agile Management Systems, Vol. 2, No. 1, pp.24–32.

46. Clemmons, S. and Simon, S.J. (2001) 'Control and coordination in global ERP configuration', Business Process Management Journal, Vol. 7, No. 3, pp.205–215.

47. Cowan, E.J. and Dder, L.B. (2003) 'The transformation of AT&T's enterprise network systems group to Avaya: enabling the virtual corporation through reengineering and enterprise resource planning', Journal of Information Systems Education, Vol. 14, No. 3, pp.325–331.

48. Davenport, T.H. (2000) 'The future of enterprise system-enabled organizations', Information Systems Frontiers, Vol. 2, No. 2, pp.163–180.

49. Davenport, T.H. and Brooks, J.D. (2004) 'Enterprise systems and the supply chain', Journal of Enterprise Information Management, Vol. 17, No. 1, pp.8–19.

50. Davenport, T.H., Harris, J.G., et al. (2004) 'Enterprise systems and ongoing process change', Business Process Management Journal, Vol. 10, No. 1, pp.16–26.

51. Davis, C.H. and Comeau, J. (2004) 'Enterprise integration in business education: design and outcomes of a capstone ERP-based undergraduate e-business management course', Journal of Information Systems Education, Vol. 15, No. 3, pp.287–299.

52. Dong, L. (2001) 'Modeling top management influence on ES implementation', Business Process Management Journal, Vol. 7, No. 3, pp.243–250.

53. Dowlatshahi, S. (2005) 'Strategic success factors in enterprise resource-planning design and implementation: a case-study approach', International Journal of Production Research, Vol. 43, No. 18, pp.3745–3771.

54. Fedorowicz, J., Gelinas, U.J., et al. (2004) 'Twelve tips for successfully integrating enterprise systems across the curriculum', Journal of Information Systems Education, Vol. 15, No. 3, pp.235–244.

55. Fleisch, E., Oersterle, H., et al. (2004) 'Rapid implementation of enterprise resource planning systems', Journal of Organizational Computing and Electronic Commerce, Vol. 14, No. 2, pp.107–126.

56. Frank, L. (2004) 'Architecture for integration of distributed ERP systems and e-commerce systems', Industrial Management & Data Systems, Vol. 104, No. 5, pp.418–429.

57. Gable, G.G., Chan, T., et al. (2001) 'Large packaged application software maintenance: a research framework', Journal of Software Maintenance and Evolution: Research and Practice, Vol. 13, No. 6, pp.351–371.

58. Gardiner, S.C., Hanna, J.B., et al. (2002) 'ERP and the reengineering of industrial marketing processes: a prescriptive overview for the new-age marketing manager', Industrial Marketing Management, Vol. 31, No. 4, pp.357–365.

59. Gargeya, V.B. and Brady, C. (2005) 'Success and failure factors of adopting SAP in ERP system implementation', Business Process Management Journal, Vol. 11, No. 5, pp.501–516.

60. Gattiker, T.F. and Goodhue, D.L. (2002) 'Software-driven changes to business processes: an empirical study of impacts of Enterprise Resource Planning (ERP) systems at the local level', International Journal of Production Research, Vol. 40, No. 18, pp.4799–4814.

61. Gattiker, T.F. and Goodhue, D.L. (2004) 'Understanding the local-level costs and benefits of ERP through organizational information processing theory', Information and Management, Vol. 41, No. 4, pp.431–443.

62. Gefen, D. (2002) 'Nurturing clients' trust to encourage engagement success during the customization of ERP systems', Omega, Vol. 30, No. 4, pp.287–299.

63. Gefen, D. (2004) 'What makes an ERP implementation relationship worthwhile: linking trust mechanisms and ERP usefulness', Journal of Management Information Systems, Vol. 21, No. 1, pp.263–288.

64. Ghoshal, S. and Gratton, L. (2002) 'Integrating the enterprise', Sloan Management Review, Vol. 44, No. 1, pp.31–38.

65. Gosain, S., Lee, Z., et al. (2005) 'The management of cross-functional inter-dependencies in ERP implementations: emergent coordination patterns', European Journal of Information Systems, Vol. 14, No. 4, pp.371–387.

66. Robey, D., Ross, J.W., et al. (2002) 'Learning to implement enterprise systems: an exploratory study of the dialectics of change', Journal of Management Information Systems, Vol. 19, No. 1, pp.17–46.

67. Robinson, B. and Wilson, F. (2001) 'Planning for the market? Enterprise resource planning systems and the contradictions of capital', The Data Base for Advances in Information Systems, Vol. 32, No. 4, pp.21–33.

68. Rolland, C. and Prakash, N. (2000) 'Bridging the gap between organizational needs and ERP functionality', Requirements Engineering, Vol. 5, No. 3, pp.180–193.

69. Rom, A. and Rohde, C. (2006) 'Enterprise resource planning systems, strategic enterprise management systems and management accounting: a Danish study', Journal of Enterprise Information Management, Vol. 19, No. 1, pp.50–66.

70. Rosemann, M. (2000) 'Using reference models within the enterprise resource planning lifecycle', Australian Accounting Review, Vol. 10, No. 3, pp.17–30.

71. Ross, J.W. and Vitale, M.R. (2000) 'The ERP revolution: surviving vs. thriving', Information Systems Frontiers, Vol. 2, No. 2, pp.233–241.

72. Rutner, S.M., Gibson, B.J., et al. (2003) 'The impacts of the integrated logistics systems on electronic commerce and enterprise resource planning systems', Transportation Research Part E: Logistics and Transportation Review, Vol. 39, No. 2, pp.83–93.

73. Sammon, D. and Adam, F. (2005) 'Towards a model of organisational prerequisites for enterprise-wide systems integration: examining ERP and data warehousing', Journal of Enterprise Information Management, Vol. 18, No. 4, pp.458–470.

74. Sarker, S. and Lee, A.S. (2003) 'Using a case study to test the role of three key social enablers in ERP implementation', Information and Management, Vol. 40, No. 8, pp.813–829.

75. Sarkis, J. and Sundarraj, R.P. (2003) 'Managing large-scale global enterprise resource planning systems: a cast study at Texas Instruments', International Journal of Information Management, Vol. 23, No. 5, pp.431–442.

76. Scheer, A-W. and Habermann, F. (2000) 'Making ERP a success – using business process models to achieve positive results', Communications of the ACM, Vol. 43, No. 4, pp.57–61.

77. Scott, J. and Kaindl, L. (2000) 'Enhancing functionality in an enterprise software package', Information and Management, Vol. 37, No. 3, pp.111–122.

78. Scott, J.E. and Vessey, I. (2000) 'Implementing enterprise resource planning systems: the role of learning from failure', Information Systems Frontiers, Vol. 2, No. 2, pp.213–232.

79. Scott, S.V. and Wagner, E.L. (2003) 'Networks, negotiations, and new times: the implementation of enterprise resource planning into an academic administration', Information and Organization, Vol. 13, No. 4, pp.285–313.

80. Sharif, A.M., Irani, Z., et al. (2005) 'Integrating ERP using EAI: a model for post hoc evaluation', European Journal of Information Systems, Vol. 14, No. 2, pp.162–174.

81. Sharma, S.K., Chen, C., et al. (2006) 'Implementation problems with ERP systems in virtual enterprises/virtual organisations', International Journal of Management and Enterprise Development, Vol. 3, No. 5, pp.491–509.

82. Sheu, C., Chae, B., et al. (2004) 'National difference and ERP implementation: issues and challenges', Omega, Vol. 32, No. 5, pp.361–371.

83. Shtub, A. (2001) 'A framework for teaching and training in the Enterprise Resource Planning (ERP) era', International Journal of Production Research, Vol. 39, No. 3, pp.567–576.

84. Sia, S.K., Tang, M., et al. (2002) 'Enterprise Resource Planning (ERP) systems as a technology of power: empowerment or panoptic control?', The Data Base for Advances in Information Systems, Vol. 33, No. 1, pp.23–37.

85. Siau, K. (2004) 'Enterprise Resource Planning (ERP) implementation methodologies', Journal of Database Management, Vol. 15, No. 1, pp.1–6.

86. Siau, K. and Messersmith, J. (2003) 'Analyzing ERP implementation at a public university using the innovation strategy model', International Journal of Human-Computer Interaction, Vol. 16, No. 1, pp.57–80.

87. Siriginidi, S.R. (2000) 'Enterprise resource planning in re-engineering business', Business Process Management Journal, Vol. 6, No. 5, pp.376–391.

88. Soffer, P., Golany, B., et al. (2003) 'ERP modeling: a comprehensive approach', Information Systems, Vol. 28, No. 6, pp.673–690.

89. Soffer, P., Golany, B., et al. (2005) 'Aligning an ERP system with enterprise requirements: an object-process based approach', Computers in Industry, Vol. 56, No. 6, pp.639–662.

90. Soh, C. and Sia, S.K. (2004) 'An institutional perspective on sources of ERP package – organisation misalignments', Journal of Strategic Information Systems, Vol. 13, No. 4, pp.375–397.

91. Soh, C., Kien, S.S., et al. (2000) 'Cultural fits and misfits: is ERP a universal solution?', Communications of the ACM, Vol. 43, No. 4, pp.47–51.

92. Soh, C., Sia, S.K., et al. (2003) 'Misalignments in ERP implementation: a dialectic perspective', International Journal of Human-Computer Interaction, Vol. 16, No. 1, pp.81–100.

93. Somers, T.M. and Nelson, K.G. (2003) 'The impact of strategy and integration mechanisms on enterprise system value: empirical evidence from manufacturing firms', European Journal of Operational Research, Vol. 146, No. 2, pp.315–338.

94. Somers, T.M. and Nelson, K.G. (2004) 'A taxonomy of players and activities across the ERP project life cycle', Information and Management, Vol. 41, No. 3, pp.257–278.

95. Somers, T.M., Nelson, K., et al. (2003) 'Confirmatory factor analysis of the end-user computing satisfaction instrument: replication within an ERP domain', Decision Sciences, Vol. 34, No. 3, pp.595–621.

96. Spathis, C. (2006) 'Enterprise systems implementation and accounting benefits', Journal of Enterprise Information Management, Vol. 19, No. 1, pp.67–82.

97. Spathis, C. and Ananiadis, J. (2005) 'Assessing the benefits of using an enterprise system in accounting information and management', Journal of Enterprise Information Management, Vol. 18, No. 2, pp.195–210.

98. Spathis, C. and Constantinides, S. (2003) 'The usefulness of ERP systems for effective management', Industrial Management & Data Systems, Vol. 103, No. 9, pp.677–685.

99. Spathis, C. and Constantinides, S. (2004) 'Enterprise Resource Planning systems' impact on accounting processes', Business Process Management Journal, Vol. 10, No. 2, pp.234–247.

100. Sprott, D. (2000) 'Componentizing the enterprise application packages', Communications of the ACM, Vol. 43, No. 4, pp.63–69.

101. Stefanou, C.J. (2001) 'A framework for the ex-ante evaluation of ERP software', European Journal of Information Systems, Vol. 10, No. 4, pp.204–215.

102. Stefanou, C.J. and Revanoglou, A. (2006) 'ERP integration in a healthcare environment: a case study', Journal of Enterprise Information Management, Vol. 19, No. 1, pp.115–130.

103. Stensrud, E. (2001) 'Alternative approaches to effort prediction of ERP projects', Information and Software Technology, Vol. 43, No. 7, pp.413–423.

104. Stensrud, E. and Myrtveit, I. (2003) 'Identifying high performance ERP projects', IEEE Transactions on Software Engineering, Vol. 29, pp.398–416.

105. Stevens, C.P. (2003) 'Enterprise resource planning: a trio of resources', Information Systems Management, Vol. 20, No. 3, pp.61–67.

106. Stewart, G. and Rosemann, M. (2001) 'Industry-oriented design of ERP-related curriculum – an Australian initiative', Business Process Management Journal, Vol. 7, No. 3, pp.234–242.

107. Stirling, M., Petty, D., et al. (2002) 'A methodology for developing integrated information systems based on ERP packages', Business Process Management Journal, Vol. 8, No. 5, pp.430–446.

108. Stratman, J.K. and Roth, A.V. (2002) 'Enterprise Resource Planning (ERP) competence constructs: two-stage multi-item scale development and validation', Decision Sciences, Vol. 33, No. 4, pp.601–628.

109. Nandhakumar, J., Rossi, M., et al. (2005) 'The dynamics of contextual forces of ERP implementation', Journal of Strategic Information Systems, Vol. 14, No. 2, pp.221–242.

110. Ndede-Amadi, A.A. (2004) 'What strategic alignment, process redesign, enterprise resource planning, and e-commerce have in common: enterprise-wide computing', Business Process Management Journal, Vol. 10, No. 2, pp.184–199.

111. Newell, S., Huang, J.C., et al. (2003) 'Implementing enterprise resource planning and knowledge management systems in tandem: fostering efficiency and innovation complementarily', Information and Organization, Vol. 13, No. 1, pp.25–52.

112. Newman, M. and Westrup, C. (2005) 'Making ERPs work: accountants and the introduction of ERP systems', European Journal of Information Systems, Vol. 14, No. 3, pp.258–272.

113. Ng, C.S.P. (2001) 'A decision framework for enterprise resource planning maintenance and upgrade: a client perspective', Journal of Software Maintenance and Evolution: Research and Practice, Vol. 13, No. 6, pp.431–468.

114. Vosburg, J. and Kumar, A. (2001) 'Managing dirty data in organizations using ERP: lessons from a case study', Industrial Management & Data Systems, Vol. 101, No. 1, pp.21–31.

115. Wagner, E.L. and Newell, S. (2004) '"Best" for whom? The tension between "best practice" ERP packages and diverse epistemic cultures in a university context', Journal of Strategic Information Systems, Vol. 13, No. 4, pp.305–328.

116. Wang, C., Xu, L., et al. (2005) 'ERP research, development and implementation in China: an overview', International Journal of Production Research, Vol. 43, No. 18, pp.3915–3932.

117. Wang, E.T.G. and Chen, J.H.F. (2006) 'The influence of governance equilibrium on ERP project success', Decision Support Systems, Vol. 41, No. 4, pp.708–727.

118. Ward, J., Hemingway, C., et al. (2005) 'A framework for addressing the organizational issues of enterprise systems implementation', Journal of Strategic Information Systems, Vol. 14, No. 2, pp.97–119.

119. Watanabe, C. and Hobo, M. (2004) 'Creating a firm self-propagating function for advanced innovation-oriented projects: lessons from ERP', Technovation, Vol. 24, No. 6, pp.467–481.

120. Wei, C-C. and Wang, M.J.J. (2004) 'A comprehensive framework for selecting an ERP system', International Journal of Project Management, Vol. 22, No. 2, pp.161–169.

121. Wei, H-L., Wang, E.T.G., et al. (2005) 'Understanding misalignment and cascading change of ERP implementation: a stage view of process analysis', European Journal of Information Systems, Vol. 14, No. 4, pp.324–334.

122. Weston, Jr., F.D.T. (2001) 'ERP implementation and project management', Production and Inventory Management Journal, Vol. 42, Nos. 3–4, pp.75–80.

123. Weston Jr., F.D.T. (2003) 'ERP II: the extended enterprise system', Business Horizons, Vol. 46, No. 6, pp.49–55.

Chapter 04

Data Collection, Observation and Interpretation

4.1 Introduction:

This chapter provides information on the research methods of this thesis. A descriptive / Qualitative / Survey Based research methodology was used for this study. A survey was administered to a selected sample from a specific Medium Scale Manufacturing Units identified by the Development Commissioner (MSME) Ministry of Micro, Small & Medium Enterprises, Mumbai and Nagpur Division.

The samples are selected on the basis of the knowledge, connection and judgment of the researcher in the Medium Scale Manufacturing industry in Maharashtra State. It is through the researchers personal and work relationships with the Individuals in medium scale manufacturing units and their references further units for same division or others to ensure the participation and completion of this survey. Most of them are Managerial, professionals and executives companies. MSME, DC-MSME, Mumbai and Nagpur, updated industry news and events, personal experience and other information all help to form the basis for the selection and ongoing maintenance of samples.

The survey will be consisted close-ended questions formulated aiming to ensure more in-depth information is provided. The questions are formulated based on the objectives, research question and hypothesis of this research.

The analysis of the survey data is processed using Microsoft Excel and the add-in software Analyze It like IBM SPSS Statistics Data Editor 2010 Ed. Collected data was compiled in MS-excel sheet, for analysis the collected data SPSS (Statistical Package for Social Sciences Ver. 20th) was used.

The statistical analyses that have been conducted include: overall multi-dimension constructs measurement towards each factor, descriptive statistics, of frequency and percentile manner. The data is analyze questionnaire wise and Reponses are get collected and interpretations done by using frequency and percentile of the frequency as compare to the total number of respondent. The Cross Tabulation or Cross Factors Analysis is used for the correlation between the industrial Zone-wise medium Scale manufacturing units towards each factor and the actual percentage of their occurrences with entire MSME and each zone wise. Tabulation and charts are provided for the ease of comparison between different categories. Other information related to respondents also designed by pie charts, Line charts and column charts for more pictorial description and analysis.

Sr. No.	Information	Types	Number of Industry (n=145)	Percentage
1	Industrial Zone of Maharashtra	Desh (Pune Div)	23	15.86%
		Khadesh (Nasik Div)	19	13.1%
		Koken (Mumbai Div)	43	29.66%
		Marathwada (Aurangabad Div)	29	20%
		Vidharabha (Nagpur Div)	21	14.48%
		Vidharabha (Amravati Div)	10	6.9%

Sr. No.	Information	Types	Number of Industry (n=145)	Percentage
2	End Product	Agricultural	28	19.31 %
		Automobile	23	15.86 %
		Chemical	11	7.59 %
		Construction Equipments	8	5.52 %
		Electrical Equipments	16	11.03 %
		Electronic Equipments	5	3.45 %
		Energy	6	4.14 %
		Food Processing	5	3.45 %
		Home Appliances	13	8.97 %
		Liquor	2	1.38 %
		Pharmaceutical	14	9.66 %
		Software	6	4.14 %
		Textiles	8	5.52 %
3	No. of Employees	Up to 50	0	0%
		51 to 150	1	0.69%
		151 to 300	100	68.97%
		More than 300	44	30.34%
4	Annual Turnover	Less Than 3 Crore	0	0%
		03 to 10 Crore	0	0%
		10 to 25 Crore	5	3.45%
		More than 25 Crore	140	96.55%

Table 4.1 General Information of Manufacturing Units

(Source: Primary data)

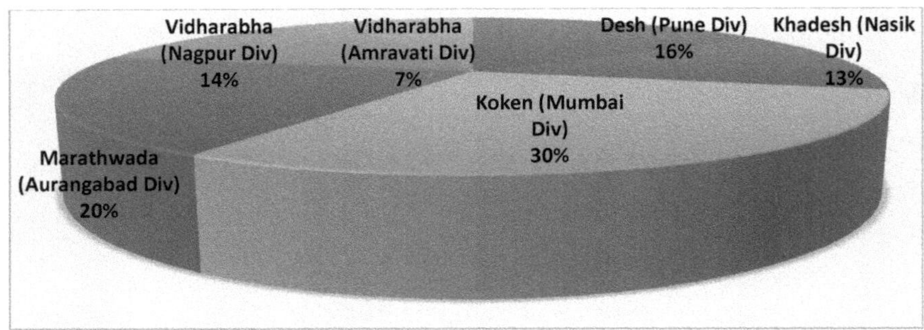

Figure 4.1 Details of Industrial Zone Wise MSMU Respondents

(Source: Primary data)

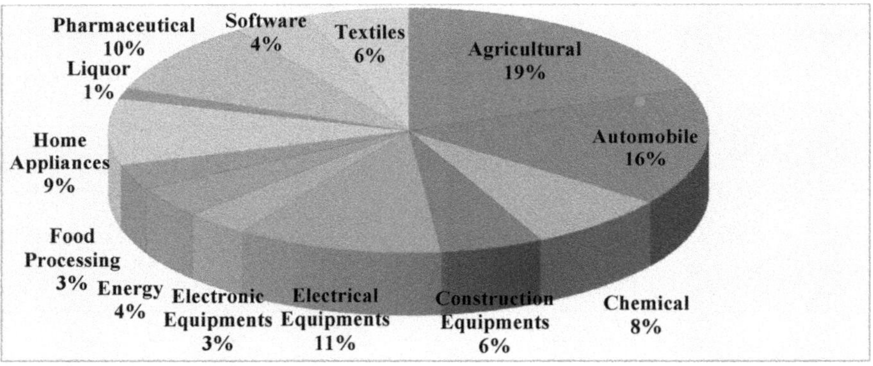

Figure 4.2 Details of End-product Wise MSMU Respondents

(Source: Primary Data)

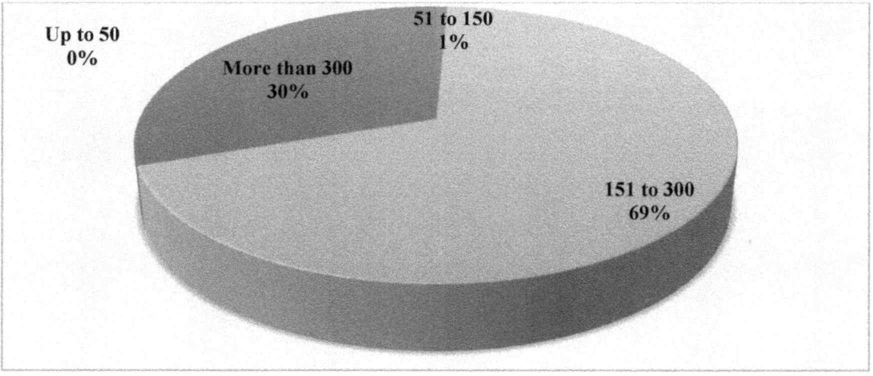

Figure 4.3 Details of No. of Employees in MSMU Respondents

(Source: Primary Data)

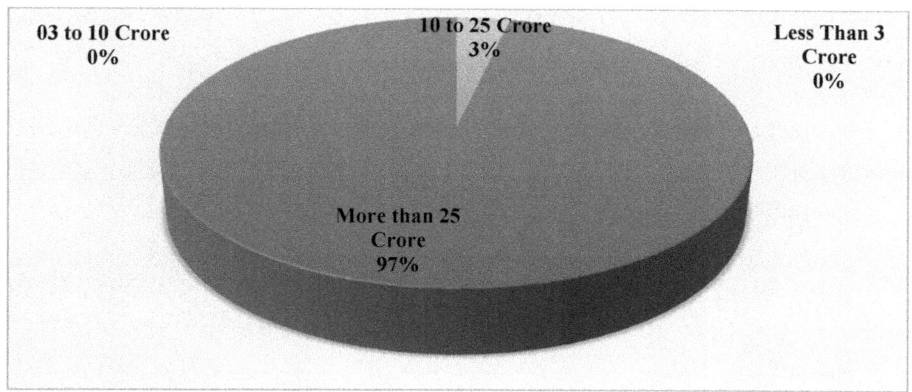

Figure 4.4 Details of Annual Turnover of MSMU Respondents
(Source: Primary Data)

The table 4.1 carried out the information about the respondent manufacturing units of Maharashtra state, whereas total 145 respondents are get consider for the interoperations and analysis. The table carries four part start with the industrial zone, end product of the MSMU, total number of employees in the MSMU and annual turnover of the manufacturing unit.

The study proves that, the respondents are belongs six different industrial zones of Maharashtra state whereas, 29.66% are from Mumbai division, Aurangabad Division with 20% and Amravati Division participated only 6.9%.

In second part of table 4.1, study enlighten that end product wise, Agricultural product manufacturing units share 19.31% of ERP implementation market whereas, automobile and electrical equipments are combined share 27% area of respondents . Liquor as a end product is only 1.38%.

The third part of the table number of employees worked in the MSMU of respondent's manufacturing unit, it gives details as, 69% almost MSMU having 151 to 300 number of employees in their firm whereas,

30.34% having employee count are than 300 and only 0.69% MSMU have employee 51 to 150 in their firm.

In last part of the study in table 4.1 is shown that, over 96% MSMU have their turnover is more than 25 crores whereas; only 3.45% MSMU having their turnover is between 10 to 25 crores.

At last the study also showed that, **no MSMU respondents having their turnover less than 10 crores who implemented ERP in their MSMU.**

Sr. No.	Information	Types	Number of Industry (n=145)	Percentage
1	Gender	Male	144	**99.31%**
		Female	1	**0.69%**
2	Designation	GM(Operation)	9	**6.21%**
		IT Head/Manager	13	**8.97%**
		Manager-Production	33	**22.8%**
		Retail Sales Manager	14	**9.66%**
		Sr. Manager	43	**29.7%**
		Sr. Engineer	18	**12.4%**
3	Work Experience	Less Than 1 Yrs	00	**00%**
		01 to 05 Yrs	40	**27.6%**
		05 to 10 Yrs	52	**35.9%**
		More than 10 yrs	53	**36.6%**
4	Income Group	Up To 05 Lacs	0	**0%**
		05 to 10 Lacs	75	**51.7%**
		More than10 Lacs	70	**48.3%**

Table 4.2 Respondent's Personal Information

(Source: Primary Data Collected)

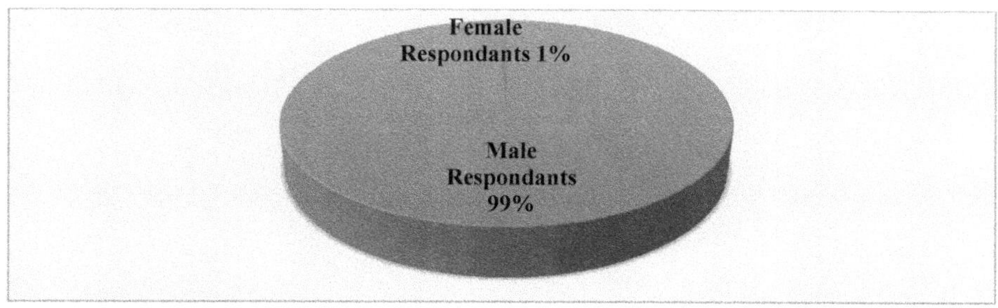

Figure 4.5 Gender details of MSMU Respondents

(Source: Primary Data)

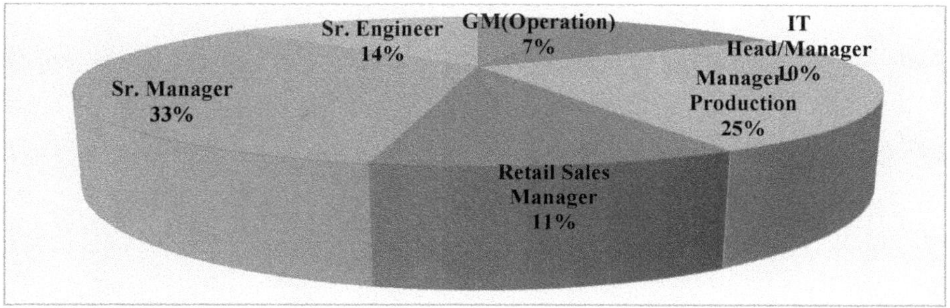

Figure 4.6 Designation details of MSMU Respondents

(Source: Primary Data)

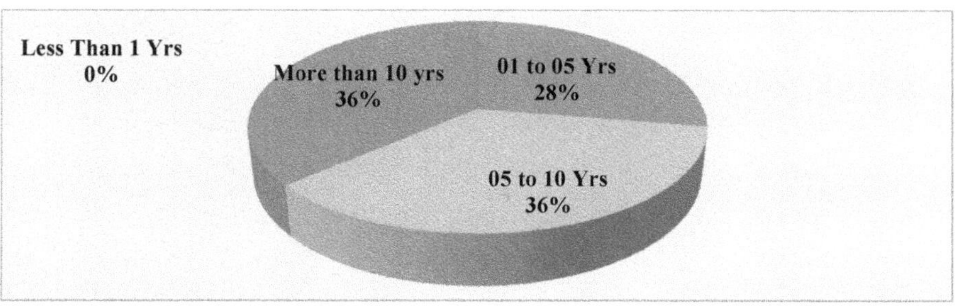

Figure 4.7 Experience details of MSMU Respondents

(Source: Primary Data)

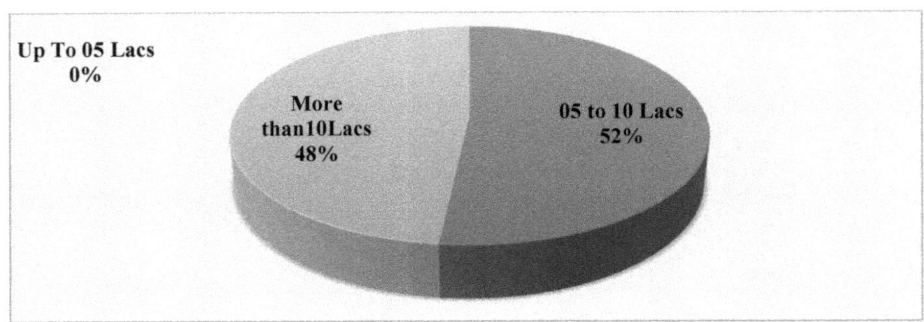

Figure 4.8 Annual Income details of MSMU Respondents

(Source: Primary Data)

The study revealed that, male respondents are 99.31% in the research whereas, only .69% i.e. 1 respondents. In second part of table 4.2 details of designation of the respondents are collected which illustrate that, 29.7% respondents are Sr. manager level and 22.8% is manager-production and only 6.21% are GM (Operation).

The research also prove that, 36.6% respondents are more than 10yrs of working experience whereas, 63.5% are having work experience between 01 yrs to 10yrs.

The study also discovered that, no respondents having less that 1 year of experience considered for the research. The research highlights on income group of respondents in last section of table 4.2 whereas, 48.3% are having their income group more than 10lacs whereas, 51.7% having their annual income between 05 to 10lacs. It also shows that no respondents in the study earn less than 5 lacs as annual income in the MSMU.

Sr. No.	Information	Types	Number of Industry (n=145)	Percentage
1	Which ERP system(s) you Manufacturing Industry currently using	SAP	140	96.55%
		Oracle	05	03.45%
2	ERP has been Used BY Respondent	Less Than 1 Yrs	18	12.4%
		01 to 03 Yrs	32	22.1%
		03 to 05 Yrs	32	22.1%
		More than 05 yrs	63	43.4%
3	Time took for ERP implementation in the industry	Under 09 months	0	0.0%
		09 months to 01 year	0	0.0%
		01 year to 1.5 years	26	17.9%
		1.5 year to 02 years	46	31.7%
		02 years to 2.5 years	4	2.8%
		2.5 years to 03 years	20	13.8%
		Over 03 years	49	33.8%
4	Need to re-engineer the business processes	Prior to the implementation	31	21.4%
		As part of the implementation	80	55.2%
		After the implementation	2	1.4%
		No re-engineering done	32	22.1%

Table 4.3 Fundamental Information of Current ERP System in Manufacturing Unit

(Source: Primary Data)

In table 4.3, the research attested that, out of many venders name only SAP and Oracle venders are more favorite venders in Maharashtra state for ERP implementation in MSMSU.

First part of the table 4.3 discloses that, 96.55% MSMU used Sap as ERP vender in their firm whereas, 03.45% MSMU dare to go with Oracle as ERP vender. No MSMU try for PeopleSoft, J.D. Edwards, BAAN, and any other ERP venders which are more popular in the globe.

In second part of table 4.3, the research made known that, 43.40% MSMU using the EERP system in their firm since last 05 yrs whereas, 44.22% MSMU using ERP system in their units between 01yrs to 05yrs. It also discovers from the study that, some MSMU in respondents are using ERP system since less than 01 year.3.

Third part of table discussed about time taken for ERP implementation in the respondents MSMU, the study investigated that, 33.8% MSMU took more than 03years for ERP implementation whereas, only 2.80% MSMU took 02 to 2.5yrs for same. 13.8% MSMU took 2.5yrs to 03yrs whereas, 49.6% MSMU implemented ERP system in their firm in-between 1yr to 02yrs span. One interesting outcome of the study is no MSMU agree for time duration for ERP implementation is less than a year.

In table 4.3, fourth and last part of the study exposed the opinion about when the BPR process need in ERP implementation. The study discloses that, 55.20% of MSMU used BPR process as a part of ERO implementations process (i.e. in-implementation phase of ERP) and 21.4% MSMU agree about BPR process done at prior to the ERP implementation. 1.4% MSMU took BPR process after the ERP get implemented in the firm. The study exposed about the BPR awareness in MSMU by the outcome as, 22.10% MSMU didn't go for ERP implementation process while they have went for ERP implementation process.

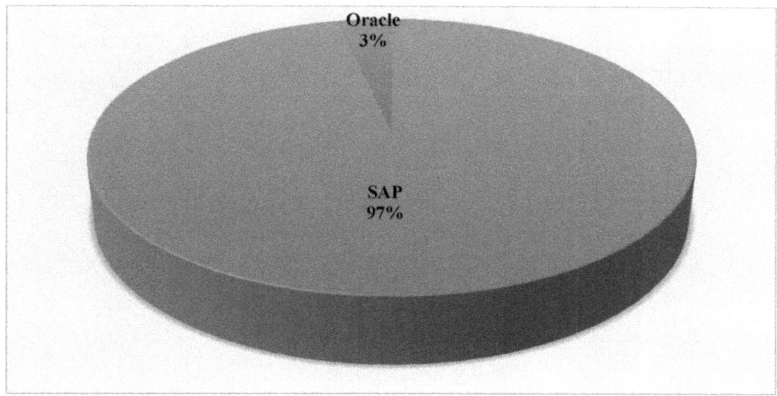

Figure 4.9 ERP venders details of MSMU Respondents

(Source: Primary Data)

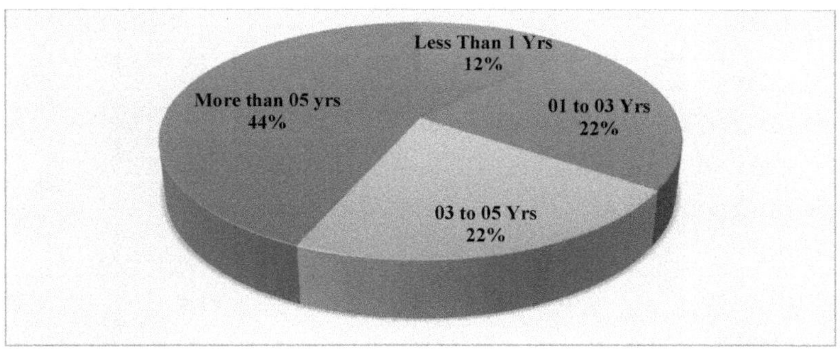

Figure 4.10 Duration of ERP system used by MSMU Respondents

(Source: Primary Data)

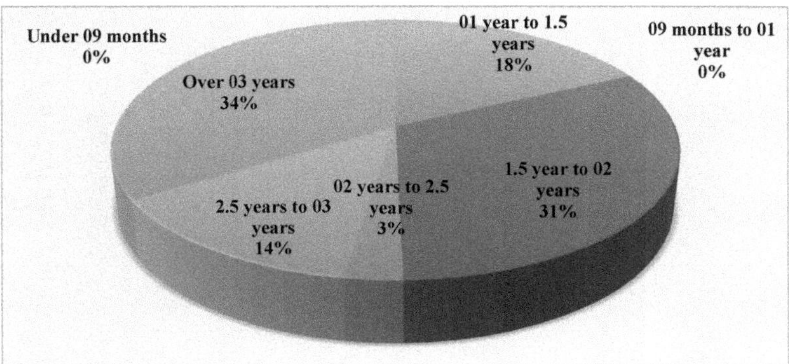

Figure 4.11 Duration of ERP implementation details of MSMU Respondents

(Source: Primary Data)

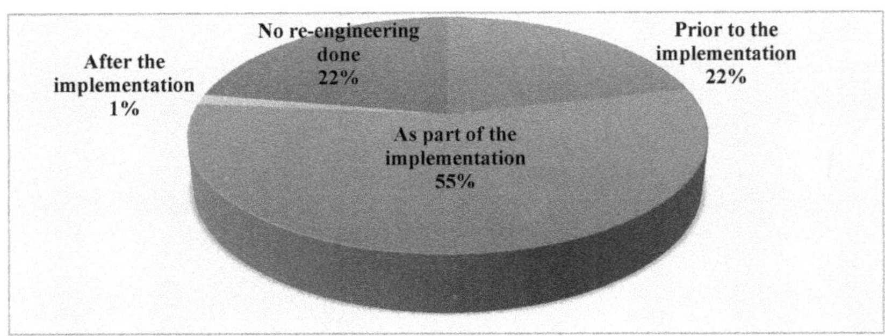

Figure 4.12 Opinion details about BPR Process in ERP implementation of MSMU Respondents

(Source: Primary Data)

Sr. No.	Information	Types	Number of Industry (n=145)	Percentage
1	Total no of computer systems in Manufacturing Unit	01 to 50	0	0%
		51 to 100	13	9.0%
		100 to 150	59	40.7%
		More than 150	73	50.3%
2	ERP Implementation Strategy	Don't know	119	82.1%
		Parallel approach	18	12.4%
		Phased approach	8	5.5%
3	Type of training is provided	Project team training	8	5.5%
		End user training/ Module Based training	96	66.2%
		Traditional training	2	1.4%
		Web-based training	0	0%
		No additional training provided	39	26.9%

Sr. No.	Information	Types	Number of Industry (n=145)	Percentage
4	Typical employee learn to the ERP Application	Mastered in a week	0	0.0%
		Mastered in a month	56	38.4%
		Mastered in 3 months	50	34.5%
		Mastered in 6 months	29	20.0%
		Rarely mastered	10	6.9%
5	Approximate training cost in terms of the overall ERP budget	Over 20%	2	1.4%
		16% to 20%	13	9.0%
		11% to 15%	16	11.0%
		6% to 10%	9	6.2%
		Below 5%	105	72.4%
		No idea	2	1.4%

Table 4.4 Fundamental Information of Current ERP System in Manufacturing Unit

(Source: Primary Data)

The table 4.4 discussed the fundamental information about the current ERP system used in respondents MEMU. The table highlighted the five different information like, total number of computers, ERP implementation strategy, type of training provided to employee, expertise while ERP learning and finally approx. training cost for ERP system. First part of table 4.4 illustrate that, 50.3% respondents MSMU having more than 150 computers in the firm whereas, 40.7% MSMU have 100 to 150 Computer system and only 9.0% respondents have less than 100 computer system and one interesting output came with the study that, no MSMU who implemented ERP system into their firm have less than 50 computers in their manufacturing unit.

The study also revealed about the ERP implementation strategy in second part of the table 4.4 that, 82.11% respondent have no idea about what ERP strategy used in their MSMU while ERP implemented in their firm.12.4% MSMU used Parallel Approach and only 5.5% used Phased Approach while implementing ERP in their firm. One last point would like to discuss in the analysis in regards of ERP implementation strategy, no MSMU used or choose for Big-Bang, Pilot Approach or any other approach.

In regards of third part of table 4.4, 66.2% MSMU used End User / Module based training to their employee whereas, 5.5% used Project team training and 1.4% used Traditional training type. 26.9% MSMU does not provided an additional training to their employee for ERP system use whereas, no MSMU provided Web based training to their end user (Employees) for using ERP system in their manufacturing unit.

Fourth part of the table provides information on how quickly employee of the MSMU learn the ERP system, the research proves that, 38.4% claim that, they can become masters in a month whereas, 34.5% agree on masters in 3months. 20% MSMU ready to accept that they can become masters in 6month of time whereas, 6.9% MSMU genuinely accepted that there are rarely some get mastery on the ERP application. No MSU dare to say about their mastery in a week on ERP system.

Last part of the table, the study highlight on approximate training cost in-terms of overall budget of ERP implementation. The study proves that, 72.4% MSMU spend less than 5% cost on training whereas, 21.4% spend more than 10% cost on training for their employee and 6.2% agreed on 6% to 10% cost on training get spend and at last 1.4% MSMU also agree about there is no idea on how much cost the organization spend on the training for ERP system, due to they think so, the cost on training for ERP system implementation is decided by the Top level management and not all MSMU respondents are belongs to the such level.

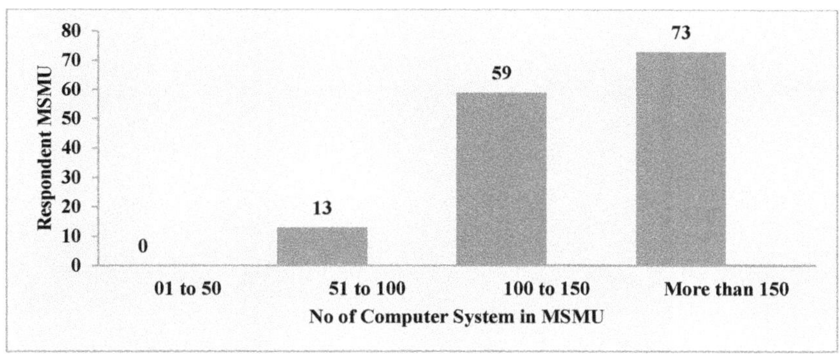

Figure 4.13 No of Computer system details of MSMU Respondents

(Source: Primary Data)

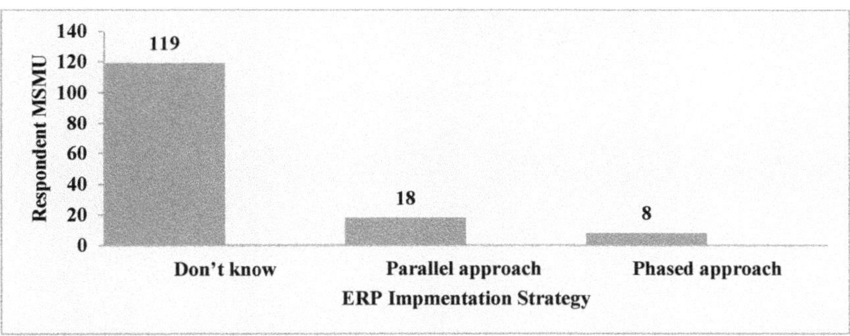

Figure 4.14 ERP Implementation Strategy used by MSMU Respondents

(Source: Primary Data)

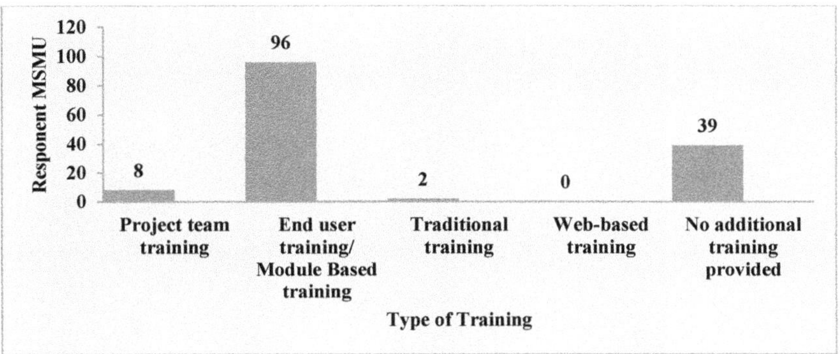

Figure 4.15 Type of Training provided to Employee by MSMU Respondents

(Source: Primary Data)

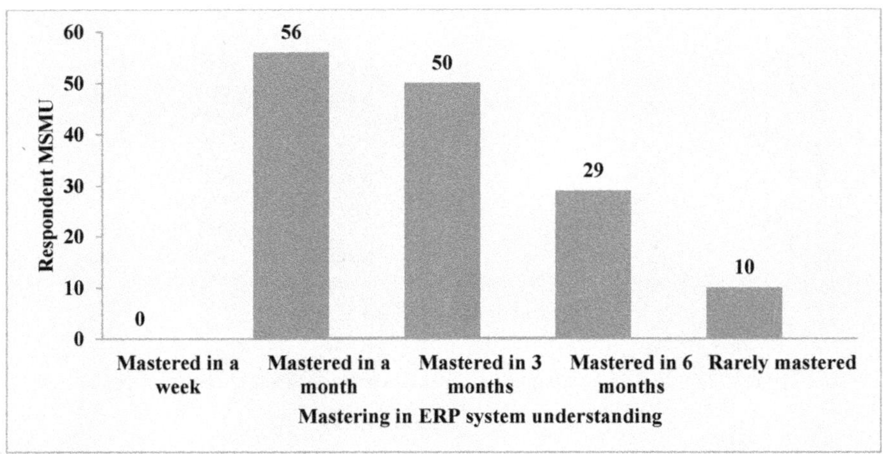

Figure 4.16 Duration for become mastery on ERP Application by MSMU Respondents

(Source: Primary Data)

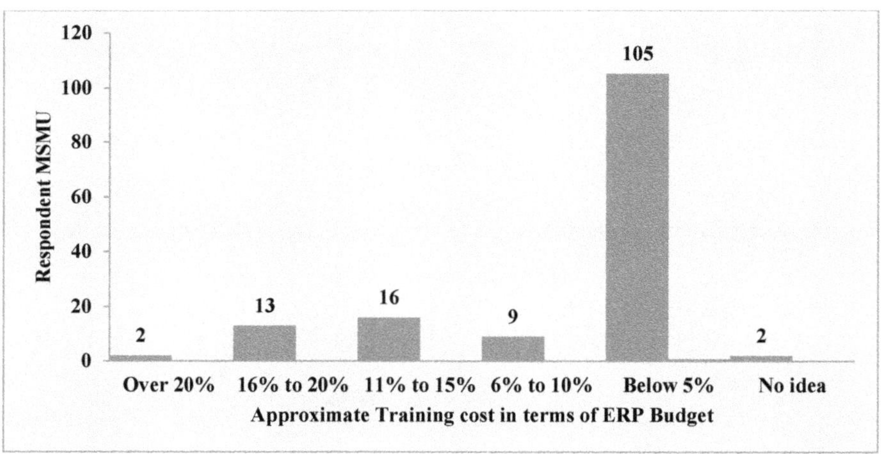

Figure 4.17 Approximate Training cost spend by MSMU Respondents

(Source: Primary Data)

Sr. No.	Need	Rank-I		Rank-II		Rank-III	
		Number of Industry (n=145)	Percentage	Number of Industry (n=145)	Percentage	Number of Industry (n=145)	Percentage
A	To Standardization of the Business Process by introducing Technical Support System	5	3.45%	21	14.48%	0	0%
B	Adoption of International best practice Business process	7	4.83%	13	8.97%	0	0%
C	To improve resource utilization within the organization	87	60%	46	31.72%	57	39.31%
D	To enabling the future growth in work Competency	25	17.24%	28	19.31%	29	20.0%
E	Increasing the firm's flexibility, acceptability and adoptability to respond new market opportunities	6	4.14%	22	15.17%	27	18.62%
F	To improve management control on Business process	15	10.34%	15	10.34%	16	11.03%
G	Other	0	0%	0	0%	16	11.03%

Table 4.5 Need of Manufacturing Industry to implement ERP System

(Source: Primary data)

- The study was found that, 60% of manufacturing units choice Rank-I to the need of ERP system implementation in their firm for improving resources utilization within the organization. As 31.72% manufacturing units Rank – II for the resource utilization as need and 39.31% units are keep as Rank-III as need to the resource utilization within the organization
- The research also revealed that, 17.24% manufacturing units given Rank-I to the need as enabling the future growth in work Competency, 19.31% units Rank-II and 20% gives Rank-III.
- The study also shows that, only 3.45% manufacturing nits consider as need "to standardization of the business process introducing technical support system" as Rank-I, some units made Rank-II to "Adoption of international best practice business process" as need and 11.03% manufacturing units decided to implement ERP system in their organization "to improve management control on the business process" and choice it as Rank-III.

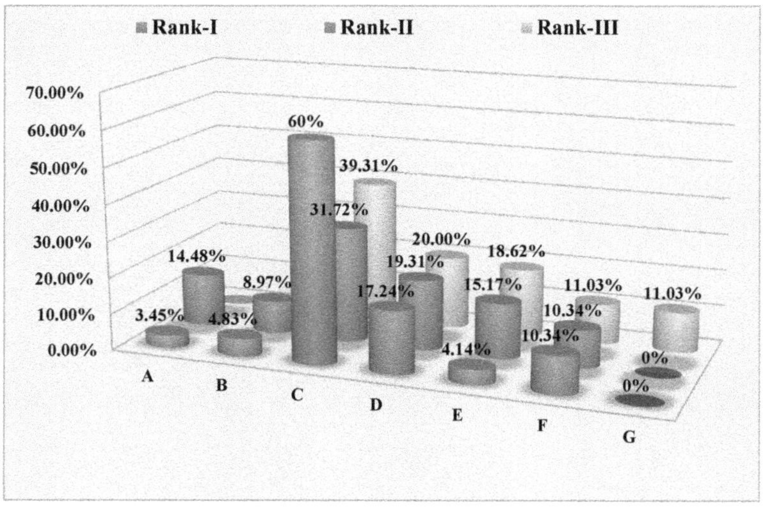

Figure 4.18 Need of ERP implementation (Rank Wise) by MSMU Respondents (Source: Primary Data)

Sr. No.	Operational Critical Success Factor Number of Industry (n=145)	Rank-I		Rank-II		Rank-III	
		Percentage	Number of Industry (n=145)	Percentage	Number of Industry (n=145)	Percentage	
A	Preliminary business process analysis (Business Process Re-Engineering)	86	59.3%	0	0%	0	0%
B	Change management	26	17.9%	8	5.5%	0	0%
C	Performance evaluation and measurement	26	17.9%	46	31.7%	8	5.5%
D	Training and education	0	0%	18	12.4%	22	15.2%
E	Project management	4	2.8%	34	23.4%	10	6.9%
F	Top Management support	0	0%	30	20.7%	14	9.7%
G	Managing Risk management	3	2.1%	6	4.1%	36	24.8%
H	Internal staff adequacy	0	0%	3	2.1%	49	33.8%
I	Make bet use of external consultant and experts	0	0%	0	0%	6	4.1%
J	Other, Please Specify	0	0%	0	0%	0	0%

Table 4.6 Operational Critical Success Factor of an ERP Implementation

(Source: Primary Data)

- The study was found that, 59.3% of manufacturing unit's choice Rank-I to the Preliminary business process analysis(Business Process Re-Engineering as Operational CSF in their firm whereas, 31.72% manufacturing units Rank – II for Performance evaluation and measurements Operational Critical success factor and 33.8% units are keep as Rank-III as Operational CSF to the Internal staff adequacy within the organization

- The research also revealed that, 35.8% manufacturing units combined agree on Change Management and Performance evaluation and measurement as Operational Critical success factor as Rank-I t whereas, 44.1% MSMU gives combined rank-II to Project Management and Top Management Support as Operational CSF and 30% MSMU gives Rank-III to Training and education with Managing Risk Management in ERP implementation as Operational Critical success factors.

- The study also shows that, only 2.1 % manufacturing units consider as Operational CSF to Managing Risk Management as Rank-I, 2.1% units made Rank-II to the Internal staff adequacy and 4.1% manufacturing units decided to gives Rank-III to Make best use of external consultant and experts as Operational Critical success Factors while ERP implementation in their manufacturing unit.

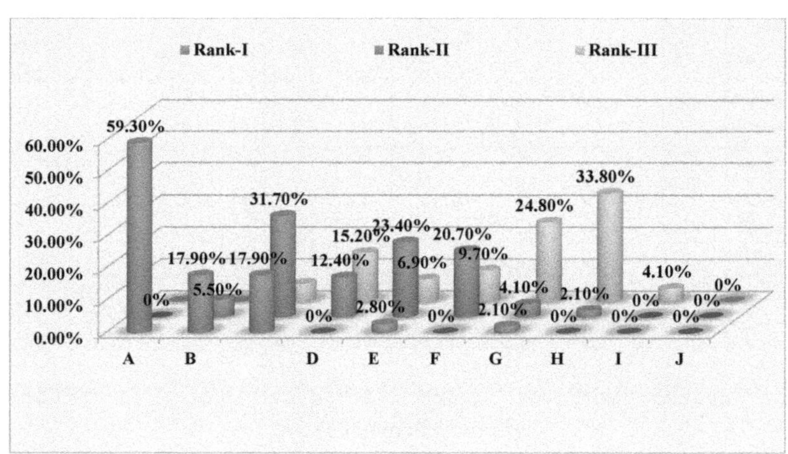

Figure 4.19 Operational CSF for ERP implementation (Rank Wise) by MSMU Respondents
(Source: Primary Data)

Sr. No.	Managerial Critical Success Factor	Rank-I		Rank-II		Rank-III	
		Number of Industry (n=145)	Percentage	Number of Industry (n=145)	Percentage	Number of Industry (n=145)	Percentage
A	Redesigning business processes to fit software	60	41.4%	0	0%	0	0%
B	Organizational commitment and leadership	43	29.7%	9	6.2%	1	.7%
C	Allocation of the responsibility and job definitions	39	26.9%	79	54.5%	6	4.1%
D	Project size	0	0%	0	0%	8	5.5%
E	Unreasonable deadlines	0	0%	0	0%	37	25.5%
F	High initial investment	3	2.1%	43	29.7%	17	11.7%
G	Dynamic Environment	0	0%	3	2.1%	18	12.4%
H	Adequate internal expertise	0	0%	11	7.6%	31	21.4%
I	Sufficient standardization and discipline	0	0%	0	0%	27	18.6%
J	Other, Please Specify	0	0%	0	0%	0	0%

Table 4.7 Managerial Critical Success Factor of an ERP Implementation
(Source: Primary Data)

- The study was found that, 41.4% of respondent units choice Rank-I to the Redesigning business processes to fit software as a managerial Critical success factor for the organization. As 54.5% manufacturing units Rank – II for the Allocation of the responsibility and job definitions and 46.9% units are keep as Rank-III combined to Unreasonable deadlines and Adequate internal expertise as Managerial CSF while implementation ERP within the organization

- The research also revealed that, 29.7% for organizational commitments and leadership and 26.9% for allocation of the responsibility and job definitions are consider for a Rank-I by respondent MSMU as managerial CSF whereas, 29.7% MSMU chosen High initial investment as Rank-II and 11.7% ranked-III as managerial critical success factor for ERP implementation.

- The study also confirm that, only 2.1% manufacturing units consider as Management CSF to high initial investment by the organization for ERP implementation as Rank-I, 2.1% units made Rank-II to Dynamic environments and 4.1%% manufacturing units decided to choice as Rank-III to Allocation of the responsibility and job definitions as managerial critical success factor for ERP implementation in their organization.

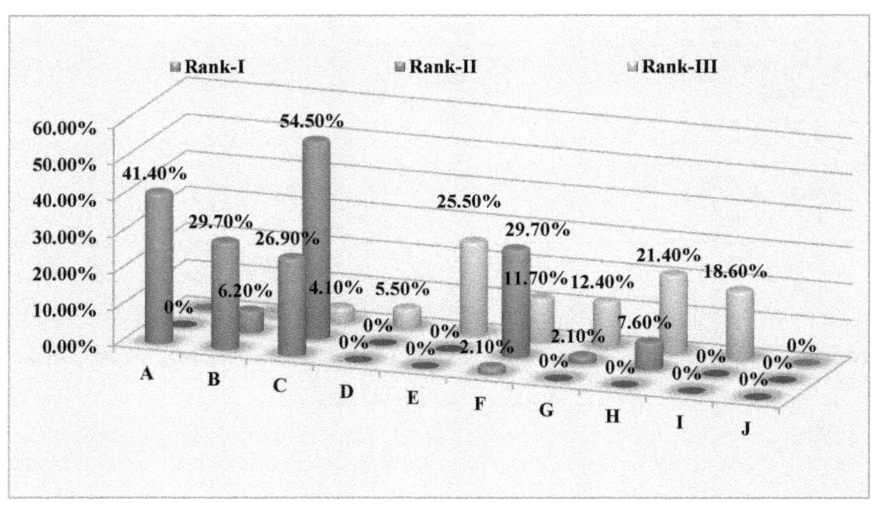

Figure 4.20 Managerial CSF for ERP implementation (Rank Wise) by MSMU Respondents

(Source: Primary Data)

Sr. No.	Technical Critical Success Factor	Rank-I		Rank-II		Rank-III	
		Number of Industry (n=145)	Percentage	Number of Industry (n=145)	Percentage	Number of Industry (n=145)	Percentage
A	Integration with software	61	42.1%	0	0%	0	0%
B	Avoiding technical bottlenecks	32	22.1%	9	6.2%	0	0%
C	Software development, testing and trouble shooting	17	11.7%	8	5.5%	2	1.4%
D	ERP architecture and system integration	31	21.4%	41	28.3%	2	1.4%
E	Put very best people in implementation team	2	1.4%	0	0%	15	10.3%
F	Data conversion and migration	0	0%	58	40.0%	33	22.8%
G	ERP customization	2	1.4%	25	17.2%	10	6.9%
H	Inadequate infrastructure and interfaces	0	0%	4	2.8%	54	37.2%
I	Unrealistic expectations of ROI (Return on Investment)	0	0%	0	0%	29	20.0%
J	Other, Please Specify	0	0%	0	0%	0	0%

Table 4.8 Technical Critical Success Factor of an ERP Implementation.

(Source Primary Data)

- The study was found that, 42.1% of respondent units choice Rank-I to the Integration with software as a Technical Critical success factor for the organization. As 40.0% manufacturing units Rank – II for Data Conversion and data migration as Technical CSF whereas, Inadequate infrastructure and interfaces CSF keep as Rank-III by 37.2% MSMU while implementation ERP within the organization

- The research also revealed that, 43.1% combined MSMU opt as Rank-I Avoiding technical bottlenecks and ERP architecture and system integration as technical CSF and 28.3% respond to ERP architecture and system integration as Rank-II whereas, 22.8% MSMU chosen data conversion and migration as Rank-III Technical critical success factor for ERP implementation.

- Only 1.4% manufacturing units consider as Technical CSF to Put very best people in implementation team and ERP customization as Rank-I, 2.8% units made Rank-II to Inadequate infrastructure and interface whereas, 1.4% manufacturing units decided to choice as Rank-III to Software development, testing and trouble shooting and ERP architecture and system integration as Technical critical success factor for ERP implementation in their organization.

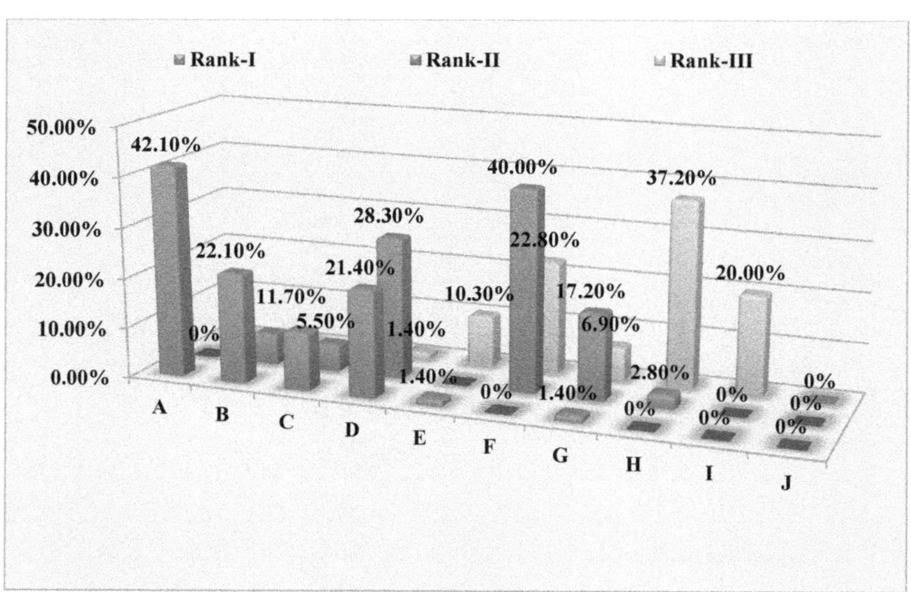

Figure 4.21 Technical CSF for ERP implementation (Rank Wise) by MSMU Respondents
(Source: Primary Data)

Sr. No.	Financial Critical Success Factor	Rank-I		Rank-II		Rank-III	
		Number of Industry (n=145)	Percentage	Number of Industry (n=145)	Percentage	Number of Industry (n=145)	Percentage
A	Ensure the project has sufficient budget	49	33.8%	0	0%	6	4.1%
B	Controlled ERP implementation cost	37	25.5%	21	14.5%	1	.7%
C	Proper planning and execution cost	40	27.6%	42	29.0%	11	7.6%
D	Change in infrastructure cost	6	4.1%	31	21.4%	0	0%
E	Miscellaneous cost	7	4.8%	20	13.8%	28	19.3%
F	Government financial policy changes	6	4.1%	8	5.5%	15	10.3%
G	Improper training cost	0	0%	10	6.9%	9	6.2%
H	Project delay cost	0	0%	13	9.0%	51	35.2%
I	Ignoring or underestimating hidden cost	0	0%	0	0%	24	16.6%
J	Other, Please Specify	0	0%	0	0%	0	0%

Table 4.9 Financial Critical Success Factor of an ERP Implementation

(Source Primary Data)

- The study was found that, 33.8% of respondent units choice Rank-I to the Ensure the project has sufficient budget as a Financial Critical success factor for the organization. As 50.0% manufacturing units Rank – II for Proper planning and execution cost and Change in infrastructure cost combined as

Financial CSF whereas, Project delay cost CSF keep as Rank-III by 35.2% MSMU while implementation ERP within the organization

- 53..1% combined MSMU opted as Rank-I Controlled ERP implementation cost and Proper planning and execution cost as Financial CSF and 14.5% respond to Controlled ERP implementation cost as Rank-II whereas, 19.3 % MSMU chosen Miscellaneous Cost as Rank-III Financial critical success factor for ERP implementation.

- Only 4.1% manufacturing units combined consider as Financial CSF to Change in infrastructure cost and Government financial policy changes as Rank-I, 5.5% units made Rank-II to Government financial policy changes whereas, 4.1% manufacturing units decided to choice as Rank-III to Ensure the project has sufficient budget as Financial critical success factor for ERP implementation in their organization.

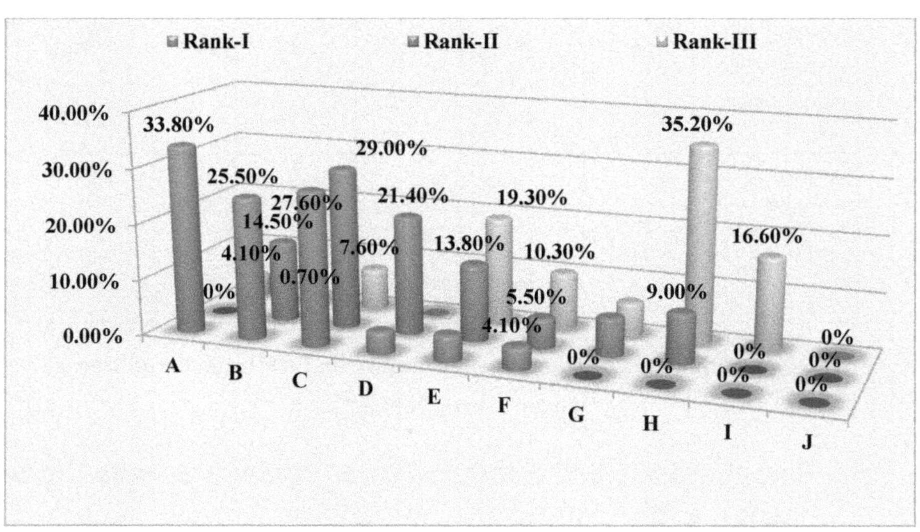

Figure 4.22 Financial CSF for ERP implementation (Rank Wise) by MSMU Respondents
(Source: Primary Data)

Sr. No.	Opinions	Number of Industry (n=145)	Percentage
1	Yes Completely	125	86.21%
2	Yes But partially	20	13.79%
3	No	0	0%
4	Never	0	0%
5	Can't say	0	0%

Table 4.10 ERP improve the resource utilization in all aspects of the organization
(Source: Primary Data)

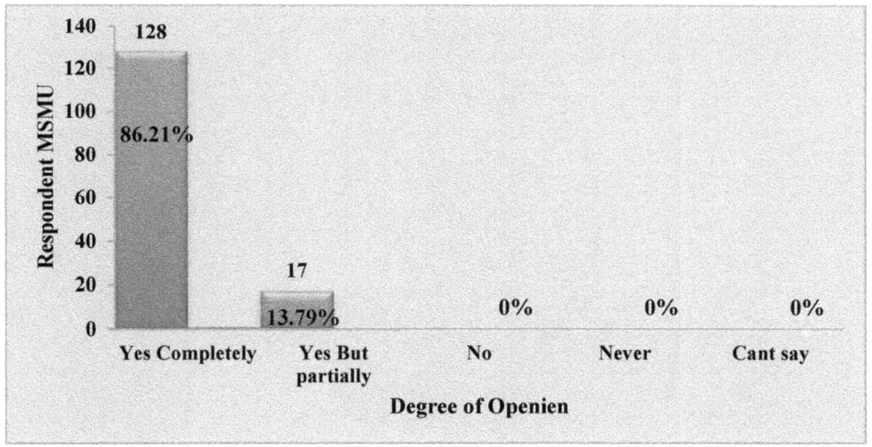

Figure 4.23 Opinions on ERP improve the resource utilization in all aspects of the organization by MSMU Respondents
(Source: Primary Data)

- The Research depict that 86.21 % manufacturing units completely agree that ERP improves the resource utilization in all aspects of the organization. Whereas, only 13.79% manufacturing units are partially agreed to the resource utilization improves in their organization due to ERP implementation.
- The study also revealed that no manufacturing units deny about the ERP improves the resource utilization in all aspects of the organization.

- Important observation found that, no MSMU disagree about ERP improve their resource utilization in all aspects of the organization.

Sr. No.	Opinions	Number of Industry (n=145)	Percentage
1	Yes Completely	99	68.3%
2	Yes But partially	46	31.7%
3	No	0	0%
4	Never	0	0%
5	Can't say	0	0%

Table 4.11 ERP improve the effectiveness and Competency of the decision process.
(Source: Primary Data)

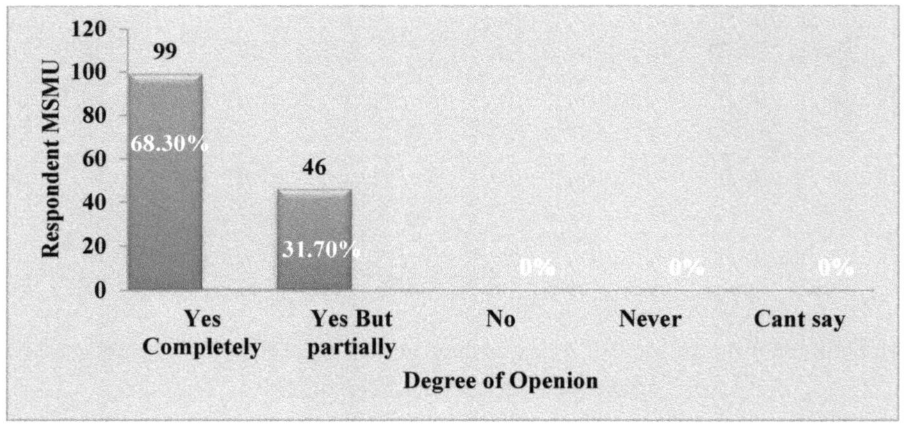

Figure 4.24 Opinions on ERP improve the effectiveness and Competency of the decision process of the organization by MSMU Respondents
(Source: Primary Data)

- The Research illustrate that, 68.30 % manufacturing units completely agree that ERP improves the effectiveness and Competency in the decision process. Whereas, only 31.7% manufacturing units are partially agreed to the effectiveness and Competency improves in their decision process in the organization due to ERP implementation.

- The study also discovered that no manufacturing units deny about the ERP improve the effectiveness and Competency of the decision process.

- No respondent MSMU have support to "NO, NEVER or Can't Say" option about ERP implementation improves Competency and effectiveness in the decision making in their organization.

Sr. No.	Opinions	Number of Industry (n=145)	Percentage
1	Yes Completely	64	44.14%
2	Yes But partially	64	44.14%
3	No	0	0%
4	Never	0	0%
5	Can't say	17	11.7%

Table 4.12 The ERP has increased the employee satisfaction and productivity and enable better choices for employees.
(Source: Primary Data)

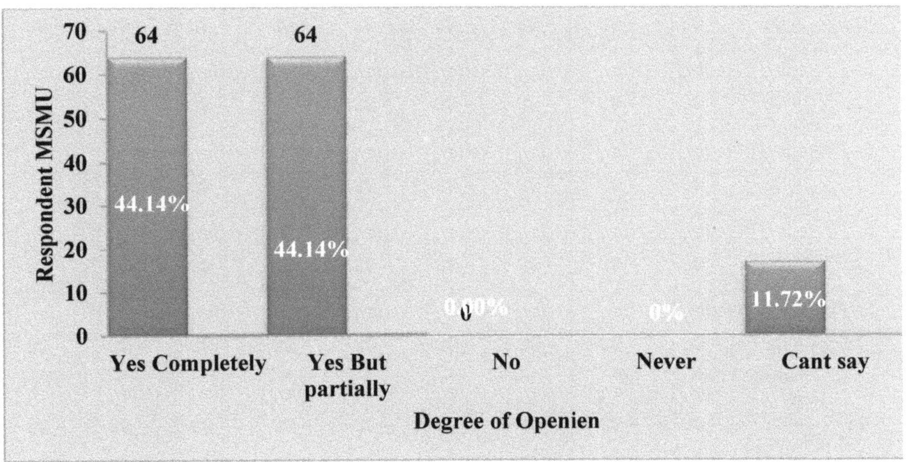

Figure 4.25 Opinions of MSMU Respondents on ERP has increased the employee satisfaction and productivity and enable better choices for employees in the organization
(Source: Primary Data)

- The Research found that 44.14 % manufacturing units completely agree that ERP has increased the employee satisfaction and productivity and enable better choices for employees in the organization, whereas, 44.14% manufacturing units are partially agreed to the same.

- The study also discovered that 11.72% manufacturing units deny that the ERP has increased the employee satisfaction and productivity and enable better choices for employees.

Sr. No.	Managerial benefits	Rank-I		Rank-II		Rank-III	
		Number of Industry (n=145)	Percentage	Number of Industry (n=145)	Percentage	Number of Industry (n=145)	Percentage
A	Increase overall productivity	18	12.4%	0	0%	0	0%
B	Speedup the management's decision making capability	38	26.2%	8	5.5%	57	39.3%
C	Improve the resource utilization ratio	61	42.1%	80	55.2%	22	15.2%
D	Timely quality control and monitoring	0	0%	0	0%	2	1.4%
E	Help to find best business process	0	0%	5	3.4%	0	0%
F	Improve production and material planning	4	2.8%	12	8.3%	4	2.8%
G	Real time reporting and data analysis	0	0%	4	2.8%	18	12.4%
H	Provides one common sight for top management	0	0%	0	0%	4	2.8%
I	Improve the information accuracy and precision in decision making	22	15.2%	36	24.8%	38	26.2%

Sr. No.	Managerial benefits	Rank-I		Rank-II		Rank-III	
		Number of Industry (n=145)	Percentage	Number of Industry (n=145)	Percentage	Number of Industry (n=145)	Percentage
J	Maintain precision in production, planning and scheduling	2	1.4%	0	0%	0	0%
K	Other, Please Specify	0	0%	0	0%	0	0%
L	Increase overall productivity	0	0%	0	0%	0	0%

Table 4.13 Managerial benefits of the ERP system for the organization

(Source: Primary Data)

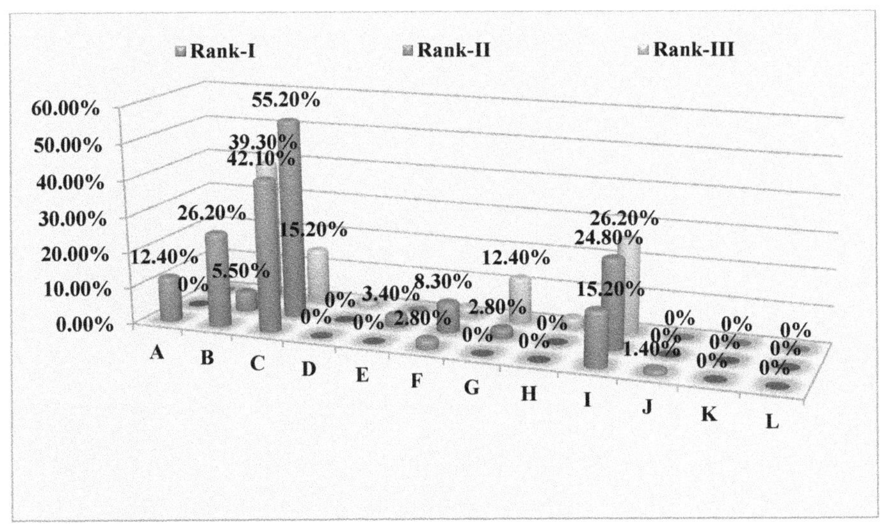

Figure 4.26 Managerial Benefits for ERP implementation (Rank Wise) by MSMU Respondents

(Source: Primary Data)

- The study was found that, for Rank-I 42.10% of manufacturing units accept the that ERP system improves resources utilization ration within the organization as managerial benefits, 26.26% agreed that the ERP system speedup the management's decision making capability and 12.4% accept that it increase the overall productivity in their units as benefits to the managerial level.

- For Rank-II, the research found that, 55.20% of manufacturing units accept the that ERP system improves resources utilization ration within the organization as managerial benefits, 24.80% agreed that the ERP system Improve the information accuracy and precision in decision making and 5.5% accept that ERP system speedup the management's decision making capability of the manufacturing units as managerial benefits.

- For Rank-III, the study depict that, 39.92% of manufacturing units accept the that ERP system speedup the management's decision making capability of the manufacturing units as benefits to the management, 26.20% agreed that the ERP system Improve the information accuracy and precision in decision making and 15.3% accept that ERP system Improve the resource utilization ratio as managerial benefits.

Sr. No.	Operational benefits	Rank-I		Rank-II		Rank-III	
		Number of Industry (n=145)	Percentage	Number of Industry (n=145)	Percentage	Number of Industry (n=145)	Percentage
A	Improves resource utilization	76	52.4%	29	20.0%	57	39.3%
B	Increasing work Competency and accuracy	69	47.6%	71	49.0%	29	20.0%
C	Reduce work head, lead time and cycle time	0	0%	24	16.6%	0	0%
D	Ease of warehousing and storage, mining scheduling and tracking	0	0%	10	6.9%	0	0%
E	Customize the executive reports	0	0%	2	1.4%	2	1.4%

Sr. No.	Operational benefits	Rank-I		Rank-II		Rank-III	
		Number of Industry (n=145)	Percentage	Number of Industry (n=145)	Percentage	Number of Industry (n=145)	Percentage
F	Provide the ready to print standard in-built reports	0	0%	1	.7%	26	17.9%
G	Support the coordination across business functionalities	0	0%	8	5.5%	0	0%
H	Linkage with the supplier and customer	0	0%	0	0%	2	1.4%
I	Eliminates duplication of work	0	0%	0	0%	0	0%
J	Seamless flow of information at all level	0	0%	0	0%	4	2.8%
K	Other, Please Specify	0	0%	0	0%	25	17.2%

Table 4.14 Operational benefits of the ERP system for the organization.

(Source: Primary Data)

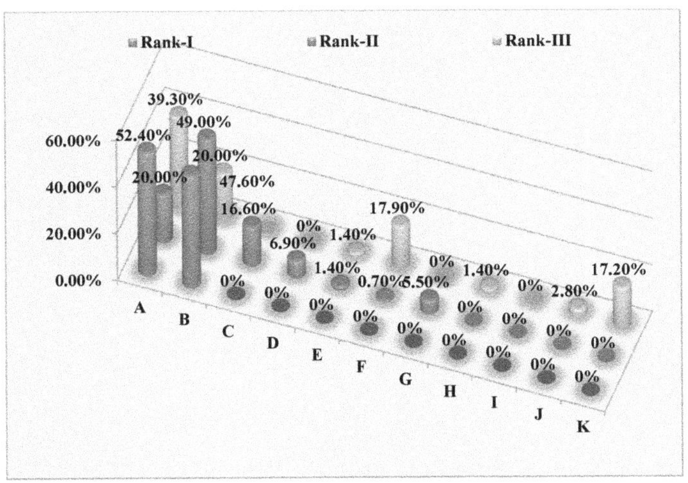

Figure 4.27 Operational Benefits for ERP implementation (Rank Wise) by MSMU Respondents

(Source: Primary Data)

- The study was found that, for Rank-I 52.42% of manufacturing units accept that ERP system improves resources utilization within the organization as an operational benefits, 47.62% agreed that the ERP system Increasing work Competency and accuracy in their units as an operational benefits.

- For Rank-II, the research found that, 49.00% of manufacturing units accept that ERP system Increasing work Competency and accuracy within the organization as an operational benefits, 20.00% agreed that the ERP system improves resources utilization of the manufacturing units as an operational benefits.

- For Rank-III, the study depict that, 39.90% agreed that the ERP system improve the resource utilization ratio as an operational benefits and 20.3% accept that ERP system increasing work Competency and accuracy in manufacturing units as an operational benefits

Sr. No.	Financial benefits	Rank-I		Rank-II		Rank-III	
		Number of Industry (n=145)	Percentage	Number of Industry (n=145)	Percentage	Number of Industry (n=145)	Percentage
A	Improve the ROI(Return on investment)	66	45.5%	52	35.9%	0	0%
B	Instant deal profitability calculations	18	12.4%	18	12.4%	2	1.4%
C	Control on payable through gem matching	19	13.1%	35	24.1%	8	5.5%
D	Controls the credit sale and account receivable	32	22.1%	9	6.2%	29	20.0%

Sr. No.	Financial benefits	Rank-I		Rank-II		Rank-III	
		Number of Industry (n=145)	Percentage	Number of Industry (n=145)	Percentage	Number of Industry (n=145)	Percentage
E	Produces timely bank re-conciliation	0	0%	13	9.0%	4	2.8%
F	Integrates cost, profit, revenue information of sales and purchased granular way	8	5.5%	0	0%	19	13.1%
G	Allows easier global integration (Currency, exchange rates etc)	2	1.4%	6	4.1%	8	5.5%
H	Reduce quality cost	0	0%	3	2.1%	23	15.9%
I	Improvement in financial management and customer services	0	0%	9	6.2%	40	27.6%
J	Reduce procurement, maintenance, transportation cost	0	0%	0	0%	12	8.3%
K	Other, Please Specify	0	0%	0	0%	0	0%

Table 4.15 Financial benefits of the ERP system for the organization.

(Source: Primary Data)

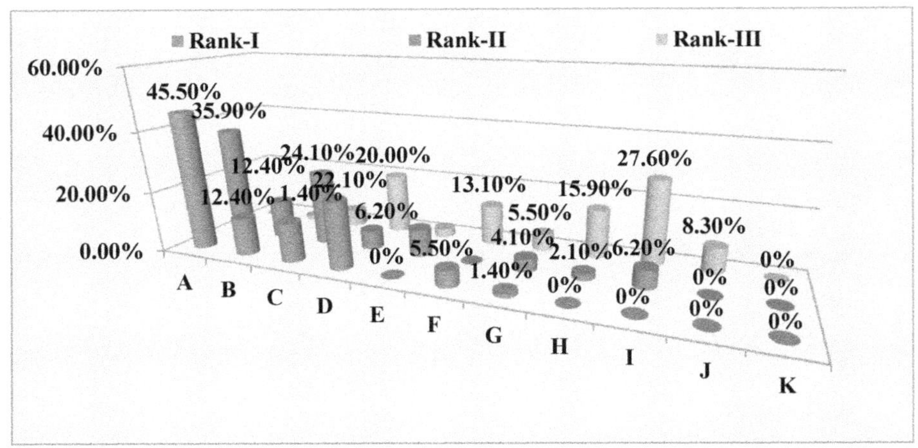

Figure 4.28 Financial Benefits for ERP implementation (Rank Wise) by MSMU Respondents

(Source: Primary Data)

- The study was found that, for Rank-I 45.5% of manufacturing units accept that Improve the ROI (Return on investment) within the organization as an Financial benefits, 22.1% agreed that the ERP system Controls the credit sale and account receivable whereas, 1.4% agree about, ERP system Allows easier global integration (Currency, exchange rates etc) in their units as an Financial benefits for Rank-I.

- For Rank-II, the research found that, 35.9% of manufacturing units accept that ERP system Improve the ROI (Return on investment) within the organization whereas, 24.1% agree on Control on payable through gem matching by EERP system, 2.1% agreed that the ERP system reduce the Quality Cost of the manufacturing units as Financial benefits.

- For Rank-III, the study depict that, 27.6% agreed that the ERP system helps in the Improvement in financial management and customer services whereas, 15.9% agree about ERP system reduce the Quality Cost and 1.4 % accept that ERP system

Provides Instant deal profitability calculation for manufacturing units as it Financial benefits.

Sr. No.	Technical benefits	Rank-I		Rank-II		Rank-III	
		Number of Industry (n=145)	Percentage	Number of Industry (n=145)	Percentage	Number of Industry (n=145)	Percentage
A	Integration of various business function	41	28.3%	0	0%	0	0%
B	Complete automation of business process	27	18.6%	17	11.7%	0	0%
C	Online availability of information at all levels	68	46.9%	7	4.8%	2	1.4%
D	Less paper work and improve the Competency	7	4.8%	87	60.0%	18	12.4%
E	Information integration with use of high and latest technology	0	0%	11	7.6%	6	4.1%
F	Common interface across the systems which contain real time information.	2	1.4%	21	14.5%	42	29.0%
G	Single application and faster transaction	0	0%	0	0%	17	11.7%
H	Web based interface	0	0%	2	1.4%	4	2.8%
I	Data security available	0	0%	0	0%	54	37.2%
J	Easy to transport, store and maintain the large data	0	0%	0	0%	2	1.4%
K	Other, Please Specify	0	0%	0	0%	0	0%

Table 4.16 Technical benefits of the ERP system for the organization

(Source: Primary Data)

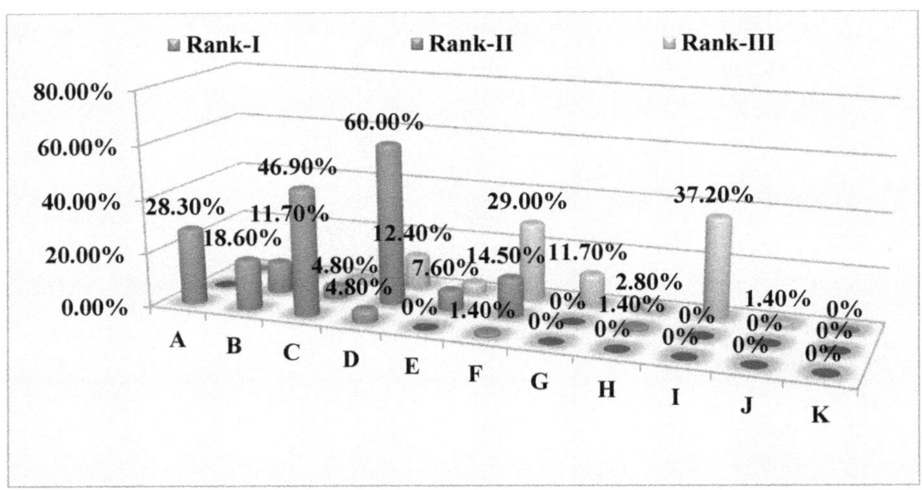

Figure 4.29 Technical Benefits for ERP implementation (Rank Wise)
by MSMU Respondents
(Source: Primary Data)

- The study found that, for Rank-I 46.9% of manufacturing units accept that due to ERP system provides Online availability of information at all levels within the organization as an Technical benefits, 28.3% agreed that the ERP system gives the Integration of various business function whereas, 1.4% agree about, ERP system Allows Common interface across the systems which contain real time information in their units as Technical benefits for Rank-I.

- For Rank-II, the research found that, 60.0% of manufacturing units accept that ERP system provides Less paper work and improve the Competency within the organization whereas, 14.5% agree that by ERP system provides Common interface across the systems which contain real time information, 1.4% agreed that the ERP system gives Web based interfaces to the manufacturing units as Technical benefits with Rank-II.

- For Rank-III, the study depict that, 37.2% MSMU agreed that the ERP system provides Data Security Availability whereas,

29.0% agree about ERP system Gives Common interface across the systems which contain real time information and 1.4 % accept that ERP system Provides Easy to transport, store and maintain the large data and Online availability of information at all levels for manufacturing units as its Technical benefits.

Sr. No.	Name of District	Total No. of Medium Scale Manufacturing Units
1	Ahmednagar	1
2	Akola	9
3	Amravati	33
4	Aurangabad	103
5	Beed	5
6	Bhandara	2
7	Buldhana	7
8	Chandrapur	3
9	Dhule	3
10	Gadchiroli	3
11	Gondiya	3
12	Hingoli	5
13	Jalgaon	8
14	Jalana	7
15	Kolhapur	11
16	Latur	5
17	Mumbai	123
18	Nagpur	91
19	Nanded	11
20	Nandurbar	4
21	Nasik	98
22	Osmanabad	4
23	Parbhani	3

Sr. No.	Name of District	Total No. of Medium Scale Manufacturing Units
24	Pune	88
25	Raigad	27
26	Ratnagiri	22
27	Sangali	4
28	Satara	13
29	Sindhadurg	2
30	Solapur	6
31	Thane	71
32	Wardha	7
33	Washim	1
34	Yewatmal	9
Total No of Manufacturing Units		**792**

Table 4.17 Medium Scale Manufacturing Units in Maharashtra (District Wise)
(Source: MSME-2018, GoM)

Sr. No	Name of Industrial Zone	Total No of Medium Scale Manufacturing Units	Percentage
1	Desh (Pune Div)	122	15.4%
2	Khandesh (Nasik Div)	114	14.39%
3	Koken (Mumbai Div)	245	30.93%
4	Marathwada (Aurangabad Div)	143	18.06%
5	Vidharabha (Nagpur Div)	109	13.76%
6	Vidharabha (Amravati Div)	59	7.45%
Total Manufacturing Units		**792**	**100%**

Table 4.18 Medium Scale Manufacturing Units in Maharashtra
(Industrial Zone Wise)
(Source: MSME-2018 report)

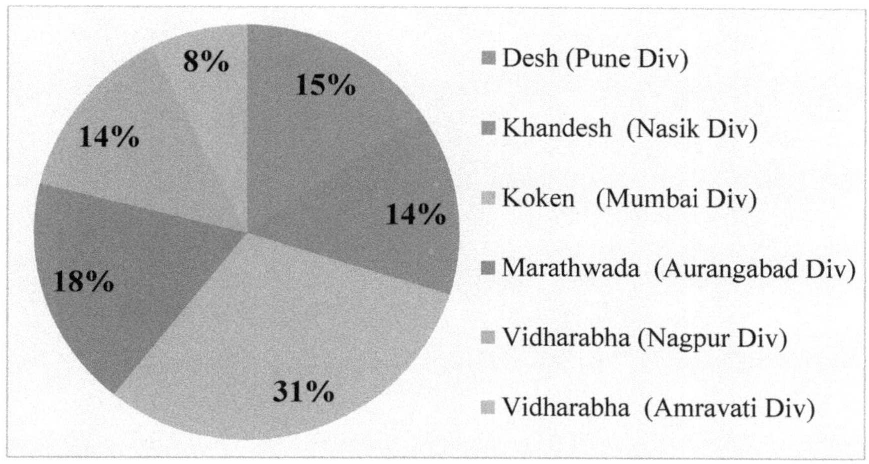

Figure 4.30 Zone wise total Medium Scale Manufacturing Units in Maharashtra State

(Source: MSME-2016)

The study found that, 31% of total medium scale manufacturing unit is situated in and around Mumbai division, where as 30% part established in Nasik and Pune division combined. Whereas 18% of medium scale manufacturing units are located in Marathwada Region and remaining 21% units are sited in Vidharabha Region (Nagpur and Amravati Combined).

Sr. No.	Name of Industrial Zone	Manufacturing Units using ERP (Response Collected)	Percentage
1	Desh (Pune Div)	23	15.86%
2	Khandesh (Nasik Div)	19	13.10%
3	Koken (Mumbai Div)	43	29.66%
4	Marathwada (Aurangabad Div)	29	20%
5	Vidharabha (Nagpur Div)	21	14.48%
6	Vidharabha (Amravati Div)	10	6.90%
Total Manufacturing Units		**145**	**100%**

Table 4.19 Manufacturing Units Who Using ERP (Selected for Study)

(Source: Primary Data)

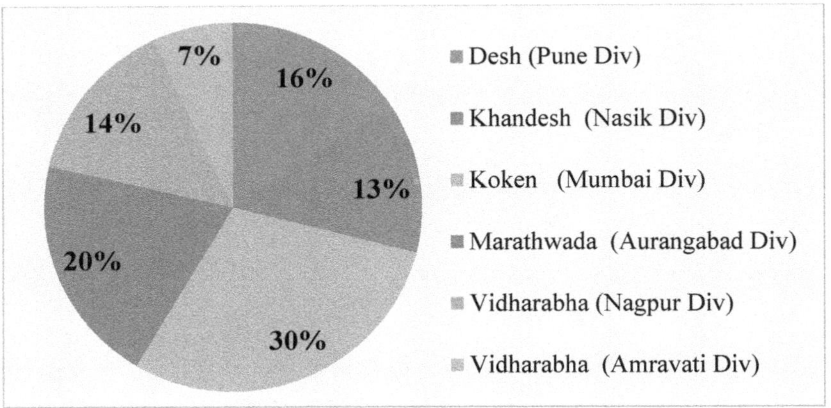

Figure 4.31 Zone wise total respondent Medium Scale Manufacturing Units in Maharashtra State
(Source: Primary Data)

The study proves that 29.66% respondents belong to Mumbai division whereas, 6.90% MSMU belongs to Amravati Division. Aurangabad division's MSMU Responded 20% and only 13.10% MSMU participated in the study. Pune Division and Nagpur division replied to the survey request as 15.86% and 14.48% respectively.

Sr. No	Name of Industrial Zone	Total No of Medium Scale Manufacturing Units	Manufacturing Units Who Using ERP	Percentage
1	Pune Div	122	44	36.07%
2	Nasik Div	114	30	26.32%
3	Mumbai Div	245	84	34.29%
4	Aurangabad Div	143	33	23.08%
5	Nagpur Div	109	35	32.12%
6	Amravati Div	59	23	38.99%
Total Manufacturing Units		792	249	31.44%
Percentage of Sample for Responses		100%	32%	32%

Table 4.20 Percentile of ERP using MSMU with Total MSMU (Zone Wise)
(Source: Primary data).

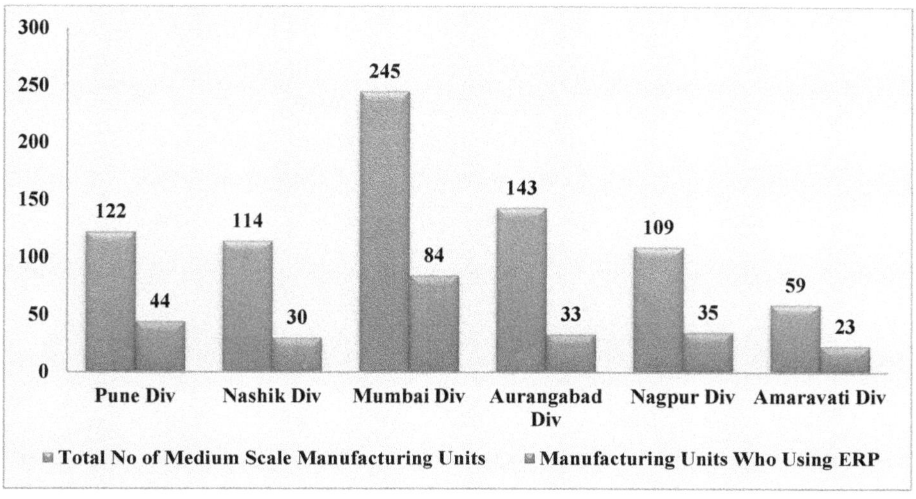

Figure 4.32 : Relationship of total MSMU with ERP using MSMU (Zone Wise)

(Source: Primary data)

The research Proves that, in table 4.20 percentile of Amravati division who using ERP system is 38.99% whereas, Pune Division secure second position in the list with 36.07%. Aurangabad division is 23.08% which is very less as compare to any other divisions and close to Nasik division which have 26.32% MSMU who using ERP system into their manufacturing unit.

Sr. No	Name of Industrial Zone	Manufacturing Units Who Using ERP	Total Responses Received from Selected Manufacturing Units	Percentage
1	Pune Div	44	23	52.28%
2	Nasik Div	30	17	56.67%
3	Mumbai Div	84	44	52.39%
4	Aurangabad Div	33	29	87.88%
5	Nagpur Div	35	19	54.29%

Sr. No	Name of Industrial Zone	Manufacturing Units Who Using ERP	Total Responses Received from Selected Manufacturing Units	Percentage
6	Amravati Div	23	13	56.53%
Total Manufacturing Units		**249**	**145**	**58.24%**
Percentage of Sample for Responses		**100%**	**58.23%**	**58.23%**

Table 4.21 Percentile of ERP used MSMU with respondent MSMU (Zone wise)

(Source: Primary Data)

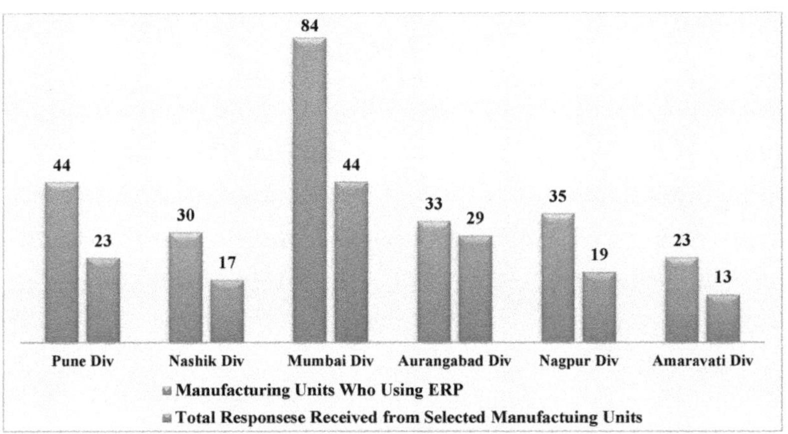

Figure 4.33 : Relationship of total ERP Using MSMU with Respondent MSMU (Zone Wise)

(Source: Primary data)

The study highlighted that, by count consideration by comparing the total number of respondents zone wise with total number of MSMU who using ERP i.e. willingness of respondents a compare to actual number of MSMU, Aurangabad division respond with 87.88% whereas, Amravati Division 56.53%, Nasik with 56.67% and 52.39% for Mumbai division replied for the survey. Total responses collected from actual ERP using MSMU are 58.24%.

End Product	Total Manufacturing Units	Percentage
Agricultural Product	28	19.32%
Automobile	23	15.87%
Chemical Product	11	7.59%
Construction Product	8	5.52%
Electrical Equipment	16	11.04%
Electronic Equipment	5	3.45%
Energy	6	4.14%
Food Processing	5	3.45%
Home Product	13	8.97%
Liquor	2	1.38%
Pharmaceuticals	14	9.66%
Software	6	4.14%
Textiles	8	5.52%
Total	**145**	**100%**

Table 4.22 Product wise Respondents MSMU details (Source: Primary Data)

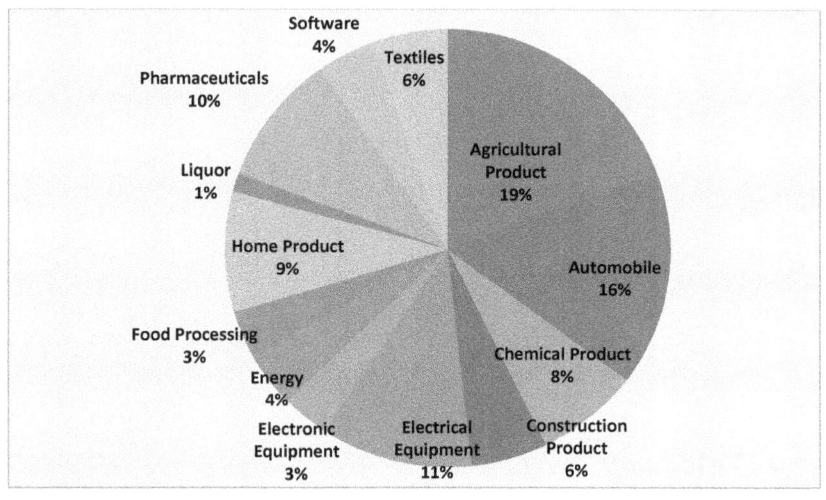

Figure 4.34 Product wise Respondents MSMU details

(Source: Primary Data)

The study gives the demonstration that, in the research 19.32% Agricultural product producing MSMU are participated whereas, 15.87% respondents MSMU manufacture Automobile end products, 11.4% MSMU have Electrical Equipments whereas, 9.66% are produce Pharmaceuticals products. The study also revealed that, liquor producing MSMU are only 1.38% whereas, Food Processing MSMU are only 3.45%

4.2 Cross Factor Analysis

		Industrial Zone						
	End Product	**Desh (Pune Div)**	**Koken (Mumbai Div)**	**Koken (Nasik Div)**	**Marathwada (Aurangabad Div)**	**Vidarbha (Amravati Div)**	**Vidarbha (Nagpur Div)**	**Total**
End Product	Agricultural Product	2	7	6	5	4	4	**28**
	Automobile	7	0	5	8	0	3	**23**
	Chemical Product	1	6	0	1	0	3	**11**
	Construction Product	0	5	0	1	0	2	**8**
	Electrical Equipment	6	7	0	3	0	0	**16**
	Electronic Equipment	0	0	1	2	0	2	**5**
	Energy	1	2	0	1	0	2	**6**
	Food Processing	0	0	1	0	3	1	**5**
	Home Product	1	4	3	2	1	2	**13**
	Liquor	0	0	0	2	0	0	**2**
	Pharmaceuticals	3	6	1	3	1	0	**14**
	Software	2	3	0	0	0	1	**6**
	Textiles	0	3	2	1	1	1	**8**
	Total	**23 (15.87%)**	**43 (29.66%)**	**19 (13.11%)**	29 (20%)	10 (6.9%)	**21 (14.49%)**	145

Table 4.23 Cross Factor Analysis on Industrial Zone with End-product of Respondent MSMU

(Source: Primary Data)

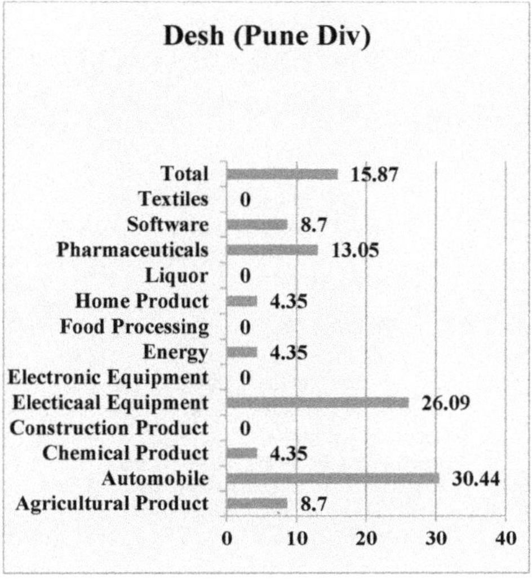

Figure 4.35.1 Pune Division with End-Product Percentile

(Source: Primary Data)

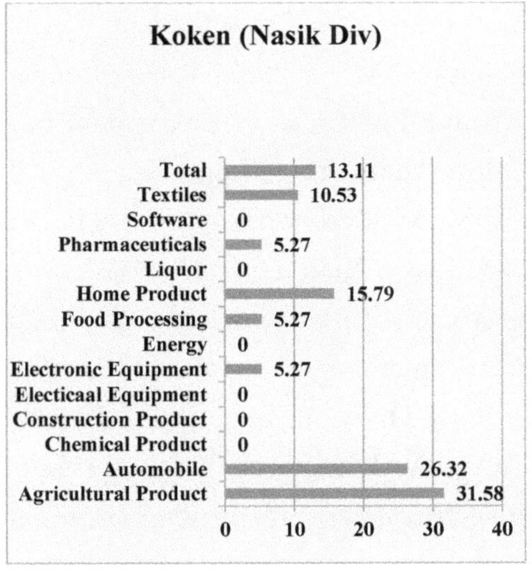

Figure 4.35.3 Nasik Division with End-Product Percentile

(Source: Primary Data)

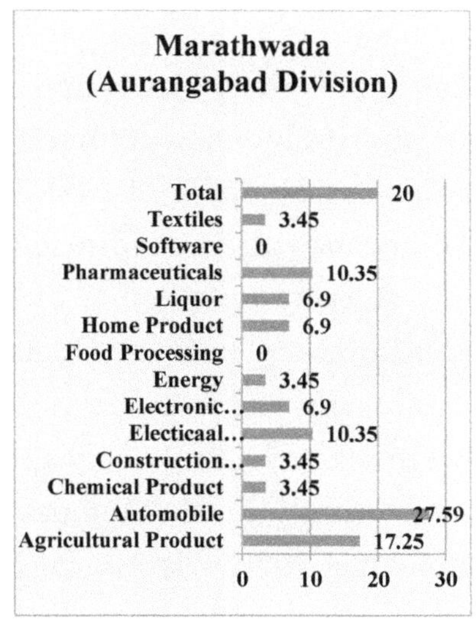

Figure 4.35.2 Mumbai Division with End-Product Percentile

(Source: Primary Data)

Figure 4.35.4 Aurangabad Division with End-Product Percentile

(Source: Primary Data)

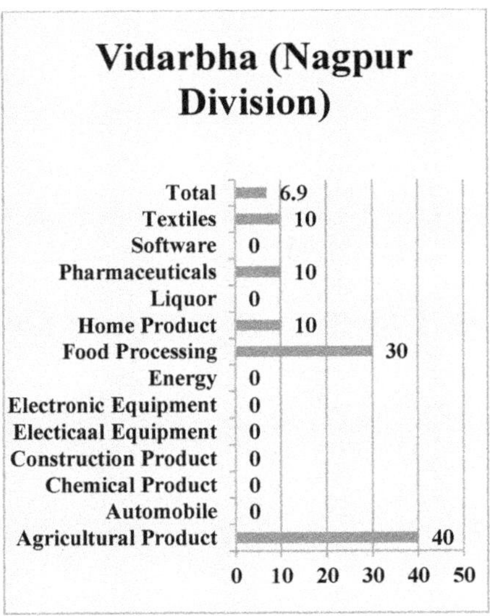

Figure 4.35.5 Nagpur Division with
End-Product Percentile

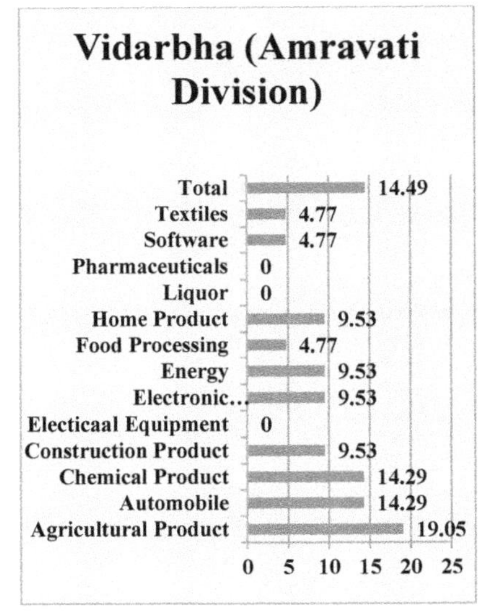

Figure 4.35.6 Amravati Division with
End-Product Percentile

(Source: Primary Data)

The Study proves that, Mumbai Division MSMU is 29.66% respondents for the study whereas, Agricultural and Electrical Equipments End-product wise share of MSMU is more than any other division, An Aurangabad division provides 20% MSMU respondent whereas, In this division Automobile MSMU are more than any other division. Pune division provides 15.87 responses with automobile, Electrical Equipments and Software MSMU of Aurangabad, Mumbai and Mumbai Divisions respectively only ahead of Pune Division. In software as end-product only Pune, Mumbai and Nagpur division avail for the ERP implementation whereas, for Pharmaceuticals as end-product Mumbai took topper position in the list. The only couple of Liquor manufacturing units are participated in this study whereas, Aurangabad is the only division in the study who have implemented ERP in their MSMU when their end-product is Liquor.

		No of Employees in Manufacturing Unit				Total
		Less than 50	51 to 150	151 to 300	More than 300	
Industrial Zone	Desh (Pune Div)	0	0	12	11	**23**
	Khandesh (Nasik Div)	0	1	12	6	**19**
	Koken (Mumbai Div)	0	0	31	12	**43**
	Marathwada (Aurangabad Div)	0	0	21	8	**29**
	Vidarabha (Amravati Div)	0	0	9	1	**10**
	Vidarabha (Nagpur Div)	0	0	15	6	**21**
Total		**0**	**1 (.69%)**	**100 (68.97%)**	**44 (30.35%)**	**145**

Table 4.24 Cross Factor Analysis of Industrial Zone with No, of Employees in respondent MSMU

(Source: Primary Data)

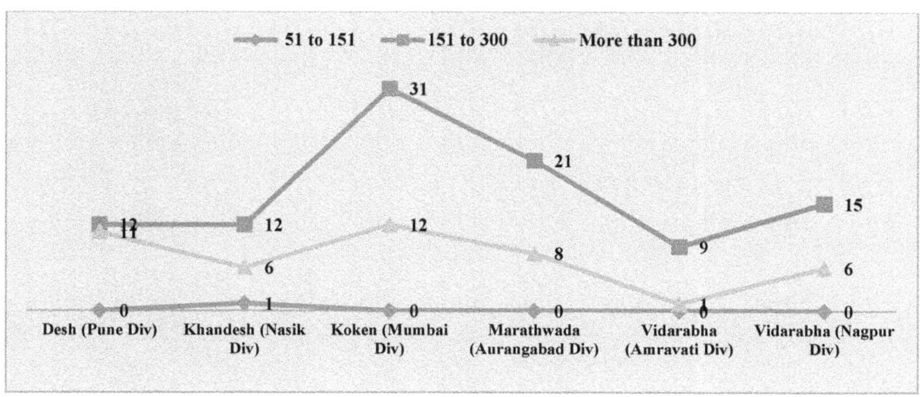

Figure 4.36 Cross factor Analysis of Industrial Zone with No. of Employees

(Source: Primary Data)

The study proves that, almost 69% MSMU who implemented ERP system they have their number of employee between 151 to 300 whereas, Mumbai and Aurangabad division combined share the 52% in this category. Amravati division having only 9% MSMU in above said category. 30.35% MSMU have their employee more than 300 and again Mumbai is at top in the list whereas, Amravati have only one MSMU in the category. One MSMU from Nasik who implemented ERP have less than 150 employees in the unit. Last important observation on table 4.23 is no MSMU who implemented ERP have their employee count less than 50.

Industrial Zone ↓ →	Annual Turnover of Manufacturing Unit			Total
	03 to 10 Crore	10 to 25 Crore	More than 25 Crore	
Desh (Pune Div)	0	1	22	**23**
Khandesh (Nasik Div)	0	0	19	**19**
Koken (Mumbai Div)	0	1	42	**43**
Marathwada (Aurangabad Div)	0	2	27	**29**
Vidarabha (Amravati Div)	0	0	10	**10**
Vidarabha (Nagpur Div)	0	1	20	**21**
Total	**0 (0%)**	**5 (3.45%)**	**140 (96.56%)**	**145**

Table 4.25 Cross Factor Analysis of Industrial Zone with Annual Turnover in respondent MSMU

(Source: Primary Data)

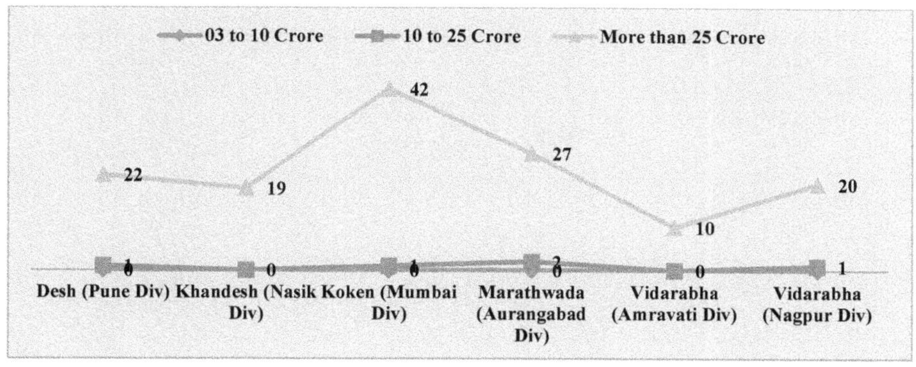

Figure 4.37 Cross factor Analysis of Industrial Zone with Annual Turnover

(Source: Primary Data)

The study provide evidence that, 96.56% MSMU who implemented ERP system in their firm are having their annual turnover more than 25 crores whereas, Mumbai and Aurangabad zone combined share 50% count of MSMU comes in the category whereas, Amravati Division have only 10 MSMU in the list. 3.45% MSMU have their turn over 10 to 25 Crores and Aurangabad Division MSMU more than any other division. Interesting finding is, no MSMU having their annual turnover less than 10 crores having ERP system in their manufacturing unit.

		ERP System Used by Manufacturing Unit (Currently)					Total
		SAP	Oracle	PeopleSoft	BAAN	J D Edwards	
Industrial Zone	Desh (Pune Div)	23	0	0	0	0	**23**
	Khandesh (Nasik Div)	18	1	0	0	0	**19**
	Koken (Mumbai Div)	42	1	0	0	0	**43**
	Marathwada (Aurangabad Div)	27	2	0	0	0	**29**
	Vidarabha (Amravati Div)	9	1	0	0	0	**10**
	Vidarabha (Nagpur Div)	21	0	0	0	0	**21**
Total		140 (96.56%)	5 (3.45%)	0	0	0	145

Table 4.26 Cross Factor Analysis of Industrial Zone with ERP venders in Respondent MSMU

(Source: Primary Data).

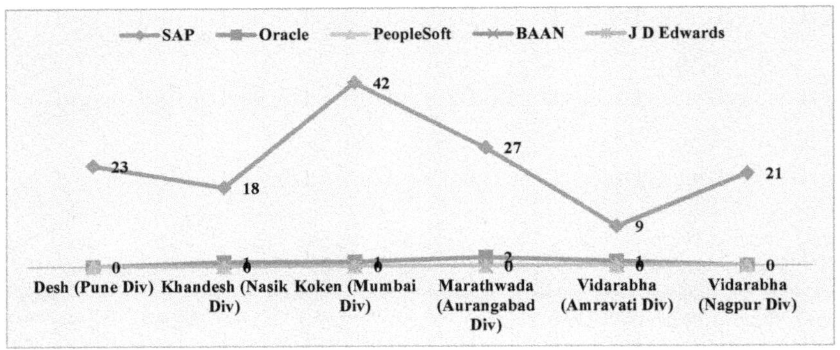

Figure 4.38 Cross factor Analysis of Industrial Zone with ERP venders in MSMU

(Source: Primary Data)

The research revealed that, 96.56% respondent MSMU follow SAP as their ERP vender whereas, only 3.45% are go with Oracle as ERP vender. Mumbai division and Aurangabad division combined cover almost 50% of total MSMU who implemented ERP in their firm with SAP vender whereas, Pune and Nagpur divisions are only implemented SAR vender's ERP into their division i.e. there are no MSMU found in the Pune and Nagpur Division who have Other than SAP as ERP vender. Attention-Grabbing factor in this study is no MSMU choose PeopleSoft, BAAN or J D Edward as their ERP venders.

		Duration of ERP System Used in Manufacturing Unit				Total
		Less than a Year	01 to 03 yrs	03 to 05 yrs	More than 05 yrs	
Industrial Zone	Desh (Pune Div)	3	6	4	10	23
	Khandesh (Nasik Div)	3	2	6	8	19
	Koken (Mumbai Div)	4	12	11	16	43
	Marathwada (Aurangabad Div)	3	9	6	11	29
	Vidarabha (Amravati Div)	2	3	0	5	10
	Vidarabha (Nagpur Div)	3	0	5	13	21
Total		18 (12.42%)	32 (22.07%)	32 (22.07%)	63 (43.45%)	145

Table 4.27 Cross Factor Analysis of Industrial Zone with ERP Using Duration in Respondent MSMU

(Source: Primary Data).

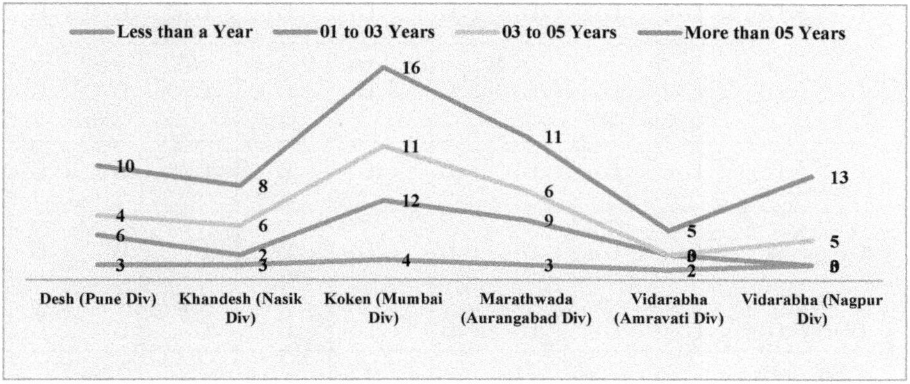

Figure 4.39 Cross factor Analysis of Industrial Zone with Duration of ERP using by MSMU

(Source: Primary Data)

The research highlighted that, 43.45% MSMU using the ERP system More than a 05 yrs whereas, Mumbai and Nagpur share more than 35% combined in the category. 44.14% MSMU using ERP from 01 yrs to 05yrs whereas Mumbai and Aurangabad combined share almost 60% of the range. Only 12.42% MSMU are newborn in the era of ERP implementation manufacturing units as they are adopted and using the ERP system in their firm since less than a year and Mumbai division is at top and Amravati division at last in the list.

	Duration of ERP System Implementation in Manufacturing Unit							Total
↓ →	Under 09 months	09 months to 01 year	01 year to 1.5 years	1.5 year to 02 years	02 years to 2.5 years	2.5 years to 03 years	Over 03 years	
Desh (Pune Div)	0	0	3	7	4	7	2	23
Khandesh (Nasik Div)	0	0	3	9	1	6	0	19
Koken (Mumbai Div)	0	0	5	16	11	10	1	43
Marathwada (Aurangabad Div)	0	0	4	12	7	6	0	29
Vidarabha (Amravati Div)	0	0	2	0	3	5	0	10
Vidarabha (Nagpur Div)	0	0	3	5	0	12	1	21
Total	0	0	20	49	26	46	4	145

Table 4.28 Cross Factor Analysis of Industrial Zone with Duration of ERP implementation the Respondent MSMU

(Source: Primary Data)

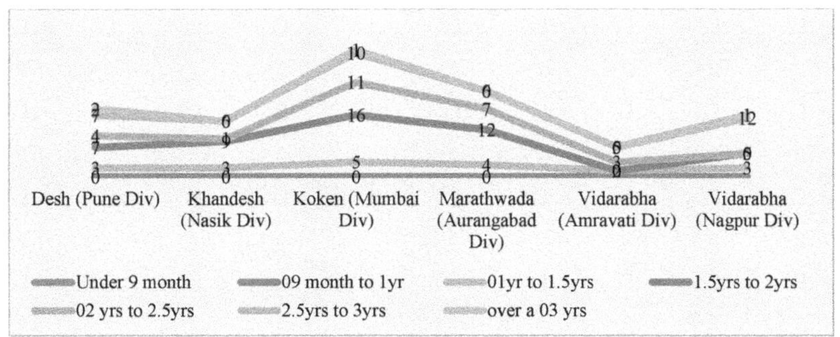

Figure 4.40 Cross factor Analysis of Industrial Zone with Duration of ERP implementation by MSMU

(Source: Primary Data)

2.76 MSMU took more than 3yrs for ERP implementation whereas, no MSMU from Nasik, Aurangabad, and Amravati division comes in this category. 33.8% MSMU took 1.5 yrs to 02yrs whereas; Mumbai and

Aurangabad division 56% combined comes in this range. No division took less than a year to implement ERP system into their MSMU.31.73% MSMU took 2.5yrs to 03yrs whereas, Nagpur division have 24% of entire 31.73% and Mumbai division 18% and Pune division 8% in this range.

		When to Perform Re-engineering the business processes in Manufacturing Unit				Total
		Prior to the implementation	As part of the implementation	After the implementation	No BPR done	
Industrial Zone	Desh (Pune Div)	7	12	0	4	**23**
	Khandesh (Nasik Div)	2	9	0	8	**19**
	Koken (Mumbai Div)	10	25	1	7	**43**
	Marathwada (Aurangabad Div)	7	14	1	7	**29**
	Vidarabha (Amravati Div)	4	6	0	0	**10**
	Vidarabha (Nagpur Div)	1	14	0	6	**21**
Total		31 (21.38%)	80 (55.18%)	2 (1.38%)	32 (22.7%)	145

Table 4.29 Cross Factor Analysis of Industrial Zone with BPR process details in ERP implementation by Respondent MSMU

(Source: Primary Data)

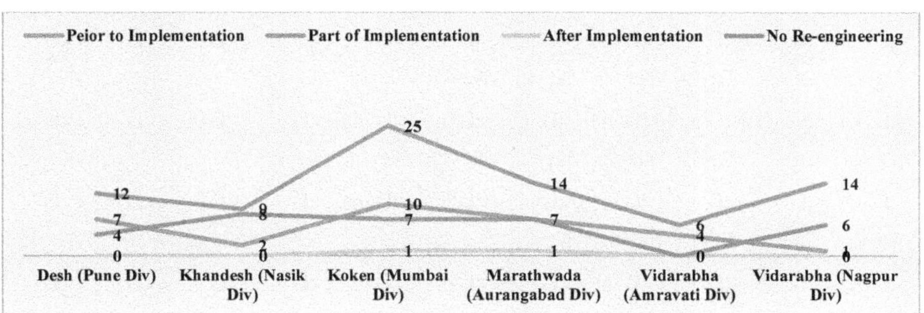

Figure 4.41 Cross factor Analysis of Industrial Zone with BPR process in ERP implementation by MSMU

(Source: Primary Data)

The study illustrate the BPR process used during the ERP implementation by various MSMU according to their zone, 55.18% MSMU done BPR In-Implementation Phase whereas, Mumbai division alone share 30% of it. 21.38% MSMU done BPR at very prior phase of ERP implementation whereas only 1.38% MSMU done it as post implementation Phase. Amravati Division is the only division who done BPR process mandatory while implementing ERP implementation whereas, 22.07% MSMU don't done any re-engineering process while implementing ERP system into their organization, Nasik division at top who avoid to do BPR process where as Mumbai and Aurangabad division are at top in the list of BPR process successfully done while ERP implementation.

		Which ERP implementation strategy Used by Manufacturing Units					Total
		Don't know	Parallel approach	Phased approach	Big bang approach	Pilot approach	
Industrial Zone	Desh (Pune Div)	13	7	3	0	0	23
	Khandesh (Nasik Div)	18	1	0	0	0	19
	Koken (Mumbai Div)	38	3	2	0	0	43
	Marathwada (Aurangabad Div)	22	4	3	0	0	29
	Vidarabha (Amravati Div)	8	2	0	0	0	10
	Vidarabha (Nagpur Div)	20	1	0	0	0	21
Total		119	18	8	0	0	145

Table 4.30 Cross Factor Analysis of Industrial Zone with BPR process details in ERP implementation by Respondent MSMU

(Source: Primary Data)

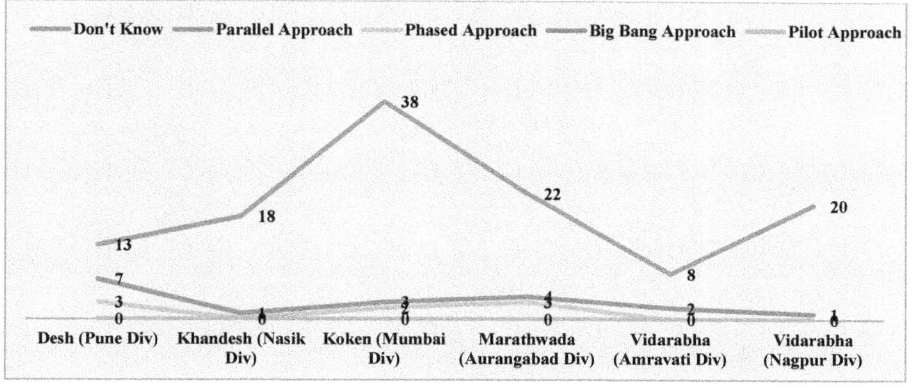

Figure 4.42 Cross factor Analysis of Industrial Zone with ERP implementation strategy used by MSMU

(Source: Primary Data)

The study optimizes the facts that, no MSMU or division used Big-Bang or Pilot Approach for the ERP implementation whereas; only 5.52% MMSU used Phased Approach. 82.07% MSMU don't know which strategy used by them and in this list Mumbai and Aurangabad division combined share more than 50% share whereas, Amravati division have only 6% of awareness. The study also proves that, 12.42% MSMU used Phased Approached strategy used while ERP get implemented into their MSMU. Out of it Pune division prefer Parallel approach more than Phased approach. The research also highlighted that Nasik, Amravati and Nagpur division have not yet used Phased Approach strategy for their ERP implementations. As percentage wise concern with 94.73% Nasik divisions and 95.23% Nagpur Division's MSMU are less aware about their ERP implementation strategy. If consider the awareness ratio then 44% MSMU for Pune division are aware about their implementation strategy.

		Which Type of Training Provided to Employees in Manufacturing Units					Total
		Project team training	End user training/ Module Based training	Traditional training	Web-based training	No additional training provided	
Industrial Zone	Desh (Pune Div)	2	11	1	0	9	**23**
	Khandesh (Nasik Div)	0	16	1	0	2	**19**
	Koken (Mumbai Div)	2	28	0	0	13	**43**
	Marathwada (Aurangabad Div)	3	17	0	0	9	**29**
	Vidarabha (Amravati Div)	0	10	0	0	0	**10**
	Vidarabha (Nagpur Div)	1	14	0	0	6	**21**
Total		**8 (5.52%)**	**96 (66.21%)**	**2 (1.38%)**	**0**	**39 (26.9%)**	**145**

Table 4.31 Cross Factor Analysis of Industrial Zone with Type of Training Provide to employees by Respondent MSMU

(Source: Primary Data)

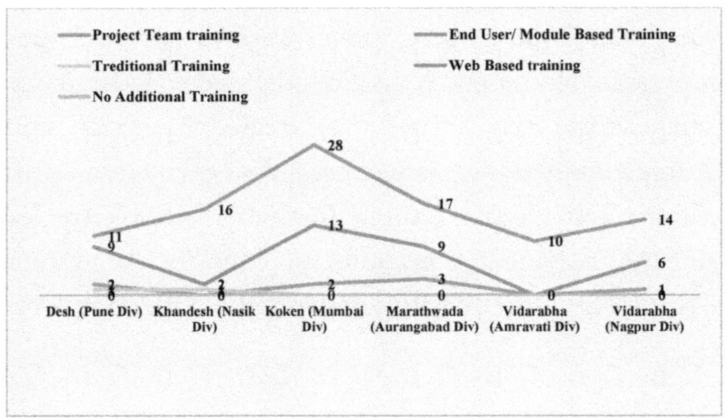

Figure 4.43 Cross factor Analysis of Industrial Zone with Types of Training provided to Employee by MSMU

(Source: Primary Data)

The research provide the facts that, 66.21% MSMU provided end-user to module based training to their employee whereas, Mumbai and Aurangabad division combined reserve 49% of the total MSMU comes in this category. Only 1.38% MSMU still provided traditional training whereas, 26.9% MSMU does not provided any type of training to their end-users whereas, Mumbai division is at top in list and Pune with Aurangabad division secure second place with 30% each of the total MSMU who doesn't provided any training category. Project team training provide by 5.52% whereas, Amravati and Nasik division doesn't interested in this format of training.. No division other than Nasik and Pune division have provided old and traditional training to their end users. The important fact came with this study is as the MSMU claim to advance their business process through the ERP system still no single MSMU from any division provided Web-based training to their employees in regards of ERP system.

Industrial Zone		How much time User will take to get expertise ERP system in Manufacturing Units					Total
		Mastered in a week	Mastered in a month	Mastered in 3 months	Mastered in 6 months	Rarely mastered	
	Desh (Pune Div)	0	4	3	8	8	**23**
	Khandesh (Nasik Div)	0	2	4	6	7	**19**
	Koken (Mumbai Div)	0	5	8	12	18	**43**
	Marathwada (Aurangabad Div)	0	2	7	9	11	**29**
	Vidarabha (Amravati Div)	0	0	2	7	1	**10**
	Vidarabha (Nagpur Div)	0	1	5	8	7	**21**
Total		**0**	**14 (9.66%)**	**29 (20%)**	**50 (34.49%)**	**52 (35.87%)**	**145**

Table 4.32 Cross Factor Analysis of Industrial Zone with Time to be Expert in ERP system by Respondent MSMU

(Source: Primary Data)

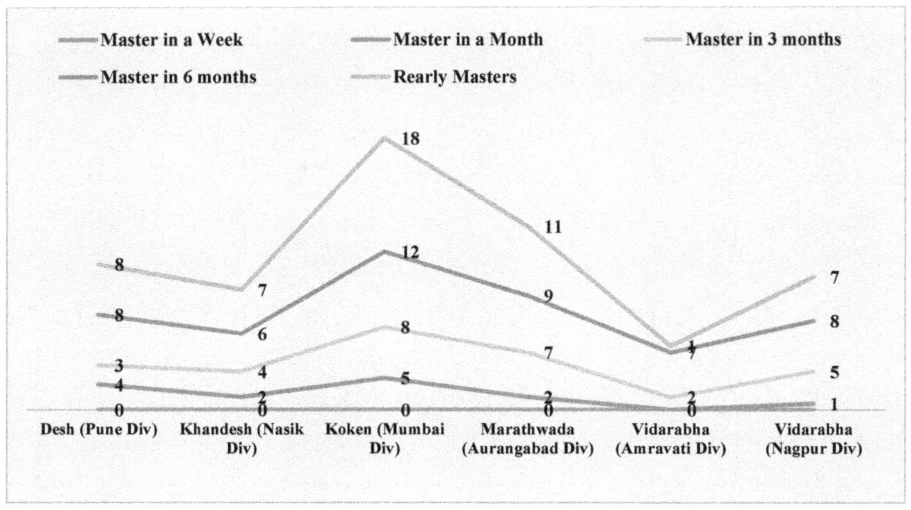

Figure 4.44 Cross factor Analysis of Industrial Zone with Types of Training provided to Employee by MSMU

(Source: Primary Data)

The study put bright light on the factors that, 35.87% MSMU accept that there is rare chances to become as masters on ERP system whereas, in this confession 52% MSMU from Mumbai and Aurangabad division. Only 1% from Amravati division accepts ERP system mastery is rarely possible. The study also revealed that 34.49% MSMU accept on the mastery in 6 months on ERP system and again Mumbai and Aurangabad combined share 45% of the MSMU. 20% MSMU support to the mastery in ERP system can possible in 3 months whereas, Only 9.66% MSMU dare to convincing about the ERP mastering possible with a month also and no Amravati division MSMU ready to agree on this point with any other division in the Maharashtra state. The interesting confession was came out with this study is no single division's MSMU claim about their mastery can possible within a week which is practical next impossible for any new user of ERP system in organization.

	Approximate training cost in terms of the overall ERP budget in Manufacturing Units						Total
	Over 20%	16% to 20%	11% to 15%	6% to 10%	Below 5%	No idea	
Desh (Pune Div)	0	3	4	0	0	16	**23**
Khandesh (Nasik Div)	0	2	1	2	0	14	**19**
Koken (Mumbai Div)	0	4	6	3	0	30	**43**
Marathwada (Aurangabad Div)	0	6	3	2	0	18	**29**
Vidarabha (Amravati Div)	0	0	0	2	0	8	**10**
Vidarabha (Nagpur Div)	0	0	2	0	0	19	**21**
Total	**0**	**15 (10.35%)**	**16 (11.04%)**	**9 (6.21%)**	**0**	**105 (74.42%)**	**145**

Table 4.33 Cross Factor Analysis of Industrial Zone with Approx. Training Cost in terms of ERP Budget spent by Respondent MSMU

(Source: Primary Data)

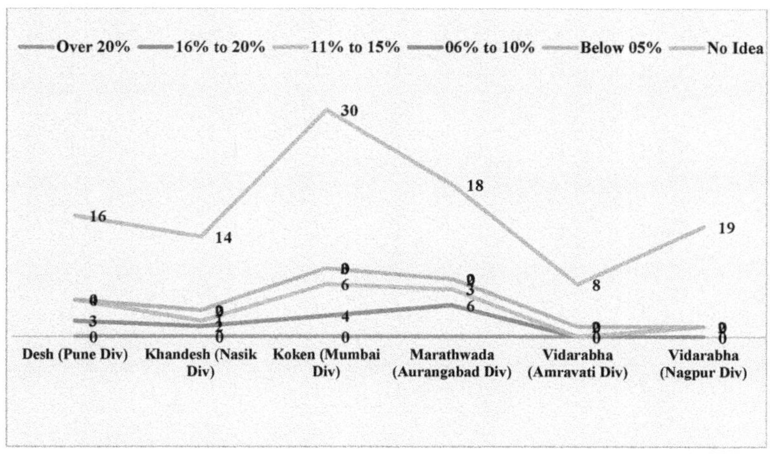

Figure 4.45 Cross factor Analysis of Industrial Zone with Approx. Training cost spent by MSMU

(Source: Primary Data)

The study is evidence that, 10.35% MSMU spent 16% to 20% of total cost of ERP budget and no division from the Vidarabha divisions i.e. Amravati and Nagpur division dare to spend the training cost in this range. With the same 11.04% MMSU spent 11% to 15% training cost whereas, Amravati this time also not ready to pay such amount on training to their MSMU end-user and Mumbai and Pune division combined share the 62.5% in this range. The research illustrate that, 74.42% MSMU have no idea about the cost concern information about the training activity whereas, Mumbai and Nagpur division are more as compare to all other MSMU in No Idea category. 90.47% MSMU from Nagpur division is more unaware on Training cost and Nasik division's MSMU are more aware about this information.

The fact which we found by this research, with special reference to this question is, respondents makes a comment like, the cost concern activity on training is depends upon the Top level management and our most of the respondents are belongs to medium or upper-medium level of the organization.

Industrial Zone	ERP improve the resource utilization in all aspects of the organization in Manufacturing Units					Total
	Yes Completely	Yes But partially	No	Never	Can't say	
Desh (Pune Div)	19	4	0	0	0	23
Khandesh (Nasik Div)	12	7	0	0	0	19
Koken (Mumbai Div)	40	3	0	0	0	43
Marathwada (Aurangabad Div)	26	3	0	0	0	29
Vidarabha (Amravati Div)	10	0	0	0	0	10
Vidarabha (Nagpur Div)	18	3	0	0	0	21
Total	125 (86.20%)	20 (13.79%)	0	0	0	145

Table 4.34 Cross Factor Analysis on Respondent MSMU's Opinions about improvement in the resource utilization due to ERP implementation (Industrial Zone wise)
(Source: Primary Data)

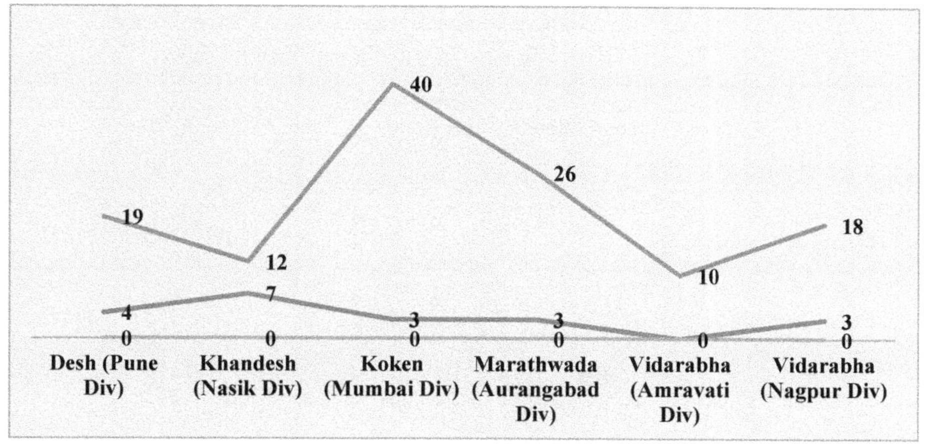

Figure 4.46 Cross factor Zone wise Analysis of MSMU's opinions on resource utilization improvement due to ERP implementation
(Source: Primary Data)

The study proves that, 86.20% MSMU completely agree for the comment that, ERP implementation improves resource utilization in all aspect of the organization whereas, Mumbai and Aurangabad division's MSMU share more than50% of the completely agree category.

As per as division wise details, Amravati is the only division who support 100% for the completely agree option whereas, other division's some percentage MSMU are partially agree also, but Amravati division is only support to completely agree option.

13.79% MSMU agree but partially on the resource utilization comment and only Amravati division has not participated in this partially agree scenario.

One of the most important outcome of the study by this question is no single MSMU from any division deny to resource utilization due to ERP implementation.

		ERP improve the effectiveness and Competency of the decision process in Manufacturing Units					Total
		Yes Completely	Yes But partially	No	Never	Can't say	
Industrial Zone	Desh (Pune Div)	19	4	0	0	0	23
	Khandesh (Nasik Div)	10	9	0	0	0	19
	Koken (Mumbai Div)	29	14	0	0	0	43
	Marathwada (Aurangabad Div)	24	5	0	0	0	29
	Vidarabha (Amravati Div)	2	8	0	0	0	10
	Vidarabha (Nagpur Div)	15	6	0	0	0	21
	Total	99 (68.28%)	46 (31.73%)	0	0	0	145

Table 4.35 Cross Factor Analysis on Respondent MSMU's Opinions about improvement in the effectiveness and Competency of the decision making process due to ERP implementation (Industrial Zone wise)

(Source: Primary Data)

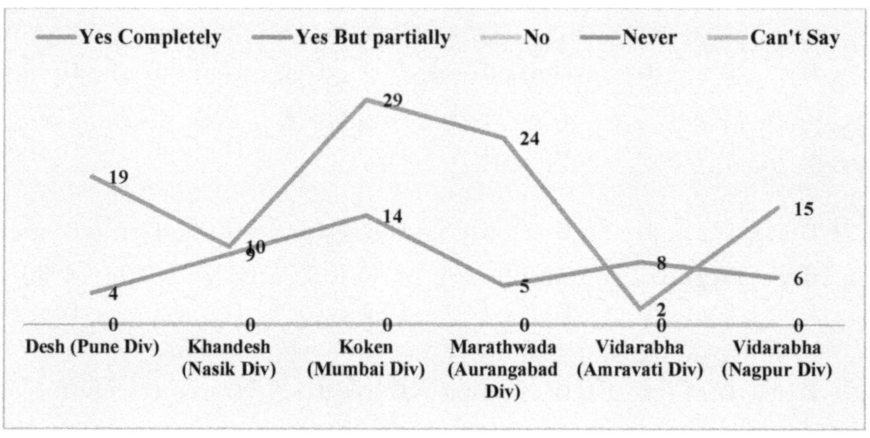

Figure 4.47 Cross factor Zone wise Analysis of MSMU's opinions on Decision making process Competency and improvement due to ERP implementation

(Source: Primary Data)

The study proves that, 68.28% MSMU completely agree for the comment that, ERP implementation improves Competency and effectiveness in the decision making process of the organization whereas, Mumbai and Aurangabad division's MSMU share more than55% of the completely agree category.

As per as division wise details, Pune and Aurangabad divisions are support more than 82% each for the completely agree option whereas, Amravati Division gives only 20% support to completely agree option.

31.73% MSMU agree but partially agree on the Competency and effectiveness in the decision making process comment and Amravati division has big support to partially agree scenario as compare to completely agree opinions.

One of the most interesting outcome of the study by this question is, no single MSMU from any division support to non-improvement in the effectiveness and Competency on the decision making process in the organization due to ERP implementation.

Industrial Zone		ERP has increased the employee satisfaction and productivity and enable better choices for employees in Manufacturing Units					Total
		Yes Completely	Yes But partially	No	Never	Can't say	
	Desh (Pune Div)	14	8	0	0	1	23
	Khandesh (Nasik Div)	8	6	0	0	5	19
	Koken (Mumbai Div)	12	27	0	0	4	43
	Marathwada (Aurangabad Div)	19	7	0	0	3	29
	Vidarabha (Amravati Div)	3	7	0	0	0	10
	Vidarabha (Nagpur Div)	8	9	0	0	4	21
Total		64 (44.13%)	64 (44.13%)	0	0	17 (11.74%)	145

Table 4.36 Cross factor Zone wise Analysis of MSMU's opinions on improvement in Employee satisfaction, productivity and enable better choice for employee due to ERP implementation. (Industrial Zone wise)
(Source: Primary Data)

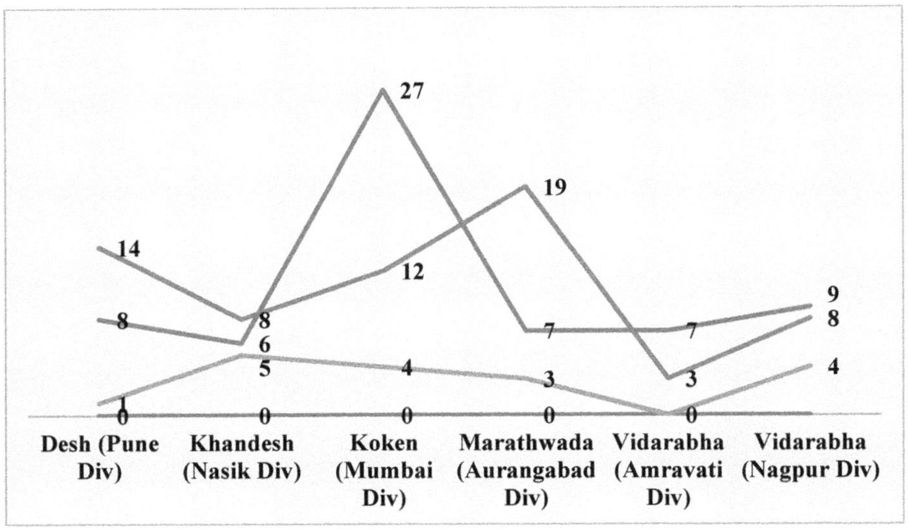

Figure 4.48 Cross factor Zone wise Analysis of MSMU's opinions on improvement in Employee satisfaction, productivity and enable better choice for employee due to ERP implementation
(Source: Primary Data)

The study shown that, 44.13% MSMU agree on ERP has increased the employees satisfaction and productivity and enable better choice for the employees in their manufacturing unit and Amravati division with 5% secure last position in the list whereas, Aurangabad Division took at top position with 65% as completely agree opinion for the comment.

44.13% MSMU are agree but in partial manner and Mumbai division participated in the category with 51.16% and Aurangabad division support the statement 24.13%.

Interesting result revealed that, 11.74% MSMU are opt the answer as **"Can't Say"** i.e. they are not in a position to say anything about the satisfaction and productivity and enabling the better choice for the employee due to ERP system, the special comment made by these respondents was, they were not confident about the entire manufacturing unit and initially they are get confused between **"partially agree"** or **"No"** option.

Only Amravati division MSMU is not opt. to **"Can't say"** option among the all industrial zones in the Maharashtra state.

No of Employee		Duration of ERP System Implementation in Manufacturing Unit							Total
	↓ →	Under 09 months	09 months to 01 year	01 year to 1.5 years	1.5 year to 02 years	02 years to 2.5 years	2.5 years to 03 years	Over 03 years	Total
	Up to 50	0	0	0	0	0	0	0	0
	51 to 150	0	0	0	1	0	0	0	1
	151 to 300	0	0	13	33	20	31	3	100
	More than 300	0	0	7	15	6	15	1	44
	Total	0	0	20	49	26	46	4	145

Table 4.37 Cross Factor Analysis for No. of Employees with Duration of ERP implementation the Respondent MSMU

(Source: Primary Data)

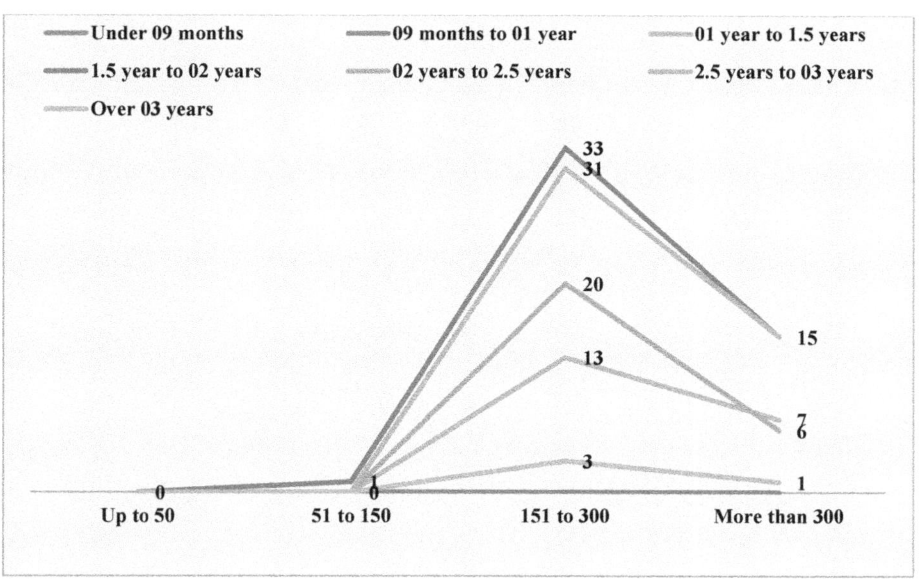

Figure 4.49 Cross Factor Analysis for No of Employee and ERP implementation duration

(Source: Primary Data)

The study proves that, no MSMU have less than 50 number of employee who implemented ERP into their firm whereas, only 1 MSMU have employees count 51 to 150. 33.79% MSMU took 1.5yr to 02yrs whereas, 151 to 300 no. of employee MSMU are 67.39% and 30% MSMU have more than 300 employees in their firm. The study also revealed that, 32% MSMU took 02yrs to 2.5yrs out of them, who have 151 to 300 employee are 67.39% and more than 300 employee counted MSMU are 32.60%. No single MSMU tool implementation duration for ERP is less than a year. 2.27% MSMU took more than 3yrs for ERP implementation into their MSMU.

No of Employee	↓ →	When to Perform Re-engineering the business processes in Manufacturing Unit				Total
		Prior to the implementation	As part of the implementation	After the implementation	No BPR done	
	Up to 50	0	0	0	0	0
	51 to 150	0	1	0	0	1
	151 to 300	19	60	1	20	100
	More than 300	12	19	1	12	44
	Total	31	80	2	32	145

Table 4.38 Cross Factor Analysis for No. of Employees with BPR process details provided by the respondent MSMU

(Source: Primary Data)

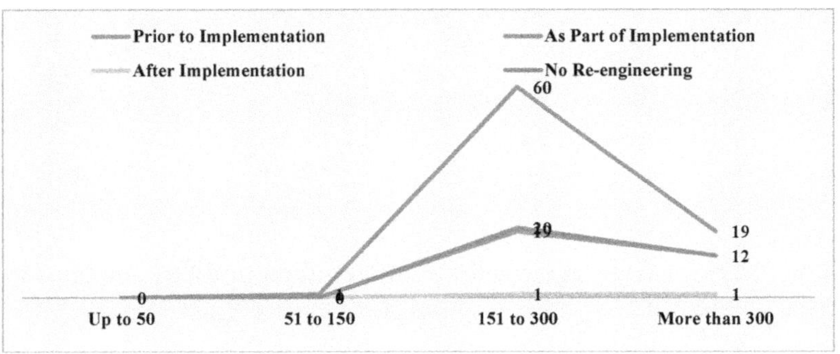

Figure 4.50 Cross Factor Analysis for No. of Employees and BPR process Details

(Source: Primary Data)

The research depict that, 55.17% MSMU done BPR process as part of ERP implementation i.e. in-implementation process for ERP, in this category only one MSMU have 51 to 151 employee in their firm and 75% MSMU have 151 to 300 ad only 24% MSMU have more than 300 employees in their manufacturing unit. Only 1.37% done the BPR Process after the ERP implementation. Only 21.37% MSMU done BPR process as prior ERP implementation process and 22.03% have not done any BPR activity in their MSMU and 65% MSMU in this list are having more than 300 employee in their firm whereas, 35% have less than 300 employees.

No of Employee ↓ →	Which ERP implementation strategy Used by Manufacturing Units					Total
	Don't know	Parallel approach	Phased approach	Big bang approach	Pilot approach	
Up to 50	0	0	0	0	0	0
51 to 150	1	0	0	0	0	1
151 to 300	80	15	5	0	0	100
More than 300	38	3	3	0	0	44
Total	119	18	8	0	0	145

Table 4.39 Cross Factor Analysis of No. of Employees with ERP implementation Strategy used by respondent MSMU

(Source: Primary Data)

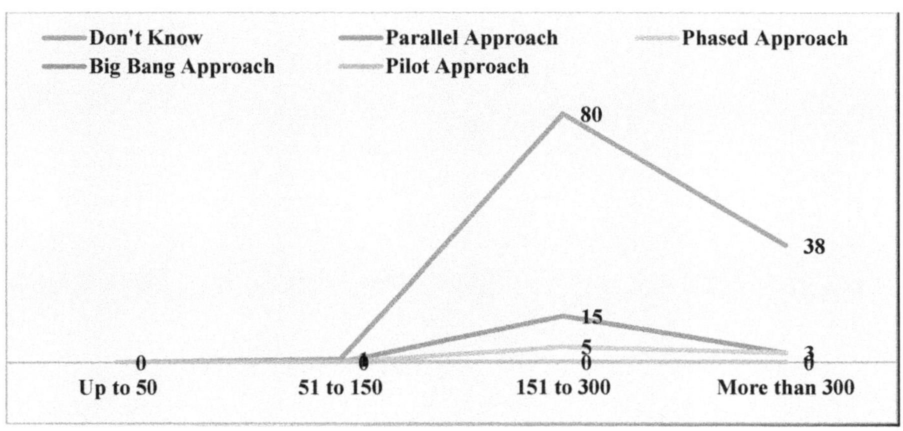

Figure 4.51 Cross Factor Analysis with ERP implementation Strategy

(Source: Primary Data)

The Study focused that, 82.06% MSMU have no idea about which ERP implementation strategy used by their organization whereas, 67.22% MSMU belongs to 151 to 300 no. of employees in their firm and 32% having more than 300 employees in their MSMU. The study also proves that, only 12.41% used parallel Approach and 5.51% used Phased approach while ERP get implemented in their MSMU whereas, almost 75% MSMU who knows about the ERP implementation strategy belongs to 151 to 300 employee count and only 25% MSMU have more than 300 employees in their firm. One interesting outcome of the study was no respondent MSMU gone for Big-Bang or Pilot Approach while ERP get implemented in their MSMU.

No of Employee		Which Type of Training Provided to Employees in Manufacturing Units					Total
		Project team training	End user training/ Module Based training	Traditional training	Web-based training	No additional training provided	
	Up to 50	0	0	0	0	0	**0**
	51 to 150	0	0	0	0	1	**1**
	151 to 300	6	71	0	0	23	**100**
	More than 300	2	25	2	0	15	**44**
	Total	**8**	**96**	**2**	**0**	**39**	**145**

Table 4.40 Cross Factor Analysis of No. of Employees with Type of Training Provided by Respondent MSMU
(Source: Primary Data)

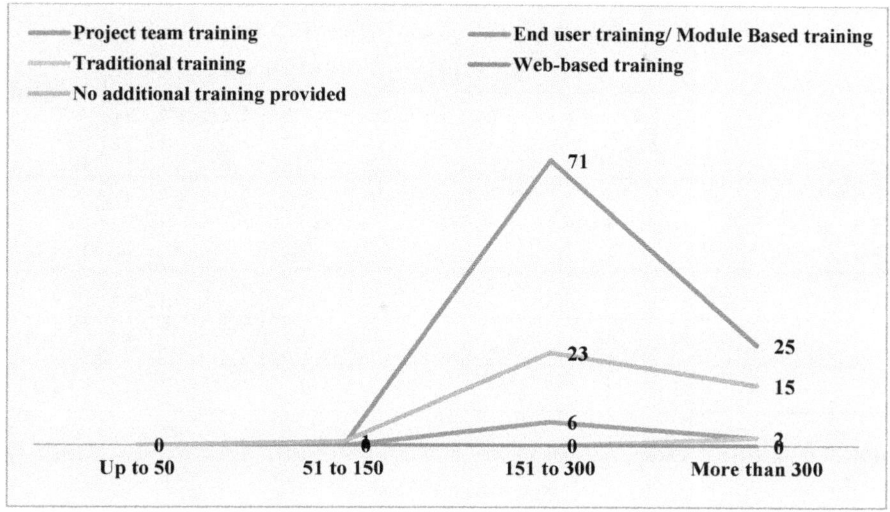

Figure 4.52 Cross Factor Analysis for No. of Employees and Type of Training Details

(Source: Primary Data)

The study observed that, end-user or module based training is more popular in 66.20% MSMU who implanted ERP whereas, 74% have 151 to 300 employees and 36% MSMU having more than 300 employees in their manufacturing unit. 5.51% MSMU used Project team training and only 1.37% MSMU used traditional training whereas, no single MSMU who have no. of employees 151 to 300. 27% MSMU have not provided any type of training to their MSMU whereas, 59% of these MSMU have 151 to 3000 employees in their firm and 37% have more than 300 employees in their manufacturing unit. The last but not list observation from table 4.39 is even-though MSMU using ERP system in their firm but still no single MSMU ready to provide Web Based Training to their user at their manufacturing unit for ERP system use.

No of Employee ↓ →	Approximate training cost in terms of the overall ERP budget in Manufacturing Units						Total
	Over 20%	16% to 20%	11% to 15%	6% to 10%	Below 5%	No idea	
Up to 50	0	0	0	0	0	0	**0**
51 to 150	0	0	0	0	0	1	**1**
151 to 300	2	9	11	7	0	71	**100**
More than 300	0	4	5	2	0	33	**44**
Total	**2**	**13**	**16**	**9**	**0**	**105**	**145**

Table 4.41 Cross Factor Analysis of No. of Employees with Training cost details by Respondent MSMU
(Source: Primary Data)

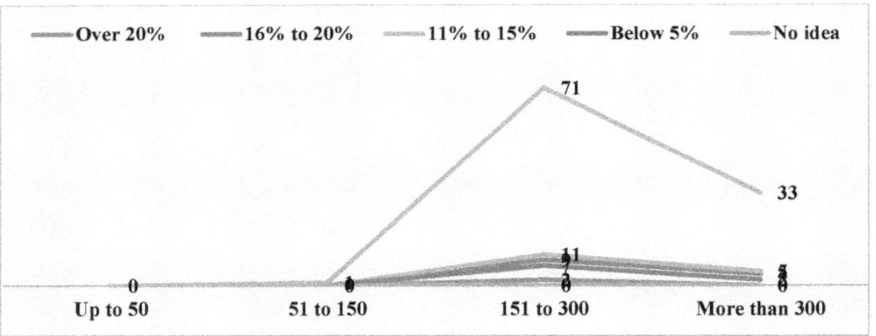

Figure 4.53 Cross Factor Analysis for No. of Employees and cost on training details
(Source: Primary Data)

The research highlight that, 1.37% MSMU spent more than 20% cost of total ERP cost on training and the MSMU who have 151 to 300 employees in their firm took the decision no their category of no. of employees category participated in this costing phase.

The resultant table has shown that, 68.90% MSMU having 151 to 300 employees and 31% MSMU having more than 300 employees in their manufacturing unit.

72.41% MSMU have no idea about the raining cost whereas, 67.61% MSMU having 151 to 300 and 31.42% having more than 300 and only

1.23% having 51 to 150 employees in their manufacturing unit. The reason about their un-awareness for training cost was, the financial decision take on the Top level and out most of the respondents are belongs to Middle level management as individual.

No of Employee	ERP improve the resource utilization in all aspects of the organization in Manufacturing Units					Total
	Yes Completely	Yes But partially	No	Never	Can't say	
Up to 50	0	0	0	0	0	0
51 to 150	0	1	0	0	0	1
151 to 300	85	15	0	0	0	100
More than 300	40	4	0	0	0	44
Total	125	20	0	0	0	145

Table 4.42 Cross Factor Analysis of Respondent MSMU's Opinions about improvement in the resource utilization due to ERP implementation MSMU (Source: Primary Data)

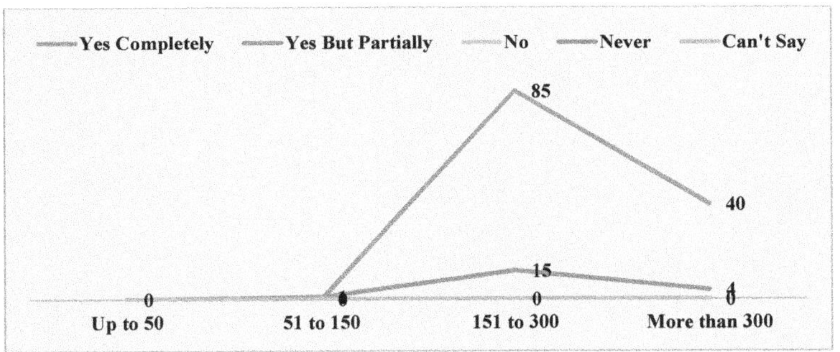

Figure 4.54 Cross Factor Analysis of Respondent MSMU's Opinions about improvement in the resource utilization due to ERP implementation MSMU (Source: Primary Data)

The research illustrate that, 86.20% MSMU completely agree for the resource utilization improvement due to ERP implementation and 68.75% MSMU are having 151 to 300 employee whereas, 31.21% MSMU are having their employee count more than 300.

It also depict that, 13.79% MSMU are partially agree on ERP improves the resource utilization and only 01 MSMU having employee count 51 to 150, 68.96 % MSMU have 151 to 300 employee count and only 30.35% MSMU have more than 300 employee.

MSMU who implemented ERP, none of them disagree on resource utilization due to ERP as nobody select the "NO, Never and Can't Say" Option as answer the question.

No of Employee		ERP improve the effectiveness and Competency of the decision process in Manufacturing Units					Total
		Yes Completely	Yes But partially	No	Never	Can't say	
	Up to 50	0	0	0	0	0	0
	51 to 150	0	1	0	0	0	1
	151 to 300	67	33	0	0	0	100
	More than 300	32	12	0	0	0	44
Total		99	46	0	0	0	145

Table 4.43 Cross Factor Analysis on Respondent MSMU's Opinions about improvement in the effectiveness and Competency of the decision making process due to ERP implementation (No of Employee wise)
(Source: Primary Data)

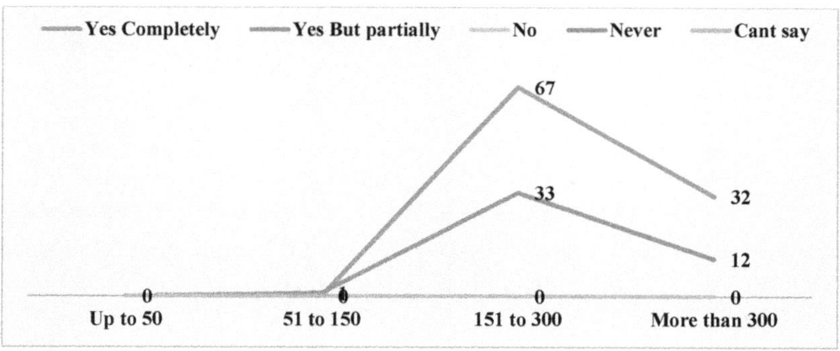

Figure 4.55 Cross Factor Analysis of Respondent MSMU's Opinions about improvement in the effectiveness and Competency of the decision making process due to ERP implementation MSMU
(Source: Primary Data)

The research illustrate that, 68.27% MSMU completely agree for the improvement in the effectiveness and Competency of the decision making process due to ERP implementation and 67.67% MSMU are having 151 to 300 employee whereas, 32.32% MSMU are having their employee count more than 300. It also depict that, 31.72% MSMU are partially agree on ERP improves effectiveness and Competency of the decision making and only 01 MSMU having employee count 51 to 150, 71.73% MSMU have 151 to 300 employee count and only 26.08% MSMU have more than 300 employee.

No of Employee	↓ →	ERP has increased the employee satisfaction and productivity and enable better choices for employees in Manufacturing Units					Total
		Yes Completely	Yes But partially	No	Never	Can't say	
	Up to 50	0	0	0	0	0	0
	51 to 150	0	0	0	0	1	1
	151 to 300	41	46	0	0	13	100
	More than 300	23	18	0	0	3	44
	Total	64	64	0	0	17	145

Table 4.44 Cross factor Analysis of MSMU's opinions on improvement in Employee satisfaction, productivity and enable better choice for employee due to ERP implementation. (no of Employee wise)
(Source: Primary Data).

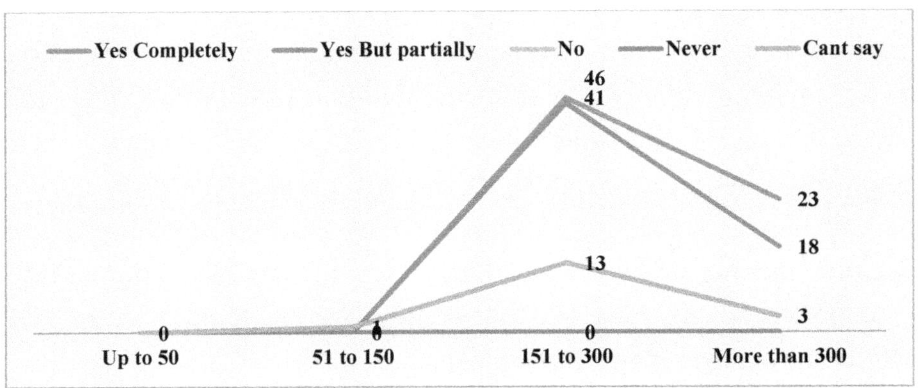

Figure 4.56 Cross Factor Analysis of Respondent MSMU's Opinions about Employee satisfaction, productivity and enable better choice for employee due to ERP implementation MSMU
(Source: Primary Data).

The research illustrate that, 44.13% MSMU completely agree for the improvement in Employee satisfaction, productivity and enable better choice due to ERP implementation and 64.06% MSMU are having 151 to 300 employee whereas, 35.93% MSMU are having their employee count more than 300. It also depict that, 44.13% MSMU are partially agree on ERP improvement in Employee satisfaction, productivity and enable better choice. 71.87% MSMU have 151 to 300 employee count and only 28.12% MSMU have more than 300 employee.

Hypothesis Validation bases on Primary Data

All the assumed Hypothesis were satisfied on basis of results which found from the research survey data collected primarily from the selected 145 medium scale manufacturing unit in Maharashtra state. This statistic can be used to determine whether there is any difference between the study groups in the proportions of the risk factor of interest. The result of the study was arranged in the tabulation format and for proving or validating the hypothesis we have used Chi-Square Testing method. The Chi-Square Test is applied when you have two categorical variables from a single population. It is used to determine whether there is a significant association between the two variables.

The study the availability of data from table no. 4.33, 4.34, and 4.35 in the same chapter (i.e., Chapter 04) and as the test could not consider the row or column with only zero values (the responses are not given or not chosen the option provided in the questionnaires) are not consider for the test as it is not applicable for testing.

The study for test the prepared the data contingency table and expected contingency table, chi-square value, degree of freedom and probability of the test variables by using online tool provided by www.chisquaretest/physics/stats.

H0: – There is No Significant Impact of ERP system in the Improvisation of the Work Competency of the Employee in the Manufacturing Units

H1: – There is Significant Impact of ERP System for Bringing the Work Competency Improvisation in the employees of the Manufacturing Units.

Industrial Zone		Improvement in the Employee Satisfaction, Productivity (Improvement in Work Competency)						Total
		Yes Completely		Yes But Partially		Can't Say		
		Actual Data	Expected Value	Actual Data	Expected Value	Actual Data	Expected Value	
	Desh (Pune Div)	14	10.2	8	10.2	1	2.70	23
	Khandesh (Nasik Div)	8	8.39	6	8.39	5	2.23	19
	Koken (Mumbai Div)	12	19.0	27	19.0	4	5.04	43
	Marathwada (Aurangabad Div)	19	12.8	7	12.8	3	3.40	29
	Vidarabha (Amravati Div)	3	4.41	7	4.41	0	1.17	10
	Vidarabha (Nagpur Div)	8	9.27	9	9.27	4	2.46	21
Total		64		64		17		145

Table 4.45 Chi-Square Test Contingency Table on Respondent MSMU's Opinions about Work Competency improvement due to ERP implementation (Industrial Zone wise)

(Source: Primary Data)

Chi-Square = 23.3
Degree of Freedom = 10.
Probability = 0.010

- In table 4.5 the ERP system implementation done in the respondent manufacturing units due to they need a future growth in work Competency and so they had opted "to enabling the future growth in work Competency" more than 56% as Rank-I, Rank-II and Rank-III as combined.

- The chi-square p-value is 0.010, which is less than 0.05, it is interpreted that, The Null Hypothesis is rejected and the Alternative Hypothesis "H1: – is statistically significant i.e. ***There is Significant Impact of ERP System for Bringing the Work Competency improvisation in the employees of the manufacturing Units.***

H0: – There is No Significant Impact on the Manufacturing unit's for obtaining Better Resource Utilization due to ERP Implementation.

H2: – There is Significant Impact on the Manufacturing unit's for obtaining Better Resource Utilization due to ERP Implementation.

Industrial Zone		ERP Obtain Better the resource utilization in all aspects of the organization in Manufacturing Units				Total
		Yes Completely		Yes, But partially		
		Actual Data	Expected Value	Actual Data	Expected Value	
	Desh (Pune Div)	19	19.8	4	3.17	**23**
	Khandesh (Nasik Div)	12	16.4	7	2.62	**19**
	Koken (Mumbai Div)	40	37.1	3	5.93	**43**
	Marathwada (Aurangabad Div)	26	25.0	3	4.00	**29**
	Vidarabha (Amravati Div)	10	8.62	0	1.38	**10**
	Vidarabha (Nagpur Div)	18	18.1	3	2.90	**21**
Total		125		20		145

Table 4.46 Chi-Square Test Contingency Table on Respondent MSMU's Opinions about Obtaining Better resource utilization due to ERP implementation (Industrial Zone wise)

(Source: Primary Data)

Chi-Square = 12.3

Degree of Freedom = 5

Probability = 0.031

In table 4.5, the study was found that, 66% MSMU Rank-I, 46% for Rank-II and 39.31% for Rank-III to the need for Implemented ERP system in their organization for improving resources utilization within the organization.

The study also revealed that no single manufacturing units deny about the ERP improves the resource utilization in all aspects of the organization.

- The chi-square p-value is 0.031, which is less than 0.05, it is interpreted that, The Null Hypothesis was Rejected and the hypothesis "H2" is statistically significant, which means ***There is Significant Impact on the Manufacturing unit's for obtaining Better Resource Utilization due to ERP Implementation***

H0: – ERP System Does Not Provided the Technology Support System That Conveys the Better Precision in the Decision Making.

H3: – ERP System provides Technology Supports System that Conveys the Better Precision in Decision Making.

Industrial Zone ↓ →	ERP System provides Technology supports system that conveys the better precision in decision making in Manufacturing Units				Total
	Yes Completely		Yes, But partially		
	Actual Data	Expected Value	Actual Data	Expected Value	
Desh (Pune Div)	19	15.7	4	7.30	**23**
Khandesh (Nasik Div)	10	13	9	6.03	**19**
Koken (Mumbai Div)	29	29.4	14	13.6	**43**
Marathwada (Aurangabad Div)	24	19.8	5	9.2	**29**
Vidarabha (Amravati Div)	2	6.83	8	3.17	**10**
Vidarabha (Nagpur Div)	15	14.3	6	6.66	**21**
Total	**99**		**46**		**145**

Table 4.47 Chi-Square Test Contingency Table on Respondent MSMU's Opinions about ERP System provides Technology supports system that conveys the better precision in decision making in Manufacturing Units (Industrial Zone wise) (Source: Primary Data).

Chi-Square = 18.0
Degree of Freedom = 5.
Probability = 0.003.

In table no. 4.13 more than 55% of the medium scale manufacturing units accept the that ERP system speedup the management's decision-making capability of the manufacturing units as benefits to the management, and agreed that the ERP system Improve the information accuracy and precision in decision making and mark them as Rank-I, more than 34% as Rank-II and More than 65% as Rank-III as Managerial Benefits for the Organization for ERP implementation.

The chi-square p-value is 0.003, which is less than 0.05, it is interpreted that, the Null Hypothesis is Rejected and hypothesis "H3" is statistically significant, which state that, ***ERP System provides Technology supports system that conveys the better precision in decision making.***

Chapter 05

Conclusions & Suggestions

5.1 Introduction:

As the study get reached its destination where the results need to get discussed and providing some guidelines on the bases of data analysis and interpretations, here this chapter highlighted the said final task on the study. It may not be an end of the study as it may open new doors for another walk on new paths for the other researchers for future study.

The study highlighted the impact of ERP in medium scale manufacturing units in Maharashtra state. With the sample questionnaires distributed among the selected respondent medium scale manufacturing units, the final data get extracted and interpreted in the chapter 04 with the details. This chapter is final words on the research as the concluding remarks on the bases of the study, data analysis and interpretation. The chapter get divided into mainly three parts, in very first part the conclusions and major finding on the research get discussed whereas, next part the limitation of the study get mentioned and at final phase of this chapter some suggestions and recommendations are get made for the medium scale manufacturing units as well as the stake holders of the ERP system for their future work and goals in concern with their manufacturing units in the concern of ERP system.

The major finding section revealed some result of the studies, which get observed and proves on the bases of the primary data get collected and analyzed in the chapter 04. The section discussed the closing remarks on the study like the ERP process, ERP system, the factors affecting on the ERP system like internal and external types, advantages and disadvantages, improvements in the manufacturing unit's resource utilization, better work efficiency, improvement in the decision making process etc. The last part of this section some cross factor analysis of the factors get conclude by keeping some factors constant like industrial zones and total number of employees in the medium scale manufacturing units.

In second part of this chapter limitation of the study get discussed where, the constraints and their impact on the study get concluded, like geographical, financial and technical limitation as well as some constraints need to put intentionally.

In the last part of the chapter, suggestions and recommendations are get discussed, which gives the opinions based on the current studies output and its current loopholes. The suggestions are get given to the various stakeholder of the ERP system and medium scale manufacturing units in both cases, for those MSMU who implemented ERP system as well as for those MSMU who wish to plan for ERP system in their manufacturing units. Some suggestions are also made for the MSME, State and Central Govt. for providing some motivational plan of actions for those MSMU who are implemented or who wish go for it.

5.2 Summary

Chapter 1: Research Introduction:

The first chapter discussed the Introduction of the ERP system, and industrial structure of manufacturing industries. The chapter also described the difference between service sectors and manufacturing sector, it also describe the Objective of the study, Hypothesis, Scope, limitation, Benefits of study and research. The chapter one also lighten the research methodology used in the study, where the details get described as, sampling mechanism like purposive sampling method used for identifying the total number of MSMU among the state and out of it purposefully selected more than 50% MSMU for the study, in measurement procedures section details of data collection methods like personal interview, questionnaires, personally and via e-mail etc get highlighted. In this section of chapter type of questions, total number of questions, sub-sections like information get discussed. In data collection details section the time duration i.e. Jan-2014 to June-2014 of the study was detailed and method for arranging the resultants information from the selected respondents are arranged in numerical and tabular formation to get easy usability during the data analysis. The data analysis and interpretations section provides the resultant data as knowledge based, standard formation in which, the interpretation can be getting possible. The conversion of raw data into proper formatted data as information was converted and analyze by using SPSS and MS-Excel tools. The analysis activity get possible on the bases of each factors descriptive statistic of frequency and percentile manger. Some factors are get interpreted by Cross Factor Analysis method to find out the influence of one factor on other factors are possible or not. The details of the Data Analysis and Interpretations are keep in Chpater-04.

Chapter 2: Relevant Study & Literature Reviews

The chapter will discuss the various studies done in the past and recently on the ERP implementation in manufacturing industries. The literature review will cover the research article, papers, PhD thesis; new article right from the international to national level, the review will cover last 5 and more years for the highlight the study domain on the ERP implementation system in the manufacturing industries in all over the globe .

The purpose of this chapter is to present the previous efforts and findings in related areas. It presents an overview of previous research on ERP implementation in information systems. The significant developments related to ERP system relevant for the present research has been highlighted. For clarity, the literature has been classified into seven sections. In the first section of this chapter Definitions of ERP from various authors, books and other references are presented. Second part of this chapter deals with ERP fundamentals with try to highlighting basic ERP process. In the third section BPR i.e. Business process reengineering process review get analyze and try to discuss various authors opinions about the BPR process and its impact stories on various county and organization. The fourth section of this chapter ERP implementation process in manufacturing industries are get reviewed, with their implementation strategy and experience of different research and authors. In Section Five SME scenario gets observed and discusses, it reviews the researchers and their correspondence analysis about the small and medium sale enterprises structure and overview. In Section Six the process of ERP implementation in SME get reviewed with their implementation strategies, deployment approaches and the reviewed results from various studies and research, as the theoretical frameworks for this study. In the last section the overview of Post implementation of ERP thorough literature review of all the factors has been taken. It presents a critical appraisal of the previous work published in the literature pertaining to the area of ERP implementation in SME.

Chapter 3: ERP System Fundamentals & it relevance with Manufacturing Units

The section gives the details of thee research methodology used for the study and detail of the sampling techniques and research world, where details of the sample, reason behind selecting only given sample is going to discuss. The details of the data collection and tabular formatted, chart and figures and going to be demonstrate in this section

Chapter 4. Data Collection, Observation and Interpretations:

This will be the core section of the Thesis where all the data analysis, observations and interpretations are going to be discuss, also provide some analytical tools and techniques for analysis of the given data on the various parameter on which the conclusion and recommendations are going to be discussed. This chapter provides information on the research methods of this thesis. A descriptive / Qualitative / Survey Based research methodology was used for this study. A survey was administered to a selected sample from a specific Medium Scale Manufacturing Units identified by the Development Commissioner (MSME) Ministry of Micro, Small & Medium Enterprises, Mumbai and Nagpur Division.

The samples are selected on the basis of the knowledge, connection and judgment of the researcher in the Medium Scale Manufacturing industry in Maharashtra State. It is through the researchers personal and work relationships with the Individuals in medium scale manufacturing units and their references further units for same division or others to ensure the participation and completion of this survey. Most of them are Managerial, professionals and executives companies. MSME, DC-MSME, Mumbai and Nagpur, updated industry news and events, personal experience and other information all help to form the basis for the selection and ongoing maintenance of samples.

The survey will be consisted close-ended questions formulated aiming to ensure more in-depth information is provided. The questions are formulated based on the objectives, research question and hypothesis of this research.

The analysis of the survey data is processed using Microsoft Excel and the add-in software Analyze It like IBM SPSS Statistics Data Editor 2010 Ed. Collected data was compiled in MS-excel sheet, for analysis the collected data SPSS (Statistical Package for Social Sciences Ver. 20th) was used.

The statistical analyses that have been conducted include: overall multi-dimension constructs measurement towards each factor, descriptive statistics, of frequency and percentile manner. The data is analyze questionnaire wise and Reponses are get collected and interpretations done by using frequency and percentile of the frequency as compare to the total number of respondent. The Cross Tabulation or Cross Factors Analysis is used for the correlation between the industrial Zone-wise medium Scale manufacturing units towards each factor and the actual percentage of their occurrences with entire MSME and each zone wise. Tabulation and charts are provided for the ease of comparison between different categories. Other information related to respondents also designed by pie charts, Line charts and column charts for more pictorial description and analysis.

Chapter 5: Conclusions and Recommendations:

The chapter get divided into mainly three parts, in very first part the conclusions and major finding on the research get discussed whereas, next part the limitation of the study get mentioned and at final phase of this chapter some suggestions and recommendations are get made for the medium scale manufacturing units as well as the stake holders of the ERP system for their future work and goals in concern with their manufacturing units in the concern of ERP system.

5.3 Major Findings:

5.3.1. The main objective of the study was, to understand the ERP implementation scenario in Maharashtra state medium scale manufacturing units and the study highlighted that, out of 792 medium scale manufacturing units only 245 MSMU have implemented ERP in their firm i.e. only 31.43% MSMU using ERP system whereas, 68.57% MSMU market open for the ERP venders just in Maharashtra state only.

5.3.2. The study also conclude that, most of the market of MSMU covered by SAP and Oracle as ERP venders, as compare to other options like PeopleSoft, BAAN, J D Edwards etc venders are still not have that much popularity in the MSMU of Maharashtra State.

5.3.3. In the respondent MSMU Mumbai and Aurangabad Division combined share the almost half of the respondent share in the study.

5.3.4. The research also revealed that, the conversion ratio of normal MSMU into ERP using MSMU are more in Pune and Mumbai division due to their industrial development.

5.3.5. Conversion ratio of MSMU to ERP using MSMU in Maharashtra state for Nasik and Aurangabad division is very low as compare to Pune and Mumbai division.

5.3.6. Most of the MSMU who implemented ERP system in their firm are used Parallel or Phased approached during the ERP developments whereas, most of the respondents are unknown to the ERP implementation strategy used in their firm for ERP system.

5.3.7. The overall budget of ERP implementation is very high and so the MSMU who have more than 25 Crores as their annual turnover are adopt the ERP system where as less than 25 Crores annual turnover MSMU are very few and dare to go for ERP system implementation.

5.3.8. The study highlighted that, Business Process Reengineering process is took by the MSMU very casual while ERP get implemented in their organization whereas, BPR should be the first step for ERP implementation process, because it refines and identifying the current business process and provides the factual opinions as "weather the organization should go for the ERP implementation" or "it Really needs to implement ERP system for current business process".

5.3.9. It also highlights that, Software sector and Liquor sectors are still not that much gets implemented under ERP application. As Agricultural, Automobile and Pharmaceutical products oriented manufacturing units are more interested in the ERP implementation for their end product.

5.3.10. The ERP implementations in manufacturing units are growing gradually as the numbers of industrial units get increasing day by day.

5.3.11. The conclusion also found on the bases of responses received from the selected manufacturing units that, most of the MSMU not taking the importance Training phase and its cost factor during the ERP implementation.

5.3.12. The basic need of ERP system in the Medium Scale manufacturing units is improve resource utilization within the organization whereas, very few of the MSMU are really looking for the Standardization of the Business Process by introducing Technical Support System or Increasing the firm's flexibility, acceptability and adoptability to respond new market opportunities.

5.3.13. The total number of employees in the organization influences the ERP implementation cost, Duration, Cost of Training, ERP implementation strategy, re-engineering process, type of training directly.

5.3.14. The fact which we found by this research that, respondents makes a comment like, the cost concern activity on training is depends upon the Top level management and our most of the respondents are belongs to medium or upper-medium level of the organization.

5.3.15. Research also conclude that most of the decision in regards of ERP implementation are taken by the Top Level Management whereas, the organization need to include all the operational level people must includes as these people are needed to work on the ERP system directly.

5.3.16. No single Medium Scale Manufacturing Units from any division of Maharashtra deny for improvement of resource utilization due to ERP implementation in all aspects of the organization, as nobody select the "NO, Never and Can't Say" Option as answer the question.

5.3.17. The research conclude a very interesting fact that, Not a single Medium Scale Manufacturing Unit in the Maharashtra from any division of Maharashtra state supporting to non-improvement in the effectiveness and efficiency on the decision making process in the organization due to ERP implementation, as nobody select the "NO, Never and Can't Say" Option as answer the question.

5.3.18. Interesting result revealed that, in table no 4.35 in chapter 04, 11.73% MSMU are opt the answer as **"Can't Say"** i.e. they are not in a position to say anything about the satisfaction and productivity and enabling the better choice for the employee due to ERP system, the special comment made by these respondents was, they were not confident about the entire manufacturing unit and initially they are get confused between **"partially agree"** or **"No"** option.

5.3.19. All the results which found from the research survey data collected primarily from the selected 145 medium scale manufacturing unit in Maharashtra state supportive evidences to assumed Hypothesis were satisfied.

5.3.20. Manufacturing units implemented the ERP system in their manufacturing units in the need as enabling the future expansion in job competency.

5.3.21. Manufacturing Units are agreed that, the ERP system growing work competence and accuracy in their units as operational benefits in rank-II.

5.3.22. The Medium Scale Manufacturing units were accepts that, ERP system increasing work efficiency and accuracy in manufacturing units as operational benefits.

5.3.23. The study was found that, the manufacturing units Implemented ERP system in their organization in the need of improving resources utilization within the organization.

5.3.24. Manufacturing units completely agree or partially agreed that ERP improves the resource utilization in all aspects of the organization.

5.3.25. The study also revealed that no manufacturing units deny about the ERP improves the resource utilization in all aspects of the organization.

5.3.26. Most of the medium scale manufacturing units accept the that ERP system speedup the management's decision making capability of the manufacturing units as benefits to the management, and agreed that the ERP system

Improve the information accuracy and precision in decision making

5.3.27. Manufacturing units agreed that the ERP system get better for the information correctness and precision in decision making; also accept that ERP system accelerate the management's decision making ability of the manufacturing units as managerial benefits.

5.3.28. In today's emerging business environment, large companies have no options to avoid such massive IT packages. Basically its aim is to mechanize work flow and generate cost savings.

5.3.29. For the present competitive scenario, lagging ERP technology seems to be unsuccessful for a firm. Thus ERP systems have the possibility either to confine or expand the organization's capabilities and lead a pathway to competitiveness.

5.3.30. Many organizations are not giving the importance to the security constraints of organizational database and information.

5.3.31. In third chapter lists the important issues in the regards of ERP security which creates huge problem in organization to prevent the important and vital data. The ERP security plays a vital role in the organization and taking attackers or hackers serious can solve the problem of ERP security at some level.

5.3.32. The Study also underscores the list of some key security issues which many organizations not considering into their account while deal with the data during the process, it helps by considering some of the countermeasures as mention in sixth section to overcome the problems or issues in the given research.

5.3.33. The chapter 03 concludes the importance or Data security and information protection mechanism in ERP systems and some of the fundamental and simple resolution to the problems which help the organization to feel safe in protective hand of technology called ERP.

5.3.34. The study highlights the BPR process as micro-level activity which plays a very important and un-ignorable activity for the organization those want to go for ERP implementation.

5.3.35. As the BPR process is time consuming and costly process most of the organization goes for it. This research also summarized the BPR process step by step.

5.3.36. By listing and elaborating the factors affecting on the BPR process the study also gives the idea to consider the different areas to the organization those planned to go for the BPR process before ERP implementation in their organization.

5.3.37. Dividing the factors in the four different categories gives the idea to the development team of the BPR process to focus on the crucial areas in organizational category during the implementation of BPR process.

5.3.38. The risk factors in various organizational function mentions in the study like Operational, Managerial etc. with the same in future the study can help to keep the eye open for the top level and strategy management people to not control the risk 100% but, at the certain level which can reduce the impact of the risk on ERP system.

5.3.39. The study highlights the SWOT analysis is the process as eye opener for the organization which gives idea about the factors affecting on organization during the ERP implementation.

5.3.40. The SWOT analysis creates new path for the organization on which business can go longer, profitable and reach the success in ERP implementation.

5.3.41. It also describes the some factors divided into internal and external factors.

> **5.3.41.1.** The internal factors affecting by inside environment which more controllable by the organization itself. The internal factors includes the Strengths and Weaknesses of the organization, which describe the Strength as main weapon of the organization present inside on the organization and Weakness as some non-favorable factors as a disadvantages to the organization and it must overcome to achieve the goals.
>
> **5.3.41.2.** The external factors like Opportunities and Threats which provide the favorable situation where the organization can convert their strengths into profit for the organization. The threats just creates the trouble to the organization in the form of Competitors, Advance Technology, Change in customer mood etc where the organization need to face positively to achieve the goals set by the top level management.

5.4 Limitation of the Research

5.4.1. The study is limited to the selected Manufacturing Industrial units who have implemented the ERP and shown their willingness to participate in the research.

5.4.2. The study is conducted only in the region of Maharashtra state only.

5.4.3. The data collected only for the analysis aspect, not for development aspect.

5.4.4. The collected information of the study was based on only personal interview with the respondent and no documentation evidences were verified during the data collection.

5.4.5. The main concern of conducting this survey research is the Sampling. Due to limited resources and time, only small portions of the Medium Scale Manufacturing Units in Maharashtra state are implemented ERP system are requested to participate in the survey. It is only through the researchers personal and work relationships with the MSMU to ensure the participation and completion of this survey.

5.4.6. Most of them are professionals and executives of units. The sample size may not accurately represent all MSMU, although most of the respondents are professionals and managerial level and therefore are more likely to have in-depth knowledge of the subject to provide accurate reflections.

5.4.7. The resources from previous research and studies are very limited. There is very little information available on the subject of ERP implementation in medium scale manufacturing units and very less MSMU implemented ERP in their unit.

5.4.8. There are other ERP implementation features and activities that are also concerns of MSMU world-wide that are not discussed in this thesis. The aim of this thesis is to provide the general impact of ERP system implementation on Medium scale manufacturing units with more insightful information.

5.4.9. It is hoped that this thesis could provide more references for individuals' MSMU in decisions making and ERP implementation process for the manufacturing units for advancement in their managerial, Operational, Technical and Financial Factors evaluation and improvement.

5.5 Suggestions:

5.5.1. Awareness Programs, exhibitions arranged by the MSME & MIDC for SME:

Agricultural, Automobile, Chemical, Pharmaceutical and Electrical Equipments are the main core areas of manufacturing units are implemented and successfully deployed but there are other sectors of the manufacturing products where ERP are not too much popular, so, I recommend it that the awareness programs must be conducted by the MSME or MIDC for which the manufacturing units who have not yet set the goals to have ERP in their firm they at least planned to go for it.

5.5.2. Financial Support for promote the Medium Scale Manufacturing units for ERP Implementation:

The study revealed that, approximate 30% of the manufacturing consider that high initial investment is the Managerial critical success factor for the ERP implementation so, it is understand that many organization who are medium scale not financial capable to take such a high financial risk, although they are ready for ERP implementation, so special policies must me introduce by the financial institute of state as well as central of the country to support, encourage them for ERP implementation

5.5.3. Cloud Based ERP Implementation:

30% Medium Scale Manufacturing Units are considering ERP implementation is very costly and time consuming process, 37.2% units are assume that change in technical infrastructure is the technical critical success factor for ERP implementation, but now a days the technology for ERP system was changed since 2005, the Cloud ERP system is introduce and due it software can be as service, infrastructure etc options are made available in the market, many venders are available in the market who support Cloud ERP system.

5.5.4. Get the Help from the MSME and MIDC with various govt. Schemes:

Following are some schemes are designed and introduce from the MSME and MIDC offer the Medium scale manufacturing units which can help financially, technically and operationally for the technical enhancement and operational improvement.

- Package Scheme of "Incentives-2007"
- TECHOLOGY MISSION FOR MSMEs
- Promotion of ICT in Indian Manufacturing Sector
- National Manufacturing Competitiveness Program

The medium scale manufacturing units must keep awareness of these schemes and get the benefits of it for technical advancement.

5.5.5. Go for alternatives of SAP and ORACLE:

As the study shown, 96.55% of manufacturing units are using SAP ender for ERP system and 3.45% are using ORACLE vender for ERP systems. No doubt these are the top most ERP venders available in the market with extraordinary experience and reputation in the ERP venders domain, but due to their quality of service and features provided by the vender the implementation cost is quite high, so it is recommending to the medium scale units to go for some local level ERP vender who customize the ERP system according to the manufacturing industries requirement and which can reduce high initial cost for the ERP implementation in the firm.

5.5.6. Do the market survey before moving towards the ERP implementation in their manufacturing industries:

"Prevention is better than cure" the statement applied for the manufacturing industries who which to implement ERP system in their firm. The market survey provides the good platform for the manufacturing units who wish to move their current traditional business process towards the ERP system. This will gives opportunities to their business analyst to create of change their plan of action for ERP implementation. This will reduce their failure chances as well as may affect the time and budget while going for ERP implementation.

5.5.7. Use ERP Customization, or Mini ERP:

As the study show the ERP comes with lots of financial and technical aspects, the organization can implement Customized ERP or MINI ERP systems in the firm as they are required. If the organization less bother about the production plans and inventory planning so, the firm can reduce these module from the ERP packages provided by the ERP vender and select only those module which are need desperately by the manufacturing industries. This will definitely reduce the initial development cost over the ERP implementation in the firm.

5.5.8. Insurance Schemes if ERP Failure:

As the ERP implementation comes with lot of money investment for infrastructure, technical manpower etc, what will happen if the ERP system fails to achieves the objective and goals of the organization after the implementation?. To answer this question the study recommending to MSME and MIDC or Medium Scale Manufacturing units to have some provision of assurance from the ERP venders a assurance for ERP success at least at some initial period after the implementation, so medium scale manufacturing units are also happily join the group of ERP implemented organization in the market.

5.5.9. Improve the Business Plans More efficient:

It can be expected that if more effort is made in developing a business case, the ERP implementation would be more successful in terms of client satisfaction, perceived quality and implementation process. However, when business case is strictly defined as a predictor variable of the project success measures, as in the regression analysis, it turns out that it only has a significant contribution to the implementation process success.

5.5.10. Entrepreneurs Motivation for the ERP system:

Entrepreneurs should also be encouraged to go for training and re-training to ensure a wider knowledge about their business process and importance of ERP system with some success stories. This will help in ensuring that entrepreneurs have the right attitude that can help in improving their productivity and enhancing sustainability by upgrading old and traditional production and business process schemes.

5.5.11. Entrepreneurs inspirational strategy designing for the ERP system Implementation and Adoption:

The entrepreneurs will need to diversify their production unit and their team to understand technical advancement creates drastic improvements in their firms and productivity for new product development to meet the demand of consumers. They can be done through market survey to find out current technological trends for improving business process which important for products as well as manufacturing unit's improvement.

5.5.12. Create Industrial Research Center for each Industrial Zone:

Industrial research centers will play a huge role in this aspect through development of product varieties to meet the need of every age group in the society. Industrial research centers can also help in the development of appropriate inter-media technology that can make production easier and cost effective. They should also organize seminars and workshop for workers to upgrade and update their skills.

5.5.13. Central and State Government Motivation (Operational and Financial):

The state and local government should unify their tax collection, lower task and to also encourage emerging SMEs by giving them a tax exemption for a number of years. Taxation should be more business friendly and less costly. Government and nongovernmental organization should provide fund for investment to stimulate the economy. They should also provide financial subventions and set up economic commission that will oversee the activities and operation of SMEs in order to model and design them to be growth oriented.

5.5.14. Annual Gathering, Conferences, reports and magazines need to share for industrialist:

The idea behind this suggestion is to share the information about the technology updates importance and view among the other entrepreneurs by viewing some standards documentation supports, which may encourage the organization for ERP implantation in their firm.

5.5.15. **Share the ERP implementation success stories to others for motivating them for the same:**
The discussion forums need to develop between ERP implemented MAMU with non-ERP implemented MSMU, where the successful ERP implementation stories and overall journey of the MSMU while implementing the ERP system in their firm. This will encourage the other non-ERP MSMU for advancement in their business process by using ERP systems.

5.5.16. **Motivation and encouragement for local or domestic level ERP venders:**
It is not possible for all the medium scale manufacturing units to have branded or standard level ERP venders due to many reasons specially cost, development lifecycle, customized business process etc, so some many entrepreneurs need to think about the local and domestic level ERP venders for the ERP implementation in their firm. This thought can gives them more closure solution for their business process according to their factors and budgeting constraints.

5.5.17. **Design the ERP for Small and close to medium Scale manufacturing units:**
The ERP system may get designed for the large and medium scale manufacturing industries as a package but, if the venders planed to design low level or limited functional or less expensive ERP system for small and close to medium scale manufacturing industries (manufacturing industries who have not yet recognized as complete medium scale manufacturing industries). This makes good market for venders who can provided better ERP solution for their small and less complex business process and according to their budget.

5.5.18. Provide the Central or State Government modular certification or vocational Short term Courses for ERP systems:

As we are in a position to make a good comment on the ERP impact on the manufacturing industries and their importance, the central and state government has to consider this is good employment opportunity for the young IT professionals to make their career in the ERP domain. The cost for becoming professional or make a career in ERP system from any private institutes and training organizations for providing training and certification courses are very high and expensive level. If the Central and State level government's technical institutes provides the same contents and certification or short term vocational courses to young generations with minimum cost, it gives more ERP professional in market. This will increase the overall benefits to all manufacturing units and also as individual by providing good employment opportunities in the market.

5.5.19. Collaborative course of action between researchers and industrialist for ERP implementation:

The researchers are providing good technical and operational supports to the industrialist by providing market survey reports, literature reviews, research papers, the doctorial thesis time to time. This can help the industry as preventive requirement gathering information before moving towards any technical enhancement in their manufacturing firm. So according to the presented research, the study suggest that, the industrialist need have some collaboration with such good analytical and experts in the domain like ERP , MIS, DSS etc; by which there are less possibility of failure get occurred while spending such huge resources on technical enhancement in the business process.

5.5.20. **Open Source ERP Systems (Development and Use)**

Today's era of technology many developers and venders are support and design the computer applications for open source community. The main problem with ERP systems are not adopted by most of the manufacturing organization is cost of the product. So there are many open source ERP system options are available in the market for those manufacturing industries, like ODOO, ERPNext, Dolibrr, Opentaps etc. Most of the open source applications are web based applications so, they may require more efficient and experience man-power to deal with it. All Open Source ERP applications listed above are free to download and easy to use, due to their development technology limitation they are very limited in the functionality and modularity but they are enough to solve the day to day problem of manufacturing units with more accuracy and efficient.

Bibliography

1. Cadili, S. and Whitley, E.A. (2005) 'On the interpretative flexibility of hosted ERP systems', Journal of Strategic Information Systems, Vol. 14, No. 2, pp.167–195.

2. Calisir, F. and Calisir, F. (2004) 'The relation of interface usability characteristics, perceived usefulness, and perceived ease of use to end-user satisfaction with Enterprise Resource Planning (ERP) systems', Computers in Human Behavior, Vol. 20, No. 4, pp.505–515.

3. Cannon, D.M., Klein, H.A., et al. (2004) 'Curriculum integration using enterprise resource planning: an integrative case approach', Journal of Education for Business, Vol. 80, No. 2, pp.93–101.

4. Granlund, M. and Malmi, T. (2002) 'Moderate impact of ERPs on management accounting: a lag or permanent outcome?', Management Accounting Research, Vol. 13, No. 3, pp.299–321.

5. Grenci, R.T. and Hull, B.Z. (2004) 'New dog, old tricks: ERP and the systems development life cycle', Journal of Information Systems Education, Vol. 13, No. 3, pp.277–286.

6. Gulla, J.A. and Brasethvik, T. (2002) 'A model-driven ERP environment with search facilities', Data & Knowledge Engineering, Vol. 42, No. 3, pp.327–341.

7. Gulledge, T. (2006) 'What is integration?', Industrial Management & Data Systems, Vol. 106, No. 1, pp.5–20.

8. Y.B. Moon Gulledge, T. and Simon, G. (2005) 'The evolution of SAP implementation environments: a case study from a complex public

sector project', Industrial Management & Data Systems, Vol. 105, No. 6, pp.714–736.

9. Gulledge, T.R. and Sommer, R.A. (2003) 'Public sector enterprise resource planning', Industrial Management & Data Systems, Vol. 103, No. 7, pp.471–483.

10. Gulledge, T., Sommer, R.A., et al. (2005) 'An introduction to basic enterprise resource planning concepts', International Journal of Management and Enterprise Development, Vol. 2, No. 2, pp.204–218.

11. Gulledge, T.R., Hayes, P., et al. (2004a) 'Aligning mySAP.com with the future logistics enterprise', Journal of Enterprise Information Management, Vol. 17, No. 1, pp.31–44.

12. Gulledge, T.R., Sommer, R.A., et al. (2004b) 'Analyzing convergence alternatives across existing SAP solutions', Industrial Management & Data Systems, Vol. 104, No. 9, pp.722–734.

13. Gupta, A. (2000) 'Enterprise resource planning: the emerging organizational value systems', Industrial Management & Data Systems, Vol. 100, No. 3, pp.114–118.

14. Gupta, M.C. and Kohli, A. (2006) 'Enterprise resource planning systems and its implications for operations function', Technovation, Vol. 26, Nos. 5–6, pp.687–696.

15. Gupta, O., Priyadarshini, K., et al. (2004) 'Enterprise resource planning: a case of a blood bank', Industrial Management & Data Systems, Vol. 104, No. 7, pp.589–603.,

16. Haines M. N. and Goodhue, D.L. (2003) 'Implementation partner involvement and knowledge transfer in the context of ERP implementation', International Journal of Human-Computer Interaction, Vol. 16, No. 1, pp.23–38.

17. Hajnal, C.A. and Riordan, R. (2004) 'Exploring process, enterprise integration and e-business concepts in the classroom: the case of petPRO', Journal of Information Systems Education, Vol. 15, No. 3, pp.267–275.

18. Hanseth, O., Ciborra, C.U., et al. (2001) 'The control devolution: ERP and the side effects of globalization', The Data Base for Advances in Information Systems, Vol. 32, No. 4, pp.34–46.

19. Hawking, P., McCarthy, B., et al. (2004) 'Second wave ERP education', Journal of Information Systems Education, Vol. 15, No. 3, pp.327–332.

20. Hawking, P., Ramp, A., et al. (2001) 'IS'97 model curriculum and enterprise resource planning systems', Business Process Management Journal, Vol. 7, No. 3, pp.225–233.

21. Hayes, D.C., Hunton, J.E., et al. (2001) 'Market reactions to ERP implementation announcements', Journal of Information Systems, Vol. 15, No. 1, pp.3–18.

22. Hedman, J. and Borell, A. (2004) 'Narratives in ERP systems evaluation', Journal of Enterprise Information Management, Vol. 17, No. 4, pp.283–290.

23. Hirt, S.G. and Swanson, E.B. (2001) 'Emergent maintenance of ERP: new roles and relationships', Journal of Software Maintenance and Evolution: Research and Practice, Vol. 13, No. 6, pp.373–397.

24. Hitt, L.M., Wu, D.J., et al. (2002) 'Investment in enterprise resource planning: business impact and productivity measures', Journal of Management Information Systems, Vol. 19, No. 1, pp.71–98.

25. Ho, C-F., Wu, W.H., et al. (2004a) 'Strategies for the adaptation of ERP systems', Industrial Management & Data Systems, Vol. 104, No. 3, pp.234–251.

26. Ho, C-T., Chen, Y-M., et al. (2004b) 'Developing a distributed knowledge model for knowledge management in collaborative development and implementation of an enterprise system', Robotics and Computer-Integrated Manufacturing, Vol. 20, pp.439–456.

27. Holsapple, C.W. and Sena, M.P. (2003) 'The decision support characteristics of ERP systems', International Journal of Human-Computer Interaction, Vol. 16, No. 1, pp.101–123.

28. Holsapple, C.W. and Sena, M.P. (2005) 'ERP plans and decision-support benefits', Decision Support Systems, Vol. 38, No. 4, pp.575–590.

29. Hong, K-K. and Kim, Y-G. (2002) 'The critical success factors for ERP implementation: an organizational fit perspective', Information and Management, Vol. 40, No. 1, pp.25–40.

30. Hsu, L-L. and Chen, M. (2004) 'Impacts of ERP systems on the integrated-interaction performance of manufacturing and marketing', Industrial Management & Data Systems, Vol. 104, No. 1, pp.42–55.

31. Huang, M-H., Wang, F-C., et al. (2004a) 'Value-added ERP information into information goods: an economic analysis', Industrial Management & Data Systems, Vol. 104, No. 8, pp.689–697.

32. Huang, S-M., Chang, I-C., et al. (2004b) 'Assessing risk in ERP projects: identify and prioritize the factors', Industrial Management & Data Systems, Vol. 104, No. 8, pp.681–688.

33. Huang, Z. and Palvia, P. (2001) 'ERP implementation issues in advanced and developing countries', Business Process Management Journal, Vol. 7, No. 3, pp.276–284.

34. Huin, S.F. (2004) 'Managing deployment of ERP systems in SMEs using multi-agents', International Journal of Project Management, Vol. 22, No. 6, pp.511–517.

35. Hunton, J.E., Lippincott, B., et al. (2003) 'Enterprise resource planning systems: comparing firm performance of adopters and nonadopters', International Journal of Accounting Information Systems, Vol. 4, No. 3, pp.165–184.

36. Hunton, J.E., McEwen, R.A., et al. (2002) 'The reaction of financial analysts to Enterprise Resource Planning (ERP) implementation plans', Journal of Information Systems, Vol. 16, No. 1, pp.31–40.

37. Hwang, Y. (2005) 'Investigating enterprise systems adoption: uncertainty avoidance, intrinsic motivation, and the technology acceptance model', European Journal of Information Systems, Vol. 14, No. 2, pp.150–161.

38. Ioannou, G. and Papadoyiannis, C. (2004) 'Theory of constraints-based methodology for effective ERP implementations', International Journal of Production Research, Vol. 42, No. 23, pp.4927–4954.

39. Jacobs, F.R. and Bendoly, E. (2003) 'Enterprise resource planning: developments and directions for operations management research', European Journal of Operational Research, Vol. 146, No. 2, pp.233–240.

40. Jaiswal, M.P. and Kaushik, A. (2005) 'Realising enhanced value due to business network redesign through extended ERP systems: case study

of HLLNet', Business Process Management Journal, Vol. 11, No. 2, pp.171–184.

41. Johnson, T., Lorents, A.C., et al. (2004) 'A customized ERP/SAP model for business curriculum integration', Journal of Information Systems Education, Vol. 15, No. 3, pp.245–253.

42. Jones, M.C. and Price, R.L. (2004) 'Organizational knowledge sharing in ERP implementation: lessons from industry', Journal of Organizational and End User Computing, Vol. 16, No. 1, pp.21–40.

43. Jones, M.C., Cline, M., et al. (2006) 'Exploring knowledge sharing in ERP implementation: an organizational culture framework', Decision Support Systems, Vol. 41, No. 2, pp.411–434.

44. Joseph, G. and George, A. (2002) 'ERP, learning communities, and curriculum integration', Journal of Information Systems Education, Vol. 13, No. 1, pp.51–58.

45. Kalling, T. (2003) 'ERP systems and the strategic management processes that lead to competitive advantage', Information Resources Management Journal, Vol. 16, No. 4, pp.46–67.

46. Kallinikos, J. (2004) 'Deconstructing information packages: organizational and behavioral implications of ERP systems', Information Technology & People, Vol. 17, No. 1, pp.8–30.

47. Kawalek, P. and Wood-Harper, T. (2002) 'The finding of thorns: user participation in enterprise system implementation', The Data Base for Advances in Information Systems, Vol. 33, No. 1, pp.13–22.

48. Kelle, P. and Akbulut, A. (2005) 'The role of ERP tools in supply chain information sharing, cooperation, and cost optimization', International Journal of Production Economics, Vols. 93–94, No. 8, pp.41–52.

49. Kennerley, M. and Neely, A. (2001) 'Enterprise resource planning: analyzing the impact', Integrated Manufacturing Systems, Vol. 12, No. 2, pp.103–113.

50. Kumar, V. (2002) 'ERP systems implementation: best practices in Canadian government organizations', Government Information Quarterly, Vol. 19, No. 2, pp.147–172.

51. Kumar, V., Maheshwari, B., et al. (2002) 'Enterprise resource planning systems adoption process: a survey of Canadian organizations',

International Journal of Production Research, Vol. 40, No. 3, pp.509–523.

52. Kumar, V., Maheshwari, B., et al. (2003) 'An investigation of critical management issues in ERP implementation: empirical evidence from Canadian organizations', Technovation, Vol. 23, No. 10, pp.793–807.

53. Kwon, O.B. and Lee, J.J. (2001) 'A multi-agent intelligent system for efficient ERP maintenance', Expert Systems with Applications, Vol. 21, No. 4, pp.191–202.

54. Lea, B-R., Gupta, M.C., et al. (2005) 'A prototype multi-agent ERP system: an integrated architecture and a conceptual framework', Technovation, Vol. 25, No. 4, pp.433–441.

55. Lee, J., Siau, K., et al. (2003) 'Enterprise integration with ERP and EAI', Communications of the ACM, Vol. 46, No. 2, pp.54–60.

56. Lee, J.C. and Myers, M.D. (2004) 'Dominant actors, political agendas, and strategic shifts overtime: a critical ethnography of an enterprise systems implementation', Journal of Strategic Information Systems, Vol. 13, No. 4, pp.355–374.

57. Lee, T., Moon, Y.B., et al. (2006) 'Enterprise Resource Planning survey of Korean manufacturing firms', International Journal of Management and Enterprise Development, Vol. 3, No. 6, pp.521–533.

58. Lee, Z. and Lee, J. (2000) 'An ERP implementation case study from a knowledge transfer perspective', Journal of Information Technology, Vol. 15, No. 4, pp.281–288.

59. Lengnick-Hall, C.A., Lengnick-Hall, M-L., et al. (2004) 'The role of social and intellectual capital in achieving competitive advantage through Enterprise Resource Planning (ERP) systems', Journal of Engineering and Technology Management, Vol. 21, No. 4, pp.307–330.

60. LeRouge, C. and Webb, H.W. (2004) 'Appropriating enterprise resource planning systems in colleges of business: extending adaptive structuration theory for testability', Journal of Information Systems Education, Vol. 15, No. 3, pp.315–326.

61. Liang, H. and Xue, Y. (2004) 'Coping with ERP-related contextual issues in SMEs: a vendor's perspective', Journal of Strategic Information Systems, Vol. 13, No. 4, pp.399–415.

62. Light, B. (2001) 'The maintenance implications of the customization of ERP software', Journal of Software Maintenance and Evolution: Research and Practice, Vol. 13, No. 6, pp.415–429.

63. Light, B. (2005) 'Going beyond misfit as a reason for ERP package customisation', Computers in Industry, Vol. 56, No. 6, pp.606–619.

64. Light, B., Holland, C.P., et al. (2001) 'ERP and best of breed: a comparative analysis', Business Process Management Journal, Vol. 7, No. 3, pp.216–224.

65. Lim, E.T.K., Pan, S.L., et al. (2005) 'Managing user acceptance towards Enterprise Resource Planning (ERP) systems – understanding the dissonance between user expectations and managerial policies', European Journal of Information Systems, Vol. 14, No. 2, pp.135–149.

66. Loarne, S.L. (2005) 'Working with ERP systems – is big brother back?', Computers in Industry, Vol. 56, No. 6, pp.523–528.

67. Loh, T.C. and Koh, S.C.L. (2004) 'Critical elements for a successful enterprise resource planning implementation in small-and medium-sized enterprises', International Journal of Production Research, Vol. 42, No. 17, pp.3433–3455.

68. Luo, W. and Strong, D.M. (2004) 'A framework for evaluating ERP implementation choices', IEEE Transactions of Engineering Management, Vol. 51, No. 3, pp.322–333.

69. Mabert, V.A., Soni, A., et al. (2000) 'Enterprise resource planning survey of U.S. manufacturing firms', Production and Inventory Management Journal, Vol. 41, No. 2, pp.52–58.

70. Mabert, V.A., Soni, A., et al. (2001) 'Enterprise resource planning: measuring value', Production and Inventory Management Journal, Vol. 42, Nos. 3–4, pp.46–51.

71. Mabert, V.A., Soni, A., et al. (2003a) 'Enterprise resource planning: managing the implementation process', European Journal of Operational Research, Vol. 146, No. 2, pp.302–314.

72. Mabert, V.A., Soni, A., et al. (2003b) 'The impact of organization size on Enterprise Resource Planning (ERP) implementations in the US manufacturing sector', Omega, Vol. 31, No. 3, pp.235–246.

73. Mandal, P. and Gunasekaran, A. (2002) 'Application of SAP R/3 in on-line inventory control', International Journal of Production Economics, Vol. 75, Nos. 1–2, pp.47–55.

74. Mandal, P. and Gunasekaran, A. (2003) 'Issues in implementing ERP: a case study', European Journal of Operational Research, Vol. 146, No. 2, pp.274–283.

75. Markus, M.L., Axline, S., et al. (2000a) 'Learning from adopters' experiences with ERP: problems encountered and success achieved', Journal of Information Technology, Vol. 15, No. 4, pp.245–265.

76. Markus, M.L., Petrie, D., et al. (2000b) 'Bucking the trends: what the future may hold for ERP packages', Information Systems Frontiers, Vol. 2, No. 2, pp.181–193.

77. Markus, M.L., Tanis, C., et al. (2000c) 'Multisite ERP implementations', Communications of the ACM, Vol. 43, No. 4, pp.42–46.

78. Marnewick, C. and Labuschagne, L. (2005) 'A conceptual model for Enterprise Resource Planning (ERP)', Information Management & Computer Security, Vol. 13, No. 2, pp.144–155.

79. Martin, I. and Cheung, Y. (2005) 'Business process re-engineering pays after enterprise resource planning', Business Process Management Journal, Vol. 11, No. 2, pp.185–197.

80. McAdam, R. and Galloway, A. (2005) 'Enterprise resource planning and organisational innovation: a management perspective', Industrial Management & Data Systems, Vol. 105, No. 3, pp.280–290.

81. Mensching, J. and Corbitt, G. (2004) 'ERP data archiving – a critical analysis', Journal of Enterprise Information Management, Vol. 17, No. 2, pp.131–141.

82. Metaxiotis, K., Psarras, J., et al. (2003) 'Production scheduling in ERP systems: an AI-based approach to face the gap', Business Process Management Journal, Vol. 9, No. 2, pp.221–247.

83. Metaxiotis, K., Zafiropoulos, I., et al. (2005) 'Goal directed project management methodology for the support of ERP implementation and optimal adaptation procedure', Information Management & Computer Security, Vol. 13, No. 1, pp.55–71.

84. Moller, C. (2005) 'ERP II: a conceptual framework for next-generation enterprise systems?', Journal of Enterprise Information Management, Vol. 18, No. 4, pp.483–497.

85. Moon, Y.B. and Phatak, D. (2005) 'Enhancing ERP system's functionality with discrete event simulation', Industrial Management & Data Systems, Vol. 105, No. 9, pp.1206–1224.

86. Motwani, J., Mirchandani, D., et al. (2002) 'Successful Implementation of ERP projects: evidence from two case studies', International Journal of Production Economics, Vol. 75, No. 1, pp.83–96.

87. Motwani, J., Subramanian, R., et al. (2005) 'Critical factors for successful ERP implementation: exploratory findings from four case studies', Computers in Industry, Vol. 56, No. 6, pp.529–544.

88. Nah, F.F-H., Faja, S., et al. (2001a) 'Characteristics of ERP software maintenance: a multiple case study', Journal of Software Maintenance and Evolution: Research and Practice, Vol. 13, No. 6, pp.399–414.

89. Nah, F.F-H., Lau, J.L-S., et al. (2001b) 'Critical factors for successful implementation of enterprise systems', Business Process Management Journal, Vol. 7, No. 3, pp.285–296.

90. Nah, F.F-H., Tan, X., et al. (2004) 'An empirical investigation on end-users' acceptance of enterprise systems', Information Resources Management Journal, Vol. 17, No. 3, pp.32–53.

91. Nah, F.F-H., Zuckweiler, K.M., et al. (2003) 'ERP implementation: chief information officers' perceptions of critical success factors', International Journal of Human-Computer Interaction, Vol. 16, No. 1, pp.5–22.

92. Nandhakumar, J., Rossi, M., et al. (2005) 'The dynamics of contextual forces of ERP implementation', Journal of Strategic Information Systems, Vol. 14, No. 2, pp.221–242.

93. Ndede-Amadi, A.A. (2004) 'What strategic alignment, process redesign, enterprise resource planning, and e-commerce have in common: enterprise-wide computing', Business Process Management Journal, Vol. 10, No. 2, pp.184–199.

94. Newell, S., Huang, J.C., et al. (2003) 'Implementing enterprise resource planning and knowledge management systems in tandem:

fostering efficiency and innovation complementarity', Information and Organization, Vol. 13, No. 1, pp.25–52.

95. Newman, M. and Westrup, C. (2005) 'Making ERPs work: accountants and the introduction of ERP systems', European Journal of Information Systems, Vol. 14, No. 3, pp.258–272.

96. Ng, C.S.P. (2001) 'A decision framework for enterprise resource planning maintenance and upgrade: a client perspective', Journal of Software Maintenance and Evolution: Research and Practice, Vol. 13, No. 6, pp.431–468.

97. Vosburg, J. and Kumar, A. (2001) 'Managing dirty data in organizations using ERP: lessons from a case study', Industrial Management & Data Systems, Vol. 101, No. 1, pp.21–31.

98. Wagner, E.L. and Newell, S. (2004) '"Best" for whom? The tension between "best practice" ERP packages and diverse epistemic cultures in a university context', Journal of Strategic Information Systems, Vol. 13, No. 4, pp.305–328.

99. Wang, C., Xu, L., et al. (2005) 'ERP research, development and implementation in China: an overview', International Journal of Production Research, Vol. 43, No. 18, pp.3915–3932.

100. Wang, E.T.G. and Chen, J.H.F. (2006) 'The influence of governance equilibrium on ERP project success', Decision Support Systems, Vol. 41, No. 4, pp.708–727.

101. Ward, J., Hemingway, C., et al. (2005) 'A framework for addressing the organizational issues of enterprise systems implementation', Journal of Strategic Information Systems, Vol. 14, No. 2, pp.97–119.

102. Watanabe, C. and Hobo, M. (2004) 'Creating a firm self-propagating function for advanced innovation-oriented projects: lessons from ERP', Technovation, Vol. 24, No. 6, pp.467–481.

103. Wei, C-C. and Wang, M.J.J. (2004) 'A comprehensive framework for selecting an ERP system', International Journal of Project Management, Vol. 22, No. 2, pp.161–169.

104. Wei, C-C., Chien, C-F., et al. (2005a) 'An AHP-based approach to ERP system selection', International Journal of Production Economics, Vol. 96, No. 1, pp.47–62.

105. Wei, H-L., Wang, E.T.G., et al. (2005b) 'Understanding misalignment and cascading change of ERP implementation: a stage view of process analysis', European Journal of Information Systems, Vol. 14, No. 4, pp.324–334.

106. Weston, Jr., F.D.T. (2001) 'ERP implementation and project management', Production and Inventory Management Journal, Vol. 42, Nos. 3–4, pp.75–80.

107. Weston Jr., F.D.T. (2003) 'ERP II: the extended enterprise system', Business Horizons, Vol. 46, No. 6, pp.49–55.

108. Wieder, B., Booth, P., et al. (2006) 'The impact of ERP systems on firm and business process performance', Journal of Enterprise Information Management, Vol. 19, No. 1, pp.13–29.

109. Willcocks, L.P. and Sykes, R. (2000) 'The role of the CIO and IT function in ERP', Communications of the ACM, Vol. 43, No. 4, pp.32–38.

110. Willis, T.H. and Willis-Brown, A.H. (2002) 'Extending the value of ERP', Industrial Management & Data Systems, Vol. 102, No. 1, pp.35–38.

111. Wood, T. and Caldas, M.P. (2001) 'Reductionism and complex during ERP implementations', Business Process Management Journal, Vol. 7, No. 5, pp.387–393.

112. Worley, J.H., Chatha, K.A., et al. (2005) 'Implementation and optimisation of ERP systems: a better integration of processes, roles, knowledge and user competencies', Computers in Industry, Vol. 56, No. 6, pp.620–638.

113. Wu, J-H. and Wang, Y-M. (2006) 'Measuring ERP success: the key-users viewpoint of the ERP to produce a viable IS in the organization', Computers in Human Behavior.

114. Xu, H., Nord, J.H., et al. (2002) 'Data quality issues in implementing an ERP', Industrial Management & Data Systems, Vol. 102, Nos. 1–2, pp.47–58.

115. Xue, Y., Liang, H., et al. (2005) 'ERP implementation failures in China: case studies with implications for ERP vendors', International Journal of Production Economics, Vol. 97, No. 3, pp.279–295.

116. Yang, C-C., Lin, W-T., et al. (2006) 'A study on applying FMEA to improving ERP introduction: an example of semiconductor related

industries in Taiwan', International Journal of Quality & Reliability Management, Vol. 23, No. 3, pp.298–322.

117. Yeh, C-T., Miozzo, M., et al. (2006) 'The importance of being local? Learning among Taiwan's enterprise solutions providers', Journal of Enterprise Information Management, Vol. 19, No. 1, pp.30–49.

118. Yen, D.C., Chou, D.C., et al. (2002) 'A synergic analysis for web-based enterprise resources planning systems', Computer Standards & Interfaces, Vol. 24, No. 4, pp.337–346.

119. Furey, Timothy.R., (1993), A Six Step Guide To Process Reengineering., Planning Review 21 (2), Pp 20-23

120. Yasar F. Jarrar ', Abdullah Al-Mudimigh 'And Mohamed Zairi(2009) " Erp Implementation Critcal Success Factors – The Role And Impact Of Business Process Management" Icmlt Pp 122-127

121. Kedar Kulkarni (2011), " Overview Of Business Process Re-Engineering (Bpr) In Sap Implementations", Sap Community Network

122. Turan Erman Erkan (2009)," Bpr Effect On Erp Implementation: A Comparative Case Study", World Academy Of Science, Engineering And Technology. Pp 1508-1511

123. Gunasekaran A. , B. Kobu(2002) "Modeling And Analysis Of Business Process Reengineering", International Journal Of Production Research, Pp 2521-2546.

124. Furey, Timothy.R., (1993), A Six Step Guide To Process Reengineering., Planning Review 21 (2), Pp 20-23. Cardoso, J., Bostrom, R., et al. (2004) 'Workflow management systems and ERP systems: differences, commonalities, and applications', Information Technology and Management, Vol. 5, Nos. 3–4, pp.319–338.

125. Yen, H.R. and Sheu, C. (2004) 'Aligning ERP implementation with competitive priorities of manufacturing firms: an exploratory study', International Journal of Production Economics, Vol. 92, No. 3, pp.207–220.

126. Yu, C-S. (2005) 'Causes influencing the effectiveness of the post-implementation ERP system', Industrial Management & Data Systems, Vol. 105, No. 1, pp.115–132.

127. Yusuf, Y., Gunasekaran, A., et al. (2004) 'Enterprise information systems project implementation: a case study of ERP in Rolls-Royce', International Journal of Production Economics, Vol. 87, No. 3, pp.251–266.

128. Strong, D.M., Johnson, S.A., et al. (2004) 'Integrating enterprise decision-making modules into undergraduate management and industrial engineering curricula', Journal of Information Systems Education, Vol. 15, No. 3, pp.301–313.

129. Sumi, T. and Tsuruoka, M. (2002) 'Ramp new enterprise information systems in a merger and acquisition environment: a case study', Journal of Engineering and Technology Management, Vol. 19, No. 1, pp.93–104.

130. Sumner, M. (2000) 'Risk factors in enterprise-wide/ERP projects', Journal of Information Technology, Vol. 15, No. 4, pp.317–327.

131. Sun, A.Y.T., Yazdani, A., et al. (2005) 'Achievement assessment for Enterprise Resource Planning (ERP) system implementations based on Critical Success Factors (CSFs)', International Journal of Production Economics, Vol. 98, No. 2, pp.189–203.

132. Symeonidis, A.L., Kehagias, D.D., et al. (2003) 'Intelligent policy recommendations on enterprise resource planning by the use of agent technology and data mining techniques', Expert Systems with Applications, Vol. 25, No. 4, pp.589–602.

133. Tarn, J.M., Yen, D.C., et al. (2002) 'Exploring the rationales for ERP and SCM integration', Industrial Management & Data Systems, Vol. 102, No. 1, pp.26–34.

134. Tchokogue, A., Bareil, C., et al. (2005) 'Key lessons from the implementation of an ERP at Pratt & Whitney Canada', International Journal of Production Economics, Vol. 95, No. 2, pp.151–163.

135. Teltumbde, A. (2000) 'A framework for evaluating ERP projects', International Journal of Production Research, Vol. 38, No. 17, pp.4507–4520.

136. Themistocleous, M., Irani, Z., et al. (2001) 'ERP and application integration: exploratory survey', Business Process Management Journal, Vol. 7, No. 3, pp.195–204.

137. Thomas, G.A. and Jajodia, S. (2004) 'Commercial-off-the-shelf enterprise resource planning software implementations in the public sector: practical approaches for improving project success', Journal of Government Financial Management, Vol. 53, No. 2, pp.12–19.

138. Trimi, S., Lee, S.M., et al. (2005) 'Alternative means to implement ERP: internal and ASP', Industrial Management & Data Systems, Vol. 105, No. 2, pp.184–192.

139. Tsai, W-H., Chien, S-W., et al. (2005) 'Identification of critical failure factors in the implementation of Enterprise Resource Planning (ERP) system in Taiwan's industries', International Journal of Management and Enterprise Development, Vol. 2, No. 2, pp.219–239.

140. Umble, E.J., Haft, R.R., et al. (2003) 'Enterprise resource planning: implementation procedures and critical success factors', European Journal of Operational Research, Vol. 146, No. 2, pp.241–257.

141. Van Everdingen, Y., Van Hillegersberg, J., et al. (2000) 'ERP adoption by European midsize companies', Communications of the ACM, Vol. 43, No. 4, pp.27–31.

142. Van Stijn, E. and Wensley, A. (2001) 'Organizational memory and the completeness of process modeling in ERP systems: some concerns, methods and directions for future research', Business Process Management Journal, Vol. 7, No. 3, pp.181–194.

143. Verville, J., Bernadas, C., et al. (2005) 'So you're thinking of buying an ERP? Ten critical factors for successful acquisitions', Journal of Enterprise Information Management, Vol. 18, No. 6, pp.665–677.

144. Verville, J. and Halingten, A. (2002a) 'A qualitative study of the influencing factors on the decision process for acquiring ERP software', Qualitative Market Research: An International Journal, Vol. 5, No. 3, pp.188–198.

145. Verville, J. and Halingten, A. (2002b) 'An investigation of the decision process for selecting an ERP software: the case of ESC', Management Decision, Vol. 40, No. 3, pp.206–216.

146. Verville, J. and Halingten, A. (2003a) 'A six-stage model of the buying process for ERP software', Industrial Marketing Management, Vol. 32, No. 7, pp.585–594.

147. Verville, J. and Halingten, A. (2003b) 'Information searches: a two-dimensional approach for ERP acquisition decision', Journal of Information Science, Vol. 29, No. 3, pp.203–209.

148. Volkoff, O., Strong, D.M., et al. (2005) 'Understanding enterprise systems-enabled integration', European Journal of Information Systems, Vol. 14, No. 2, pp.110–120.

149. Voordijk, H., Stegwee, R., et al. (2005) 'ERP and the changing role of IT in engineering consultancy firms', Business Process Management Journal, Vol. 11, No. 4, pp.418–430.

150. Voordijk, H., Van Leuven, A., et al. (2003) 'Enterprise Resource Planning in a large construction firm: implementation analysis', Construction Management and Economics, Vol. 21, No. 5, pp.511–521.

151. Abraham Stub "Enterprise resource planning (**ERP**): the dynamics of operations".

152. Ng, C.S.P., Gable, G.G., et al. (2002) 'An ERP-client benefit-oriented maintenance taxonomy', Journal of Systems and Software, Vol. 64, No. 2, pp.87–109.

153. Ng, J.K.C. and Ip, W.H. (2003) 'Web-ERP: the new generation of enterprise resources planning', Journal of Materials Processing Technology, Vol. 138, Nos. 1–3, pp.590–593.

154. Nicolaou, A. (2004) 'Quality of postimplementation review of enterprise resource planning systems', International Journal of Accounting Information Systems, Vol. 5, No. 1, pp.25–49.

155. Nikolopoulos, K., Metaxiotis, K., et al. (2003) 'Integrating industrial maintenance strategy into ERP', Industrial Management & Data Systems, Vol. 103, No. 3, pp.184–191.

156. Noguera, J.H. and Watson, E.F. (2004) 'Effectiveness of using an enterprise system to teach process-centered concepts in business education', Journal of Enterprise Information Management, Vol. 17, No. 1, pp.56–74.

157. O'Leary, D.E. (2002) 'Knowledge management across the enterprise resource planning systems life cycle', International Journal of Accounting Information Systems, Vol. 3, No. 2, pp.99–110.

158. O'Leary, D.E. (2004) 'On the relationship between REA and SAP', International Journal of Accounting Information Systems, Vol. 5, No. 1, pp.65–81.

159. Okrent, M.D. and Vokurka, R.J. (2004) 'Process mapping in successful ERP implementations', Industrial Management & Data Systems, Vol. 104, No. 8, pp.637–643.

160. Olhager, J. and Selldin, E. (2003) 'Enterprise resource planning survey of Swedish manufacturing firms', European Journal of Operational Research, Vol. 146, No. 2, pp.365–373.

161. Palaniswamy, R. and Tyler, F. (2000) 'Enhancing manufacturing performance with ERP systems', Information Systems Management, Vol. 17, No. 3, pp.43–55.

162. Park, K. and Kusiak, A. (2005) 'Enterprise Resource Planning (ERP) operations support system for maintaining process integration', International Journal of Production Research, Vol. 43, No. 19, pp.3959–3982.

163. Parr, A. and Shanks, G. (2000) 'A model of ERP project implementation', Journal of Information Technology, Vol. 15, No. 4, pp.289–304. Peslak, A.R. (2005) 'A twelve-step, multiple course approach to teaching enterprise resource planning', Journal of Information Systems Education, Vol. 16, No. 2, pp.147–155.

164. Pollock, N. and Cornford, J. (2004) 'ERP systems and the university as a "unique" organisation', Information Technology & People, Vol. 17, No. 1, pp.31–52.

165. Poston, R. and Grabski, S. (2001) 'Financial impacts of enterprise resource planning implementations', International Journal of Accounting Information Systems, Vol. 2, pp.271–294.

166. Puschmann, T. and Alt, R. (2004) 'Enterprise application integration systems and architecture – the case of the Robert Bosch Group', Journal of Enterprise Information Management, Vol. 17, No. 2, pp.105–116.

167. Rajagopal, P. (2002) 'An innovation – diffusion view of implementation of Enterprise Resource Planning (ERP) systems and development of a research model', Information and Management, Vol. 40, No. 2, pp.87– 114.

168. Rao, S.S. (2000) 'Enterprise resource planning: business needs and technologies', Industrial Management & Data Systems, Vol. 100, No. 2, pp.81–88.

169. Yusuf, Y., Gunasekaran, A., et al. (2006) 'Implementation of enterprise resource planning in China', Technovation.

170. Zafiropoulos, I., Metaxiotis, K., et al. (2005) 'Dynamic risk management system for the modeling, optimal adaptation and implementation of an ERP system', Information Management & Computer Security, Vol. 13, No. 3, pp.212–234.

171. Zhang, Z., Lee, M.K.O., et al. (2005) 'A framework of ERP systems implementation success in China: an empirical study', International Journal of Production Economics, Vol. 98, No. 1, pp.56–80.

172. Zheng, S., Yen, D.C., et al. (2000) 'The new spectrum of the cross-enterprise solution: the integration of supply chain management and enterprise resource planning systems', Journal of Computer Information Systems, Vol. 41, No. 1, pp.84–93.

173. Scott Hamilton "Maximizing your **ERP** system: a practical guide for managers".

174. Travis Anderegg "ERP A-Z Implementer's Guide for success"

175. Daniel E.O. Leary "Enterprise Resource Planning Systems System, Lifecycle, Electronic Commerce and Risk".